12/19/97

B   Chamberl
Nietzsche
C   Nietzsch

25,00

DATE			

NIETZSCHE
in Turin

NIETZSCHE
in Turin

AN INTIMATE BIOGRAPHY

LESLEY CHAMBERLAIN

PICADOR USA
NEW YORK

3 4873 00158 7054

Picador® is a U.S. registered trademark and is used by St. Martin's Press under license from Pan Books Limited.

ISBN 0-312-18145-0

First published in Great Britain by Quartet Books

First Picador USA Edition: January 1998

10   9   8   7   6   5   4   3   2   1

ACKNOWLEDGEMENTS

Generous assistance towards the making of this book came from The Authors' Foundation administered by The Society of Authors. The Swiss Tourist Office helped the author retrace Nietzsche's days in Sils Maria.

CONTENTS

NIETZSCHE'S LIFE AND WORKS

A Comparative Chronology

1819 Arthur Schopenhauer, *The World as Will and Idea*
1839 Ludwig Feuerbach, *On Philosophy and Christianity*
1841 Søren Kierkegaard, *The Essence of Christianity* and *The Concept of Irony*
1844 Arthur Schopenhauer, *The World as Will and Idea* (2nd edition)

1844 Birth of Nietzsche

1845–6 Karl Marx, *The German Ideology*
1847 Karl Marx, *The Poverty of Philosophy*
1848 Karl Marx and Friedrich Engels, *The Communist Manifesto*

1849 Death of Nietzsche's father, Carl

1859 Charles Darwin, *The Origin of Species*
1867 Karl Marx, *Das Kapital* (vol. 1)

1865 Nietzsche a student in Bonn
1865–6 Nietzsche a student in Leipzig
1867–8 Military service ends with riding accident

1869 Eduard von Hartmann, *Philosophy of the Unconscious*

1869 Nietzsche appointed Professor of Classical Philology in Basel
1869–76 Enjoys close friendship with the Wagners
1870 Serves as medical orderly in Franco-Prussian War
1871 First major period of illness

1872 THE BIRTH OF TRAGEDY
1873–6 UNTIMELY REFLECTIONS

1876–8 Break with Wagner

1877 HUMAN, ALL TOO HUMAN

1879 Nietzsche, dogged by ill-health, resigns from Basel University
1880 First of three winters (1880–83) in Genoa establishes pattern for an itinerant life, with later winters in Nice and summers in Swiss Alps

1880 THE WANDERER AND HIS SHADOW
1881 DAYBREAK
1882 THE SCIENCE OF JOY

1882 Nietzsche meets Lou Salomé and pursues passionate friendship

1883 Friedrich Engels, *Socialism Utopian and Scientific*

1883 Death of Wagner
1883–4 Nietzsche alienated from mother and sister over failed love for Lou

1883–5 THUS SPAKE ZARATHUSTRA

1885 Elisabeth Nietzsche marries Bernhard Förster

1886 BEYOND GOOD AND EVIL
1887 THE GENEALOGY OF MORALS

1886 Elisabeth and Forster emigrate to Paraguay
1888 Nietzsche moves from Nice to Turin (April)

1888 THE WAGNER CASE
TWILIGHT OF THE IDOLS
THE ANTICHRISTIAN
Friedrich Engels, *Ludwig Feuerbach and the Outcome of Classical German Philosophy*
1889 ECCE HOMO
NIETZSCHE CONTRA WAGNER
THE DIONYSUS DITHYRAMS
1890 Sigmund Freud, *The Interpretation of Dreams*

1900 Death of Nietzsche

1904 Sigmund Freud, *The Psychopathology of Everylay Life*
1919 Friedrich Engels, *Principles of Communism*
1930 Sigmund Freud, *Civilisation anl its Discontents*

NIETZSCHE
in Turin

In England, for a long time they had
discredited Nietzsche by giving out not
only that he lost his reason after
publishing his books, but that he had
lost it even while writing the most
important of them.

Oscar Levy

There are no philosophies, only
philosophers.

Nietzsche

PREFACE

This book is an attempt to befriend Nietzsche. Philosophers may smile, other readers may doubt the efficiency of my social behaviour. But it seems to me important to know, approximately, what it was like to walk down the road with this strained, charming, malicious and misunderstood thinker so important to the present age. He was perhaps the most original European philosopher of the nineteenth century. Despite being a closet metaphysician, he wrestled with problems 'near at hand', problems of pain and loneliness and joy and uncertainty, in a thoroughly advanced way. He wondered at the inadequacy of science and the Christian church to make everyday life meaningful. He hated everything from big towns to newspapers, from nationalism to mesmerizing and narcotic modern art: anything that compromised the freedom of the human spirit – and of course all these things you may see and may still want to weigh up in the street today.

Our late-flowering encounter, not the first but the most substantial, began in a Turin square where I was reading his direct, warm and surprisingly unsolemn letters of 1888. The square was small and shady, surrounded by the quiet back entrances of commercial buildings, lock-up garages and a few dwellings, not far from the cathedral which guards a piece of cloth absurdly identified as Christ's shroud. A long low wall down one side of this tranquil triangle provides a familiar place for local people to gather. I happened upon it by chance and not caring to sightsee, I sat down on a bench and read the Turin letters (London Library copy, Schlechta edition). A madman entered and began jesting. The local audience, who knew him well, and waved at him dismissively for my benefit, showered him with laughter. Meanwhile another piece of theatre began. *'Vieni a casa! Vieni a casa!'* called a tanned and wrinkled old-seeming man. 'Come home with me for a few September sexual pleasures before lunch!' Nietzsche wandered Turin, loveless, remembering love, dissecting culture, already mad in the vernacular sense. These mad, erotic charades might have been dedicated to him. They seemed like tantalizing symbolic distractions outside the theatre where I would eventually dramatize my interpretation of his life.

Nietzsche has long excited writers more than philosophers. Too long a question hung over him: was he indeed a philosopher? 'You ask if I am a philosopher. Is that of any consequence?' he blustered in one of those 1888 letters. Actually he had been asking himself that question for twenty years. It hurt him, and he often laughed over it. He was once a university professor of philology, lecturing on Plato and Aristotle and the pre-Socratic philosophers. A reputation for militant atheism precluded his success in obtaining any similar post in later years.[1] His books were too original and too shocking for the philosophical and classical establishments to acknowledge him as one of their own. A thinker of exemplary moral high-mindedness and subtlety, he was indeed different.

As a philosopher, his fate was ghastly, though hardly untypical. No sooner was he dead in 1900 than all manner of *non*-philosophers poured in to plunder his intellectual creation and put it to *non*-philosophical uses. His sister Elisabeth, a queer mixture of intermittent loyalty, constant power-mongering and utter fatuousness, someone who entirely lacked self-knowledge, the way her brother entirely possessed it, was a famous culprit, inventing merits in Nietzsche to appeal to the National Socialists. As a writer his lot was gentler: writers loved him. They made what use of him they could.[2]

4

I would like to see Nietzsche known and praised widely for his real and lasting qualities. Not that I am alone. A Nietzsche reinterpretation industry exists at the end of the twentieth century to which perhaps some future intellectual historian will devote a study of our present weaknesses. For every idea expressed in this book there exist whole books to which the sufficiently fascinated reader may want to turn: on Nietzsche's style, his view of art, the nature of his metaphors; his views on politics, history and morality; his relation to the German tradition of aesthetic play; his situation in relation to Hegel and Marx, and ultimately to any other philosopher you care to name; and his influence on writers and poets from Yeats to D.H. Lawrence and André Gide. The core attraction of Nietzsche at the end of a century ravaged by ideology is that he provides no positive doctrines nor answers, and even made a fetish out of so doing, or not doing. So we make a fetish out of him. The number of new books devoted to Nietzsche is dizzying. What to do about it? Keep reading Nietzsche himself, I suspect. He writes so well, and, despite being uncommon and disregarded in his own time, it is right that he has gradually emerged as the outstanding critic of the modern age.

His rebelliousness against all moral and religious and scientific absolutes and his radical desire to emancipate the body in thought have been provoking some readers since the beginning of the century. He has helped successive generations find their own way through the usual conflict of instinct versus self-preservation which brings such an abrupt and cruel end to youth. Yeats and Lawrence and Gide, Joseph Conrad, Thomas Mann, Jean-Paul Sartre and Michel Foucault all explicitly owe Nietzsche a creative debt, and there are many others. Instinct coupled with fresh intellectual discovery runs up against received pieties and stagnant institutions. The young perhaps ought not to read Nietzsche, who can be wild and seem recklessly violent, too soon. But so much Nietzsche is good, and looks even better from the standpoint of middle age. He is implicitly inimical to any form of political correctness or mass ideology. He always lacked that idealization of human nature and its ability to progress which variously underpinned socialism and imperialism and nineteenth-century positivism. Instead he was quite sure:

Man is something which must be overcome.

Everyone knows now: the ideas of the *Übermensch* (the Superman, the Over-Man) – the Will to Power, the exhortation: live dangerously! – all of them reduced to slogans, must be recovered within the whole Nietzsche corpus if they are to have any meaning in future. Extracted from it in the past, in the wretchedly ideological twentieth century, they have been pressed into service where they least deserved to go. Nietzsche was not a proto-Nazi, not a nihilist, not an anarchist. The truest things about Nietzsche the philosopher lie embedded in his method and style. It is probable that it was because those qualities are almost impossible to extract from the books that the adulterating simplifications took their place. Historical irony, he would have said.

He was a peculiar writer, of course, and probably more peculiar than most, though also kinder, at least in life. His isolation sometimes encouraged a manic sense of counter-determination to make himself effective. His downtrodden position in life encouraged pride and a sense of superiority, so much so that he recognized the affinity between himself and the oppressed protagonists of the Russian novelist Dostoevsky.

Yet Nietzsche was too ironic a spirit to see himself as a simple hero or rebel and he laid no claim to moral sympathy as an underdog. What is important is that he never wanted to become a leader, a figurehead, or an evangelist. He did not want a graven image of himself to form in the reader's mind and the effect shines forth in a style replete with false trails and wordplay and notions of dreaming and conjuring. The tension between meaning and non-meaning, between picture and painter and perceiver, holds Nietzsche's work together like an experimental novel.

I mean that as a vital pointer. To read Nietzsche one has to appreciate the way he writes; to follow him a little down his path of professional philologist, or as we might say, writer and critic. Writing is the medium through which Nietzsche claims to be a singer and a dancer, a philologist and a doctor. He creates verbal music, lightens burdens, undercuts the manipulative power of other men's words and thoughts, and urges a too long repressed humanity to accept the body with pleasure. His attention to detail gladdens the heart. As he once said of Wagner, he is a great miniaturist.

Life for Nietzsche was the language he used to invent it, a language which was always musical and pictorial. Life itself was invented shape. The books, so close to that life, have an improvised feel; they are asymmetrical, discontinuous, tightly concentric while without an obvious centre. They are the product of a fierce mind and a divergent personality. They stand to be read for their flashing insights, sudden illuminations, patterns and fleeting pleasures. The style consists of elaborate and often brilliant mental snapshots.

What is deceptive though is the sudden leap from style to opinion. Suddenly the books strike out. Nietzsche abjured half of ancient and most of modern civilization, if I have not mis-understood *Twilight of the Idols*. He would have lived happily only in the Italian Renaissance or pre-Socratic Greece. How to say that entertainingly? The idea struck him in his first book, *The Birth of Tragedy*, published when he was twenty-seven. He more or less invented the Greek god Dionysus to keep his eye on his self-appointed task: how to save life from the great and monstrous idealizers who came in between. From Platonists, Christians and German idealists, thinkers along a single devastating life-destructive line, might the god Dionysus save him! And perhaps he did. Nietzsche went mad believing he was that god, signing his name.

Nietzsche's contribution to philosophy was in one sense devastatingly simple; he made the *cathedrae* tremble. He questioned whether Western philosophy since Plato had any meaning in the face of the absurd and irrational forces underlying human life, symbolized by Dionysus. See the beginning of *Twilight of the Idols*, under the heading 'The Four Great Errors', for the answer that there were no answers, only errors. They were interesting errors though, decorative dalliances with meaning along the way. That fact alone suggests why the philosopher *must* become a writer, an artist, a stylist, if he is to survive the collapse of truth around him. At least that is the way the philosopher Friedrich Nietzsche had to move.

For Nietzsche the history of Western thought was an ongoing fancy-dress party, attended by the dogmas and religions of the world dressed as harlequins. Now he was host, now wardrobe master, now guest. He dressed and painted the harlequins, playing with long-established truths like baubles. He walzed with them to giddy music. *Beyond Good and Evil* seems like a costume jewel stuck on to the dying body of Christian Europe. I am allowing myself a little sub-Nietzschean bombast here to make the point. Philosophy for him was a vital, charming and desperate business, in which he far preferred writing metaphors than concocting footnotes to Plato. It was fun, for instance, to picture the solemn Immanuel Kant, purveyor of transcendental reason and absolute moral duty, in a Chinese hat. The alert reader will find many more such instances.

Nietzsche wrote as a lover of life and as a man with enough intelligence and humility to see that mankind was not necessarily the point and centre of life on this 'pitiful little planet called Earth'. Any fixed beliefs filled him with distrust, for at base there were only two sensations: pleasure and pain. (This fundament Freud would borrow and build upon.) Nietzsche watched his feelings and analysed his thoughts for the psychology and physiology they revealed. What difference did it make to a man's thoughts if he had a happy childhood or generally a sluggish metabolism? Rather a lot. That frankness which seems to us gratifyingly post-Freudian is one of the delights in reading Nietzsche today.

Another delight of Nietzsche's style is its companionship, with which I come back to my initial aim. The style leads to the man, even if he insists he is wearing a mask. (He is like a child here: of course we can see him *and* the mask.) Love, gratitude and elegance shaped all he had to say together with immense, overriding pain and hurt. If ever you wished to love Wagner, you should read Nietzsche's loving criticism of him in the original. If you ever doubted Nietzsche's sympathy for the figure of Jesus then look again, in the original, at the unqualified love at the centre of *The Antichristian*, a book which would be best named 'Against the Christian Church'. Nietzsche I feel was often acting out the wisdom of Christ, facing the whole world angrily, as if he had found the moneychangers in the temple. Indeed he loved to hate all 'counterfeiters'. He also hated intellectual corruption, manipulation and lies; he abhorred pettiness, meanness, envy and vengefulness; he loathed mediocrity. Though he could be defensive, blunt, obsessive and quick to take offence, Nietzsche combined a high, austere intellect with a boundless religious need and a striking sweetness of heart. He was endlessly self-questioning and self-critical.[3]

Not least, Nietzsche aimed to be European, not German, in spirit, an absence of national narrowness we can delight in these days, and delight in with a timeless relish too, because a European *style* was part of Nietzsche's campaign. His fierce criticisms of scientific, moral and religious certainty he set down with great economy, poetry and panache, in startling contrast to the classical German philosophers. Meanwhile he hammered away at the chauvinism of the new German Reich.

Nietzsche is well translated. And yet I must say I have never found him a *joy* to read in English. The vocabulary is too abstract and the continuity sometimes menacingly absent because so much is suggested by verbal nuance. But to read him in German is to feel oneself in the company of an acute, witty and passionate mind. Nietzsche never expresses himself long-windedly or inelegantly and his manner is always direct and down-to-earth, however learned and allusive. The ideas flow easily from one to the next. The books seem substantially shorter, more joyful and more gripping than their coldly modernist and fragmentary reflections in English. Nietzsche, unlike Freud, has not been mistranslated. But his essence, his *Heiterkeit* – a peculiar intellectual serenity which frequently breaks out into exuberance and anger, scorn and rhapsody – does not reproduce in any other medium but German. In that tongue he pioneered a refinement and psychological depth that would attract a century of German thinkers and critics and poets.

So much for verbal translation. An even greater problem opens up now as I translate from the letters of April 1888 to January 1889, the dramatic last ten months of Nietzsche's sane life. But, as I say, I have tried to befriend him, and give a sympathetic rendering of his being and his thoughts.

1

FORTY-THREE YEARS BEHIND ME AND JUST AS ALONE AS WHEN A CHILD ...

Nietzsche's friend the composer Henrich Köselitz gave him the idea of Turin in the springtime. Nietzsche, who suffered from headaches, never knew quite where he wanted to live, only that he should avoid extreme sunlight, heat and cold. Summers he spent in the Swiss Alps, winters on the French Riviera. In April and May he knew of nowhere that particularly suited him. Köselitz thought the Piedmontese capital at the foot of the Alps an ideal station between seaside resort and high mountain. Others praised its mild, dry air, its grand regular perspectives and the long stone-covered porticoes which would allow sheltered walks in the open air. From Nice where he had spent the winter Nietzsche made up his mind at the last minute. He wrote a flurry of letters saying he would move on to Turin by train on Monday, 2 April.

It was a matter of less than a day's transit, across what had only recently ceased being one country, the kingdom of Savoy. But true to Nietzsche's neurotic fears, everything went wrong on the journey along the north Mediterranean coast, and inland via Alessandria and Asti. He lost his luggage, got into the wrong train at his one connection point in Savona, then felt so ill at the ensuing complications he had to rent a room in Sampierdarena, just outside Genoa, for two unscheduled nights. He made an unplanned visit then to the old centre of Genoa before finally proceeding to Turin on Thursday, 5 April.

In Savona he probably misread a platform sign, or the destination on the side of a train. He spoke only a few words of Italian and was three-quarters blind without his spectacles. He put himself and his hand luggage in the Genoa train, instead of the one bound for Turin. Hurt by his own incompetence he turned his rage on the Sampierdarena locals, accusing them of exploiting him with high prices he could neither afford nor avoid. The result was an immobilizing migraine attack. This, he told another old friend, Franz Overbeck, was his worst journey ever.

'Apparently just a little trip, it was perhaps the most unfortunate I have [ever] made. A deep weakness overcame me on the way, so that I did everything wrong and stupidly . . . I ought not to risk travelling alone any more.'[1] What was important here, for a philosopher who was going to make himself understood, was that he didn't lack the gift of self-dramatization.

The drama continued when he arrived in Turin, tired and for the first few days in his new rented accommodation unable to sleep. Also the weather disappointed him. It was dull and raining and the temperature fluctuated uncomfortably. 'Not even old yet! Just a philosopher, just someone on the fringe of things, compromisingly only on the fringe of things!' he groaned. He was a terrible hypochondriac – within a week he was feeling almost normal.[2]

On the other hand what he had just rehearsed were the two experiences of pain which structured his inner life and by which he gave himself, Friedrich Nietzsche, shunned German writer, loveless professor, a profound meaning. The first was a melodrama of loneliness, compounded by a sense of himself as a genius and a prophet unheard. The second was the tragic cycle of sickness and recovery which would make Turin his last conscious home. He did feel shaken. He was living in a strange place, surrounded by strangers speaking a foreign tongue. Memories crowded in from the past.

Loneliness was his destiny after he retired from Basel University in 1879. He was only thirty-four. He cited sickness and lack of sufficient time to pursue his own work as reasons for inviting solitude. He had that *Machtgefühl*, a sense of what he must do with his talents and powers. Without severing himself from a demanding institution he probably wouldn't have written the majority of the books – all those after *Human, All Too Human* – which made his mark in history. But he was also wretchedly ill, and therefore most vulnerable, when he took up the itinerant writing life. He had to be prepared to suffer.

To strike out alone was at least a way of life symbolically suited to his intellectual calling as a cosmopolitan Renaissance thinker. We might take a mental snapshot of him now, as a brilliant wanderer in search of passing princely patronage, somehow strayed into the modern world. As much as he was influenced by the tragic Greeks, Nietzsche, thanks to the renowned Swiss scholar Burckhardt, also loved Italian Renaissance culture. Jacob Burckhardt spoke of the quattrocento humanists living off 'the abundance of neutral intellectual pleasure which is independent of local circumstances'. Nietzsche heard him with enormous pleasure in Basel and ever after loved and venerated a man who could see the intellectual joy in not belonging.[3]

Ubi bene, ibi patria. Before Turin, in almost ten years of wandering, Nietzsche had lived in Sorrento, Genoa, Venice, the Swiss Alps, Zurich and Nice. Becoming a Wanderer, talking to his Shadow, gave him common experience with exiles from Diogenes to Dante. What glory it was to be homeless and how it deepened his sense of being European! His unique, powerful attacks on Western tradition he framed sitting in small boarding-houses in fashionable European resorts and cities. Like Nietzsche's life they are truncated, fragmentary and portable. Intellectually, except for their language, they easily cross borders. In that sense the wandering life made him.

But he was lonely and isolated and socially impotent. How can we take such pleasure in his plight? He turned on the Sampierdarena locals because he had a headache, because he was panicking over his inability to organize his life and because he was also desperately hard up. The books earned him nothing. Only the previous year he had paid for *The Genealogy of Morals* to be published and he had to borrow where he could. He depended on a small pension from Basel, the kindness of friends and the company of strangers. All these things, lack of money, isolation, lack of friends encouraged a sense of self-consciousness and powerlessness in Nietzsche's inner world.

The pressures had all worsened too by 1888. His sister Elisabeth for seven years before her marriage had often acted as his housekeeper and travelling companion. Since she emigrated to Paraguay with her husband in 1886 Nietzsche had been doubly alone. His friendships depended on correspondence and he belonged to no institutions. As a writer he had no public to speak of. Indeed he felt positively hated or at least ignored by the German public – the standard way, he said, in which the Germans showed dislike, for it happened to Schopenhauer too. He could retreat into his imagination, and books, but to the sense of being outcast there was only one real counterweight: his memory of friendship with Richard and Cosima Wagner in the early Basel years. Nietzsche was never happier as a German, an artist and a man than when in their stimulating company. The memory of this great artistic and personal intimacy kept resurfacing through 1888. It lived on despite Wagner's death in 1883, the great psychological and geographical distance and the passing of the years. To be sure, Nietzsche remembered the Tribschen—Bayreuth era as a time when he struggled to define his intellectual character against Wagner. Still the Wagners, their music, their personalities, their passionate relationship inspired him, because through all those means they brought him to experience love. That best felt life he kept rehearsing in Wagner's music, which he would play to himself wherever he found a piano.

In a similar, lesser vein of subconscious remembrance, Nietzsche also worked continually on a piece of music which had been with him through most of his compositional life, as a hymn to friendship, and to the joyful acceptance of life despite pain. Halfway through the career of what would finally be the *Hymn to Life*, Nietzsche's greatest female love, Lou Andreas Salomé, provided the words. The words then of his musical work-in-hand

14

dated from 1882. It was the case, contributing to the growing apocalyptic atmosphere of 1888, that now he could only live on memories.

He was never one to conceal or deny his loneliness. He had relished the sociable life with the Wagners and the celebrity his precocious brilliance as a classical scholar won him in Leipzig and, initially, in Basel. But he grew up, grew into his more difficult self, found his course. His conscience over religion, over art, over Bismarck's Imperial Germany compelled him to dissociate himself from Wagner and what seemed like Christian nationalist humbug. In fact he had always shown originality and waywardness in his writings. *The Birth of Tragedy*, dedicated to Wagner and eccentrically combining his love of the Greeks with his hopes for German music, alienated the staid academic world even when it was published in 1872. Gradually his disruptiveness became more widely known and resented. He hardly helped his position by writing an essay on the mediocrity and servility of German universities. Then illness stepped in and cut him off still further. After Wagner died and Elisabeth became engaged and the unfulfilled love affair with Lou Salomé collapsed, three disasters which all happened in the years 1882–3, Overbeck feared for his friend's well-being in such an emotional desert, when he was not yet forty.

Nietzsche himself felt it. In the autumn of 1887 he had tried to revive a relationship with Erwin Rohde, his closest friend as a student, with whom he had once shared his passion for the Greek world and Wagner. The letter ended with the pathetic words I have inscribed over this chapter: 'I have now forty-three years behind me and I am just as alone as I was when a child.' Yet the general tone of this letter was hectoring and uninviting. Nietzsche didn't necessarily want friends. He had to get on.[4]

As for the drama of ill-health, it never left him after he reached his mid-twenties. Even in childhood he had suffered headaches and myopia, and the weakness seemed to run in the family since it also afflicted Elisabeth, and their father Carl Ludwig, who had died at thirty-six of a brain disease. Nietzsche gave out never to know quite what was wrong with himself, though he suspected a hereditary problem and congratulated himself on surviving beyond his father's age. Yet how can he not have known he had syphilis, with a scar close to his foreskin and a history, albeit brief, of treatment? He surely lied to Wagner's doctor, Otto Eiser. The syphilis caught from prostitutes in his student days was complicated by diphtheria and dysentery contracted as a medical orderly in the 1870 Franco-Prussian War. Nietzsche was left with a delicate stomach and poor digestion and a recurring migraine, with constant vomiting and retching maximizing the pain in his head and the disruption to work. For days he could do nothing but lie in a dark room, as now at Sampierdarena.

In Sampierdarena though, there is a double drama to examine: not only what happened to poor lonely sickly Professor Nietzsche who got into the wrong train, but how the whole experience became translated into ideas on the page. The combined pressures of sickness, penury and obscurity go part way to explain the frequency of such terms as power (*Macht*) and strength (*Kraft*), sickness (*Krankheit*), rottenness (*Verdorbenheit, Verderbnis*) and decay (*décadence, Dekadenz*) in his writing. But we come closest to Nietzsche in seeing how he transforms pain.

Sampierdarena one day signified illness and weakness and poverty; but the next day, which Nietzsche spent against his original intentions revisiting Genoa, brought a complete re-valuation of his position. He felt better, his mind was working again, and it threw up quite a different set of ideas: love, pleasure, nobility, gratitude, personal fate, will, courage and cure. He had in ordinary terms something Wagner noticed about him: the power to bounce back; the physical and spiritual capacity to be an *Übermensch*. No one was better qualified to 'overcome himself'. This I think is the physiological and psychological explanation of why revaluation lay at the heart of the intellectual project which dominated his maturity. He constantly discussed it in 1888 as the 'transvaluation of all values', *Die Umwertung aller Werte*.' The very idea of transformation invited his best capacities and the qualities in himself he most cherished.

16

Genoa is a spectacular Ligurian port built into the steep hillside, with a warren of dark narrow alleys animated by the rituals of Italian life and made startlingly beautiful by churches and palaces from rich past ages of sea-trading. Christopher Columbus was born there, and has come to symbolize Genoa's mystery, its mingling of peoples because of the proximity of the ocean, and its adventurous mercantile heart. Nietzsche absorbed the symbolism of Columbus, but for the rest was not a great external observer. Everywhere he went the inner life overwhelmingly concerned him. This or that place simply provided a backdrop. Thus Genoa, when he returned, principally evoked memories of the winter of 1880–81 when in a cold garret he wrote *Daybreak*, and souvenirs of the next visit when he conceived parts of *The Science of Joy*. His room had been on the top floor, in a row of houses descending steeply down the cobbled hillside, and very close to the Opera House. He recalled, retreading those highsided narrow streets and steep alleys, 'this hard and gloomy town' and 'a winter of incredible wretchedness, cut off from doctors, friends and relations'. *He* certainly had been hard and gloomy in Genoa, despite hearing there his beloved *Carmen* for the first time.

For half a day in April 1888 he was completely absorbed in that painful, still cherishable past. These were amongst the first words he wrote from Turin to Koselitz:

In Genoa I was so full of memories I went about like a shadow. What I used to love there, five or six chosen spots, pleased me even more this time; it seemed to me to be of an incomparable *pale nobility*, and far above anything the Riviera has to offer. I thank fate that in the years of *décadence* it sentenced me to this hard and gloomy town; every time you go out of it you go out of yourself too – the will extends itself again and one no longer has the courage to be cowardly. I was never so grateful as during that hermit's existence in Genoa.[5]

These are enigmatic words but let me try to make sense of them. In letters from the winter of *Daybreak* he described himself as wanting death but feeling exuberance. The impulse to write that book, the first wholly new work since leaving Basel, emanated from a unique combination of misery and high spirits. 'My spirit matured for the first time in those fearful days.'

That inner disposition he remembered now. The more extreme his pain, the greater his creative *élan*. He welcomed the scourge of illness which made romantic idealism and religious faith impossible. These were 'sick', 'decadent' cultural phenomena for him. The logic was, why should he want further to weaken his life? It was illness, therefore, which would give him his philosopher's insights and set him on his unique course. He would oppose all forms of cultural debility.

Daybreak shows this happening. Nietzsche began to think from a beyond which was equally close to death and to absurd gaiety. He vomited questions. What did men need to live? What help was philosophy? For instance, was it helpful to believe certain things were good and others evil? Was there a happiness available to the mind no longer able to believe in God? He posed these questions with a devilish self-confidence which cannot be adequately translated from the German word *Bosheit*, a word which has a range of meanings from naughty to malicious and sits ominously alongside the related word *böse*, meaning evil. He was to be a thorn in everyone's side, a naughty boy among the philosophers, a malicious dissident and apparent Antichrist amongst the men of the cloth.

Vomiting questions, Nietzsche sought remedies. Notorious for his amateur pharmacology, and his diets, he made himself physically strong in the face o˜ essential weakness, and that was exactly what he did in philosophy too, with his fondness for Feuerbach and Schopenhauer. Ludwig Feuerbach, who declared the next life promised by Christianity a waste of the energy of the human spirit when this life alone demanded so much, and spoke of man's need to take the divine back into himself, was a tonic to Nietzsche's whole generation. They suffered from the inheritance of Idealism which Nietzsche believed drained the individual's capacity to flourish. Arthur Schopenhauer though left a deeper and more problematic mark on the young men of the 1860s. He suggested life was essentially brutal and morality an illusion. Only art was available to compensate the clear-sighted soul forced into Buddhist-like retreat. Wagner took the view that reading Schopenhauer sapped Nietzsche's spirits, and he was probably right, because Nietzsche by the time of Genoa had turned violently against this pessimism – this 'courage to be cowardly'. He formulated what he called his 'pessimism of strength' in defiance. Still he remained a complex man who knew more pain than joy, and his 'pessimism of strength' is best understood as a tribute to the fine balance between the triumph and the collapse of the human spirit. His contribution to Schopenhauer was to assert that the perpetual illusoriness of the world was not a sufficient cause for despair.

That apparent paradox, therefore, about no longer having the courage to be cowardly, is explicable in terms of Nietzsche's refutation of Schopenhauer. Self-overcoming was literally a 'going over', an *übergehen*, a way of gaining a high vantage over that human fallibility which demands an answer to eternal questions and a release from pain. After Sampierdarena Nietzsche spoke to Köselitz in just those terms, of his 'going out of himself' and no longer fighting an inner moral battle (because that in itself was debilitating). The letter was written in a kind of code, in which Genoa's *pale nobility* stood for Nietzsche's own sickly pallor after his collapse in transit. He set his pain outside himself, he admired it for what it was, and he moved on. It was an exemplary occasion for Nietzsche's use of pain in his personal economy and his philosophy.

But what of solitude in the personal and the creative economies of this extraordinary man we have to meet today off an Italian train? At the same time as he courted solitude with the itinerant life, Nietzsche often complained about it in heartrending terms.

The year-in year-out lack of a really refreshing and healing human love, the absurd loneliness that it brings with it, to the degree that almost every remaining connection with people becomes only a cause of injury; all that is the worst possible business and has only one justification in itself, the justification of being necessary.[6]

In fact two different Nietzsches talked about loneliness. The one was his mother's son and the close friend of Franz Overbeck and Heinrich Köselitz. The other was a fearless explorer and a military strategist on his philosophical quest, one for whom solitude was powerfully symbolic. Here the transition from experience to writing could be made in any instant of his creative life. Its potential has to be borne in mind every moment we follow Nietzsche about Europe, this oddly dressed, shabby fellow with an enormous moustache and a book in his pocket, sitting in the train. Nietzsche sometimes saw himself as a Columbus ready to sail uncharted waters and a Napoleon about to conquer the world. So yes, Genoa could be a resting place for him. It had the right historical nimbus. Also Corsica. The very winter of 1888 he had been hankering after the windy Buonparte island, only deciding against it, and in favour of Turin, because he feared the weather. While lonely man simply complained then, the solitary philosopher plied an intriguing course of mental associations with every place he went, and that sustained him.

But I must finally let him arrive in majestic Turin. We have held each other up with our thoughts and complaints about the journey, which is such a simple one really. The train pulled into Turin Porta Nuova on Thursday at mid-morning. Nietzsche located the missing luggage and set off on foot, along one of the long straight parallel roads leading from the station to Piazza Castello, to find suitable accommodation for a gentleman. Bourgeois in the continental sense is what he meant. He wanted to live with a middle-class, educated family where appearances were cultivated, where cleanliness and good husbandry prevailed, and where there was time-to read and play the piano. Davide Fino, who superintended the public writing room and kept a newspaper kiosk and bookstall on Piazza Carlo Alberto, was his man. Nietzsche may have had a recommendation to contact him from someone in the extensive Italian community he had known during the winter in Nice. Fino kept pleasant rooms at a modest rent and spoke French, which was doubly useful. So Nietzsche took a room in the Finos' large house on the corner beside the Post Office. After that dreadful journey all was almost well.[7]

'My courage for life is waxing again,' he wrote to Franziska, his mother. She was still living in the Saxony town of Naumburg, where he grew up. 'Your heart told you what to advise me! This is really the town I can use now! Just the sort of place I can get hold of and it was like that almost from the first moment' were his effusive words to Köselitz. Thus it was that Turin stepped into Nietzsche's life like a person. A kind of relationship began.

It looked then, thanks to the architect Guarino Guarini (1624–83), much as it does today, a model of urban dignity without pomposity, a Baroque metropolis laid out with geometric precision, yet still with a southern air. Over the whole towered the 165-metre Mole landmark, which in Nietzsche's day had not long been built. He came to know it well, along with the name of its famous architect Antonelli. The vast domed structure with a towering spire was completed in 1878 as a synagogue but never used for worship. A not unlikeable folly, a sightseeing tower and an exhibition hall today, the Mole stands just southeast of the inner focus of the city, Piazza Castello. Almost adjacent to the vast square was Nietzsche's lodging house in Via Carlo Alberto, No 6, right on the corner. His room was on the top floor of the four-storey building.

It was about ten foot square and enjoyed good views in every direction. Nietzsche looked directly out over the small, elaborate Piazza Carlo Alberto, where a large equestrian statue of the first Savoy king of Piedmont and Sardinia after Napoleon strutted pompously before his weak eyes. To the right stood the

Carignano Palace, with its imposing municipal façade, while on the left stood another bureaucratic temple, housing the Finance and Tax Office. The older part of the Carignano Palace, a rather menacing dark grey building giving onto the adjacent Piazza Carignano, was built by Guarini, but Nietzsche's view was of the new southeastern elevation, altered when the palace was expanded to house the first United Italian Parliament in 1861. Since very quickly – in 1870 – the newly created Italian capital moved from Turin to Rome the palace's original function was already redundant by the time of Nietzsche's visit. But it continued to house national state organizations and to look splendid. He loved this city instantly, and one reason why he did was its grandeur coupled with an effortless accommodation of nature. It was a matter for celebration that from the small strip of balcony outside his window he could also see *la collina* – the green Turin hills – to the southeast and, on a clear day, the Alps to the northwest.

As in Genoa, Nietzsche had to live close to music. In Nice too his room had been a few hundred yards from the Opera House. Now the Fino house was within a stone's throw of the Carignano Opera and Music Theatre. Via Carlo Alberto 6 was also only a few paces from the imposing, if hardly beautiful, early eighteenth-century Palazzo Madama, the Teatro Regio – the national drama theatre – and the seventeenth-century Royal Palace, all in the Piazza Castello. Nietzsche's access to this vast square was through the newly built Galleria dell'Industria Subalpina, where the Carignano Theatre orchestra played at weekends, just beneath his window. The Galleria, an elegant, glass-roofed, two-storey arcade of shops and offices, with fountains, statuary and a splendidly tiled stone floor, is unchanged today. The soft chandeliers, polished wood and upholstery of the then Caffè Romano, now the Baratti and Milano, seen through generous ground-floor windows, offer an enchanting vision of urbanity.

The reclusive philsopher could hardly resist. His central situation quite plunged him into the reality of a historic city, which in turn almost overcame his phobia about the weather and his own nervous lack of sleep. Here in full is the central part of that first letter to Köselitz in which he reported his positive emotion.

Turin! My dear friend, let me congratulate you! Your heart told you what to advise me! This is really the town I can use now! Just the sort of place I can get hold of and it was like that almost from the first moment, despite the dreadful circumstances of my first days. Above all miserable nerve-racking wet weather, with freezing, fluctuating rain, and humid half-hours in between. But what a dignified and serious city it is! It has nothing of the capital city, and nothing modern, as I feared: it is rather more a residence from the seventeenth century, which had the court and the nobility, and a single prevailing taste in everything. Aristocratic tranquillity is what has been preserved here in everything: there are no squalid suburbs; a unity of taste, which extends even to the colour (the whole city is yellow or reddish brown). And for the feet as for the eyes it is a classical place! What safety, what pavements, not to speak of the omnibuses and trams, which are so well run they evoke wonder! It seems to me cheaper to live here than in the other large Italian towns I know; and no one has cheated me yet. I am regarded as *ufficiale tedesco* (whereas last winter in the Nice Visitors' Directory I figured *comme Polonais*). No, what serious and splendid squares! And an unpretentious palace style; the streets clean and serious – and everything much more dignified than I had expected! The most beautiful cafés I have seen. Such a changeable climate makes these arcades rather necessary; but they are spacious, they don't feel oppressive. Evenings on the Po Bridge: superb! Beyond Good and Evil!![8]

There is an almost overwhelming amount of encoded Nietzsche in this digest of his first impressions. Yet for the moment let us not hold up the man by confronting him with his writerly words. He was, as always, anxious to get out for a walk, and he was hungry.

His first walks were not particularly adventurous. He toured the four porticoed sides of the Piazza Castello then took the similarly covered Via Po down to the river. Without marked originality he judged the city to be 'aristocratic', 'tranquil' and 'not at all modern'. These days the centre of Turin can still seem calm, old and aristocratic on a Sunday morning, or during the after-lunch rest, though it is also a little dilapidated along the Via Po and too many cars rumble over its stone-paved squares and cross under its otherwise pedestrian porticoes. In the late nineteenth century Nietzsche probably saw the city at its best, and his response was straightforwardly enthusiastic. He liked the cafés. He liked the seventeenth-century buildings, the general orderliness of the city, and the stone paving he had heard so much about in advance. Also he was pleased Turin did not seem expensive.

A week into his stay he had already absorbed so much of Turin that when he told its virtues to Carl Fuchs the city resurfaced as a kind of Zarathustran paradise, resplendent with freedom and light.

That one can see from the middle of the town the Alps covered with snow! That the roads seem to run so dead straight into their midst! The air dry, sublimely clear. I never believed a town could become so beautiful through light. One can walk for half-hours at a stretch under high vaulted passageways. Everything here is tall and broad in scope so that in the centre of the town one has a proud feeling of freedom.

He sent another summary of Turin's strengths, less condensed but this time overtly subjective, to Overbeck:

The town has an indescribable appeal to me. Turin is the only big town that I like. Something peaceful and old-fashioned flatters my instincts. I walk these stately streets with delight. Where else do they have such pavements! A paradise for the feet and for my eyes too! . . . Spring is my bad season, when these eyes of mine tend to become absurdly sensitive. Here I can count on a certain energy in the air, caused by the ptoximity of the Alps; up till now I haven't been disappointed. I find the inhabitants pleasant and I feel at home.⁹

This was Nietzsche's place. It struck an immediate chord in his creative and physical being. He had a tendency to throw out superlatives of possession every time he moved house, but he had never felt his being so well encompassed by Genoa, or Nice, or Venice, or Sorrento. Soon, declaring 'this is the only place I can be', he would change his plans for the autumn to spend all possible time in Turin, which is impressive evidence of the attachment he formed on first acquaintance to a unique city.

It struck him from the first as 'almost a music place', which was praise indeed from a man who said that without music life would be a mistake. He went now and again to the inexpensive music theatre and opera and joined an audience of 2,000 to listen to brass bands from across the kingdom compete for the highest laurels. Back home at the Finos two pianos stood at his disposal. The music must have danced on in his head as he sat in cafés, browsed in bookshops and visited the public library. The Parisian *Journal des Débats* and local Italian newspapers broke into his reveries with news of political events, crimes and natural disasters. In Loescher's trilingual bookshop in Via Po, his presence in Turin was recognized by some of the more erudite customers, among them the Turin professor of philosophy Pasquale d'Ercole.

He liked to eat and he had to be economical. In the evenings he found himself under the same roof as military officers and university students in similar circumstances. There was also a trattoria in the Hotel Nazionale where the waitress liked him, he decided, because she appeared to keep back the best grapes for him. A typical meal began with soup or risotto followed by 'a good piece of roast meat, vegetables and bread – all very tasty'. We know so much about Nietzsche's eating habits because he took such pains to get his diet right, as a weapon against debility. In Turin, restaurant prices were amongst the lowest he had come across in Italy, and certainly compared favourably with the Riviera and Switzerland. The chic grandeur of the coffee houses like the Café Nazionale, where a twelve-piece band played till midnight, and which served the finest coffee and chocolate and ice cream, was comparable with Monte Carlo, he reported to his mother. Delicious cake shops sweetened his days.

Once he felt well, he set about establishing a routine. He had some books with him, though the bulk would not arrive from Nice until autumn. He rose early, sluiced himself in cold water, breakfasted and began reading and writing letters. Every day was a working day because Nietzsche had to avail himself of every moment free from illness. Impossible fate for a writer: reading and writing strained his eyes. Köselitz had been his amanuensis and had read aloud to him at the start of their friendship, but Nietzsche couldn't stand his physical proximity, so that arrangement, the editorial part of it still functioning by post, lost its main usefulness. Nietzsche bought a typewriter, quite an adventure in 1880, but it soon broke, forcing him back on his own resources. He would work for just a few hours because the words would run into each other on the page as soon as he began to tire. Then he would walk, lunch, walk again, work again, dine and walk again in the evening.

He walked along the banks of the Po to left and right of the Ponte Vittorio, into the present-day Michelotti Park on the far bank, and through the Valentino Park on the near side as far as the medieval castle. The terrain is flat and the views of a civilized city, by the river so much *rus in urbe*, without traffic, without today's dusting of exhaust fumes and an overhang of lead-darkened foliage, excited a heart so susceptible to neo-classical pastoral.

But the walking did still more for his soul and thank heaven for it, for exercise in the fresh air was the only real counterbalance to his sickness. He told the Danish critic Georg Brandes that he had conceived the whole of *Zarathustra* Book I in ten days out walking in the mountains. As a muscular, physically fit man to be out moving in the fresh air anywhere soothed and stimulated

Nietzsche. His whole work is peppered with *Wanderer*, who in German are not only itinerants but walkers for pleasure.

The general routine was frugal and practical. It does not seem particularly unusual in someone whose life was dedicated to writing and thinking, except perhaps for that emphasis Nietzsche placed on physical exercise. We know of his build and fitness from the doctors who examined him after he went mad. He practised daily gymnastics and, despite an enthusiasm for sweet things, carefully controlled that food: fat-free cocoa and low-salt salami were explicit requests in the Turin year. Only very occasionally these days did he drink alcohol.

His great human comfort was letter-writing. It has been suggested that he took the room at the Finos because it was next door to the Post Office, though I can't fit that idea into my notion of his love of walking. An odder thing about his life by correspondence was his insistence on having his letters sent *poste restante*, even after he secured a fixed address. Maybe he didn't want even his friends to know where he was, maybe he feared having his letters read by the Finos. But I think he just liked hiding, for there was a childlike theatricality lurking in Nietzsche. I have a suspicion he never forgot the first time he met Wagner in Leipzig, when the already widely celebrated composer, notorious for his adulterous affair with Cosima von Bülow, was visiting his native city incognito. Wagner asked via his sister, who knew the wife of Nietzsche's professor Friedrich Ritschl, if he might meet the young man who had been writing about him so generously in the music columns of the Leipzig press. The meeting, as dramatic as love at first sight, and complete with an absurd concatenation of circumstances which almost prevented poor eager Nietzsche from arriving, had a rare formative power. Even after it Nietzsche too affected the need to go about incognito, though no one knew who he was.

In Turin there soon arrived letters from Köselitz and Overbeck. Meanwhile he found waiting for him a letter from Resa von Schirnhofer, a young philosophy student with whom he had in recent years climbed mountains behind Nice, drunk a little vermouth and attended a bullfight. True, he would be rolling his trousers and eating a peach next, but he was such a nice man. Resa remembered him as a kind, impressive man who amongst much else urged her to read Stendhal. She loved his seriousness and relished his harmlessness. He evidently was touched. From the first days in Turin he wrote an engaging letter back to her about his new home and his latest ideas, the philosophy couched in the broadest terms and mixed with a note on his passion for Turin ice cream.

Resa von Schirnhofer later recalled: 'So unrestrained as a thinker, Nietzsche as a person was of exquisite sensitivity, tenderness and refined courtesy in attitude and manners towards the female sex, as others who knew him personally have often emphasized. Nothing in his nature could have made a disturbing impression on me.'[10]

Nietzsche is infamous for the virulent verbal attacks on women which loom up like ugly sores on the fine body of his work. A number of them have been read out of context, including his much-quoted exhortation to men going among women not to forget the whip. Many other observations about women are tender and sensitive and suggest quite a different view.

It is true that his actual relationships with women were rare. He never went to bed with a woman of his own class. He never had an erotic friendship with a woman. His stiffness, his lack of emotional maturity, invited rejection and inevitably the whole complex of relations with women humiliated him. He tended to get himself involved in triangular situations with women where he was the loser. His sexuality was unfulfilled. But once he had put himself outside the field of romantic possibility, as with Resa, he was tender and enlightened. He had a solid religious upbringing in a house which had seen three generations enter the Lutheran church, and he was a man of virtue. There were disadvantages to that household in that it was overwhelmingly female, but for the time being I bring together his religious upbringing and his tenderness in such reactionary conjunction because it was surely one of the great achievements of the

Christian church to make the male more gentle, if also to cause him inhibitions. Freud declined to analyse *post mortem* a man who left so few clues to his sexuality. But I believe overall Nietzsche feared a lack of manliness. One of his most telling requirements for the true philosopher was that he show 'rugged and unbending masculinity'.[11]

Philosophy became his masculine tool, and took on what the psychologist Adler would have called a compensatory ferocity. Marked though was Nietzsche's desire to preserve simple friendships – and especially relations with his mother and sister – from exactly this roughness, or the depredations of intellect. He hated alienating old friends through his books.

Nietzsche in 1888 therefore was a gentle, thwarted soul, with an extraordinary and for some people frightening mind. I must say this now, for with the books he would write in the Turin year, he would alienate most of the world.

2

THE BEGINNING OF THE FUTURE: THE FIRST PLACE WHERE I AM POSSIBLE

He knew he cut a strange figure publicly. His first words to Köselitz from Turin addressed the problem:

> Basically the man who, given the chance to measure himself by his own standards, *justifies* his life through his creative works, turns into a very demanding sort of person: I mean he no longer thinks about pleasing people. He is too *serious* and they sense it; there is a devilish seriousness behind someone who wants respect from his work . . .[1]

Such anxieties had filled Nietzsche since his late teens, when he became a disciple of Schopenhauer. When a few years later he analysed Schopenhauer's position as revolutionary thinker and 'saint' outside the German academic establishment, he identified the difficulties besetting a serious, original mind. Public scepticism led to loneliness and emotional sclerosis.[2] In his own case it led also to radical misunderstanding, and there is a sense in which his intellectual fate demanded he formulate a theory of masks. For Nietzsche did not want to be taken for an apostle of a new 'truth'. He was a thinker, not a purveyor of doctrines, as he tried to show in *Beyond Good and Evil*. In that book, his finest as a philosopher, Nietzsche offered a subtle appreciation of the world 'beyond good and evil', without absolute truths and judgements. He showed thinking people how to look for cover and disguise.

To preempt the fate of any thinker taken for gospel became his message.³ Nietzsche's intellectual side sought refuge from misunderstanding. Yet his retreat was not without passion. He wanted his audience to listen, and the issue of whether Schopenhauer was 'courageous' or 'cowardly', and where Nietzsche figured on the graph of bravery versus inward withdrawal was always with him.

His practical moral side was quieter. He formed the view that the world felt shortchanged by his seriousness and solitariness, which made him feel guilty. The way he expressed it to Köselitz, he felt there was a kind of guilt hanging over solitude. Since this book is interested in how Nietzsche behaved in the street, about the town of Turin, I imagine he was like a man or woman freshly divorced, but always that way: freshly alone, freshly unsettled, necessarily self-conscious though not always or even often unhappy. It would have been wonderful to be wanted. That possibility shimmered before him as real happiness when he first met Lou and told her he needed time to return to the world of other people, as a human being. But he accepted his awkward position. Where once he had regarded himself as an eligible dancing partner, as it were, others had long seen him as a tin soldier out of place at a real ball.

Now his ineligibility, compounded by illness, stared him in the face. When at forty-three he stepped out after hours of solitary thought he found it difficult to orient himself. Expressly he preferred to meet strangers or write letters. At Christmas 1887 he wrote to Gersdorff:

> Between you and me the tension under which I live, the pressure of a great task and passion is too great for anyone new to come close to me. In fact the desolation around me is monstrous: actually I can only bear on the one hand complete strangers and people I meet by chance and on the other people I've known for ages and those who belong to me from childhood. Everything else has either crumbled away or been

pushed away (that involved much of a violent and painful nature . . .)[4]

The violence of course was psychological and inflicted on himself.

Ernesto Fino, aged fourteen, thought that the family lodger hardly passed for a professor. In Basel he had been known as a dandy, but now his appearance was careless and neglected, something lack of money did not help. In Turin he would make much in a letter home to his mother of having a new suit tailormade. 'I have made a resolution to have a little respect for myself again and to set myself a target in my neglected external appearance. That seems to me also to be a sign of a certain progress in the improvement of my health. If you are shattered you don't care what you look like.'[5] But this was the end of May, and as he observed, he was looking better by then because he was feeling better. Usually his outerwear consisted of a brown overcoat and a battered hat, and when in transit he carried a plaid travelling blanket over his arm. Because of that blanket the Finos first assumed Nietzsche was English.

He was about five feet, seven inches tall and ten stone, four pounds in weight, by present standards small and slender, and walked with an agile gait. His steps though were oddly short and high, because his myopia made him fear tripping. A much reproduced photograph taken in 1890, when he was already mad, shows deep-set penetrating eyes, hooded by extraordinary bushy eyebrows and an outsize walrus moustache rolling down like a great wave from nostrils to mid-chin, with longer side fronds. This extraordinary hirsute phenomenon, which altogether obscured his perfect lips, he first cultivated around the age of twenty-two. The 1890 monochrome photograph shows the moustache and hair black, though in reality they were brown, and the eyes brownish-green. The brow was furrowed and the eyes normally half-closed. Without his thick round glasses Nietzsche resembled an eccentric sage with, according to Lou, lustreless, staring eyes. With the glasses he looked forbidding. Yet he didn't disapprove of his appearance, and even, oddly given his dislike of fixed truths, rather liked photographs. From Turin he kept writing to his mother begging her to send a good one of him to Georg Brandes, who was about to give him almost his only publicity in the world with a series of public lectures in Copenhagen.[6]

No, it wasn't his appearance that bothered him. It made him laugh the way other people misjudged it, just the way appearances ought to make a man laugh who has nothing else in the world to entertain him, that is, no meaning, no faith. I am suggesting a little vernacular madness here. Intellectually alert and mischievous, he was otherwise divorced from the world beyond his own head. Out walking he took his revenge on the impenetrable newness of his surroundings, though it was he who was impenetrable. These Turiners, fancy taking him for a German official! As for the people of Nice, it had been flattering of them to consider him a Pole last winter. In *Beyond Good and Evil* Nietzsche judged humanity to be 'manifold, mendacious, artificial and untransparent', and it seems obvious how that 'philosophical' view evolved out of his petty daily experiences. Lou also said of those deep-set, hooded eyes that 'instead of reflecting changing external impressions they only relayed what passed through his inner life'. But really they acted as a strange prism. The retreat into mind and into solitude magnified every common perception Nietzsche had of the foolishness of life, the incongruous judgements, the misunderstandings, the sheer intellectual impurity of the whole martyrous thing, and what came out on the page was laughing contempt and chuckling malice. Wasn't it clear the world was all dressed up with lies and tricks, nothing but *tromperie*, all its order fake and deceptive? It would take an idealist to fight it, and an ascetic to withdraw from it.

Wagner was probably right. Schopenhauer brought out the worst in Nietzsche. He saw it himself. In his thought, once he seemed to have freed himself from Schopenhauerian pessimism, he wanted to side with the world whatever it was like. Yet he still saw that world as essentially illusory, and he had to find a way of seeing that state of affairs positively. He did it by viewing life as a form of art, built upon wilful deceptions and incorporating transient meanings. Thus the philosopher became a purveyor of metaphors. At least they might be beautiful, the philosopher's metaphors. For nothing else meant more, or was more true, than what those metaphors expressed.[7]

Human nature was itself a metaphor, for as Nietzsche wonderfully declared: 'Man is the animal whose nature has not yet been fixed.'[8]

The power of art and the scope of human imagination took the place of tradition in Nietzsche's mind and rendered impotent the power of doctrine.

In Turin and elsewhere Nietzsche often wrote in his head while out walking, believing that 'a philosopher [is] a man who constantly experiences, sees, hears, suspects, hopes, dreams extraordinary things; who is struck by his own thoughts as if from without, as if from above and below, as by his kind of events and thunder-claps . . .' He adapted experience at every turn to generate new thoughts and images. This imaginative adaptation was Nietzsche's answer to the collapse of religious faith. It was at least as sustaining to believe man was a creature who could create his own world, as it was for other men to believe in the immortality which would give them a second chance.[9]

Yet his friends were frightened for him, chuckling to himself while living out the conclusions of a philosopher for whom all was vain except appearance. Despite the double exclamation marks there was something symptomatic about the line in his letter to Köselitz which joked of evenings in Turin being like inhabiting his own book ('Evenings on the Po Bridge: *Beyond Good and Evil*!!') – and especially *that* book, the gospel of masks. Nietzsche's manic sense of detachment from his real circumstances, and his courting of the idea in daily life that all truth was only a matter of appearance was potentially unhinging. Rohde said: 'It is as if he comes from a country where no one else lives.'[10]

Still we must think of him as a writer, and concern ourselves for the time being with his writing, otherwise this book will begin and end in too much sympathy for Nietzsche's human plight. If the tragedy of Nietzsche's position is over-stressed, the friendship this writer wants to offer him from across the span of a hundred years will be purged of its intensity and the gesture run out of energy. Nietzsche himself would not have been impressed. He took issue with Aristotle over the very business of tragic spectacle. Pain was not something you purged, but something you lived with. I continue to live with Nietzsche then in that Dionysian spirit. Come what may I will not be moved by sad pronouncements like Rohde's, even if they have the ring of prosaic truth. Also Nietzsche's love of fictiveness in life should not be made to seem so very unusual: we all more or less configure our circumstances so as to make them satisfying.

Well-adjusted children are those who can make the world work for them almost from the cradle, by saying what they need: to play, to pretend, to be cuddled, to be talked to, to be bounced in the air. Nietzsche was somewhat autistic, says Curt Janz, his German biographer. He did rely on fiction more than most of us. He fled into poetic fantasy from the kind of emotional intimacy that household of eccentric women offered: his mother, his sister, his aunt and his grandmother. Explicitly he envied Schopenhauer's more wordly origins (thanks to a father in the shipping business who wanted his son to follow suit). As the child is father to the man, the adult Nietzsche did live in his head, increasingly so. In Turin he couldn't be bothered to see Pasquale d'Ercole – his only professional contact – a second time, and while on the surface he didn't want to be thought ungrateful and impolite, underneath he quickly dredged up old excuses, heat and illness, to avoid a meeting, excuses which this time were probably not true. Elisabeth even claimed his *only* mask was illness, worn to avoid seeing people, and at least in drawing attention to her brother's instinctive hermitage she was right. He was not a madman but he preferred to be alone with his thoughts. The intellectual richness which Nietzsche developed out of his contact with the world expressed itself best on the page.[11]

Yet, as Nietzsche walked down Via Po the fact that everything around him was a potential new metaphor still tells me more about the high seriousness of his personality than it does about his as yet far-off mental breakdown. What pictures might make the world a more fulfilling place to pass through? What fairy lights of Turin might illuminate the trajectory of consciousness to nothingness? This was the profound sense in which Nietzsche deemed Turin to be his kind of city. The place already contained his thoughts and as I have suggested it came to him like another person, a person he had long sought because he or she would be, must be, close to him.

In which case what took place was a kind of love. To adapt Stendhal's famous metaphor for the process of romantic attachment, symbols began to crystallize from Nietzsche's first walks down Via Po, spinning a subjective thread between him and the town. It wasn't conventional lovers' talk though, which passed between them, rather Turin reminded Nietzsche of the attractiveness of being tough. It allowed him from the first letters to Köselitz and his mother to express two of his most cherished ideals: the military and the aristocratic. Turin was splendid, distinguished and very military.

The idea of war, warfare and military campaigns was often on Nietzsche's mind. There is no way of escaping that, and it has allowed his misuse and has lost him readers. But there is a kind of absurdity about that misunderstanding, because Nietzsche mainly used the military idea in a transformed sense, the way the Greek word *agon* is sometimes used today to signify cultural challenge. Often the military metaphor referred to his own struggle to assert 'a pessimism of strength' over the decadence of contemporary life. Or it announced a quasi-Christian combativeness on behalf of travestied ideals. He frequently organized his writing as a campaign, with fronts and periodic regroupings of already deployed forces, and he certainly felt he was fighting intellectual battles. Moreover we can be sure with his religious upbringing that the Bible affected Nietzsche's style, urging him towards metaphors of bloody warfare. But the reality concerned words. Would not Brandes agree with him, he asked from Turin, a question already posed in *The Genealogy of Morals*, that the German word *Krieger* meaning warrior derived from *gut*, the root word for good?[12]

Nietzsche, a grown-up philologist, had an almost overwhelming sense of fighting the good fight. Those who know the early life of 'the little Minister' must constantly conjure with his boyhood piety, his fidelity to rules, his desire to do the right thing. As a young man his well-drilled obsession with virtue made him weep. In the last book he would write – *Ecce Homo*, late in 1888 – he would even denounce his formation as a philologist as an unhealthy consequence of German piety. Remaining a fanatical and perverse personality, he never quite cut loose from moral balefulness. Indeed, certain experiences strengthened the tie.

When he was a soldier in 1886 he linked the discipline, valour and rigour of those months with his instinctively rigorous taste in matters of daily living and aesthetics. He told Brandes now: 'I am a brave animal, a military one even.' It pleased him that the military life was not decadent, and the combination of his own military and philosophical activity strengthened his identity with the worlds of Homer and Plato, agonistic in both the athletic and the rhetorical sense.[13]

On the other hand Nietzsche was petty enough to point out to Brandes that, during the Franco-Prussian War of 1870, when he served as a volunteer medical orderly, he lodged in Lugano with the Moltke family. He avoided specifying that the Moltke in question was the famous general's *brother*. And he was obsessed with military appearances in a way that suggests he deliberately wanted to mislead the world with that moustache of his. Even while he was a salaried professor of antiquity he looked like a Prussian military officer. In early semi-active madness he resembled no one so much as the strutting Kaiser Wilhelm II, who came to the imperial throne halfway through 1888 and acquired a hyper-military image in the newspapers. 'Officer-like' was certainly Köselitz's first impression of Nietzsche in Basel in 1875.[14]

The boost a military image gave to his confused masculinity no doubt retrospectively added to its lasting attraction. In truth he had loathed the long physical grind and discomfort of a soldier's day. Mentally he cried out from under the belly of his muddy horse: 'Help, Schopenhauer!' and longed to return to his books. But looking back he was plainly proud and pleased at his toughness. Good philosophers were masculine, if Schopenhauer was any model. Good soldiers were masculine too. One can just about see the logic of the next idea, that good philosophers might even increase their goodness by being military. Nietzsche defined his achievement by fighting pessimism, idealism and all forms of decadence. What he meanwhile hugely admired and might have wished to emulate in Stendhal was the soldier-writer.[15]

At the same time what Nietzsche experienced of real war, Prussia against France, appalled him. He brought away only disease in his body and a loathing of suffering. He participated voluntarily out of duty, but the spectacle shocked him into creative lament. A letter to Cosima Wagner told of how he was composing music in a field hospital in Erlangen.[16] Through that same bloody summer of 1870 he wrote the essay 'The Dionysian World View'. This precursor of the all too aptly named *Birth of Tragedy out of the Spirit of Music* framed the anti-Christian account of pain which armed Nietzsche for life. The Dionysian responded to what Nietzsche called in letters to his wounded friend Carl von Gersdorff, who had already lost his brother, 'the terrifying underground foundations of being . . ., the whole, endless realm of wretchedness . . .' Taking up the thread again against the background of their shared belief in Schopenhauer, he wrote:

What enemies for our faith are growing up now out of the bloody ground of this war! I've braced myself for the worst in this matter, at the same time I'm confident that from beneath an excess of pain and horror [*dem Übermass von Leid und Schrecken*] now and again the night flower of knowledge will raise its head. Our struggle lies before us - and that's why we must stay alive.[17]

Schopenhauer's *The World as Will and Idea* appeared in its second revised and expanded edition in the year of Nietzsche's birth, 1844, and after several decades of obscurity, it gripped and consoled the generation which matured just as Prussia declared war on France. Nietzsche remembered its impact in his 'Schopenhauer as Teacher' and from Turin commented to Brandes that anyone interested in Nietzsche should understand the personal importance of that 1875 essay. At the same time the experience of real war marked the limits of Schopenhauer's influence on Nietzsche. Between letters of consolation to Gersdorff in September and December 1870, Nietzsche sent his Dionysian essay to Wagner in November. Schopenhauer's solution was equally artistic, but Nietzsche wanted a more positive answer to misery.

The readiness to espouse the Dionysian was there even in 1870. Nietzsche's love of beauty and of the beauty of mental constructs was always more colourful, more celebratory, more energetic and abandoned than Schopenhauer's. He now believed that there could be, as there once had been, an art form capable of embracing life's horrors and irrationalities without needing to explain them or sublimate them or lessen the furious pace of their attack. In this sense pain could be directly confronted and celebrated without loss of present vitality and without what we would surely call today 'repression'. Otherwise, without the Dionysian, Nietzsche, as an intelligent, sensitive human being who did not believe in God, had no way of explaining the suffering he had witnessed.[18]

We ought to pause here to wonder at the violent and terroristic image which has clung so long to Nietzsche, who really was so sensitive to pain. This *Reizbarkeit*, which he would also attribute in excessive measure to Christ when he wrote such a sweet paean to Him in *The Antichristian*, seems to me to cancel out his braggardly superficial declarations of desirable war. We are left with two features of his inmost personality. The first, commendable to the point of saintliness, is his passionate preoccupation with the relief of suffering. The second is a petty fondness for things military, particularly things expressed in military terms, which springs from his subconscious, expresses deep-rooted anxieties, and is not sufficiently mediated by his conscious self to have any attraction or real meaning for the reader. Arthur Danto has suggested in another context that much of Nietzsche is given over to in-jokes and remarks only he himself could appreciate; to eccentric illustrations of his thought which wilfully obscure its message. He talks to his subconscious. The military affectation was that kind of 'joke', and it proved disastrous to his reputation.[19]

Yet Turin does have a military quality and that is why Nietzsche as a philosopher 'who is struck by his own thoughts as if from without' was so excited to discover it. From the top of the Mole or the hilltop landmark known as the Superga the city appears perfectly planned. Its immaculate grid of straight roads has often been remarked upon, not only by Nietzsche. Its name even today, in the more erudite tourist brochures, is 'the metaphysical city' and Nietzsche was living right in its old heart.

The city was renowned in ancient times as the butt of Hannibal's wrath. When the Carthaginian warrior crossed the Alps in 218 BC *en route* to attack the Romans from the north, he found, at the foot of the mountains, a conglomeration of insubordinate plain-dwellers, whose city, favourably placed between the Rivers Dora and Po, he consequently razed to the ground. The Romans, interested in the city's strategic position, later rebuilt it, renamed it Augusta Taurinorum and used it as a base for fighting the Gauls. The collapse of the Roman Empire let in the Goths and Lombards, who remained until Christendom drove them out. The year 774 was a landmark date when the Turin area became a Frankish palatinate under Charlemagne. In the eleventh century control passed by marriage to the counts of Savoy, and they ruled for around 350 years over what became a dukedom with Turin as its walled capital. Absolutism kept the peace, but civil wars and local discords brought progress. The seventeenth century was the scene of much suffering as the city rebounded from medieval conflict and grew. (Gibbon, the very opposite of Nietzsche, was one later visitor who loathed what he saw of this crucial expansion.)

Carlo Emanuele II, Duke of Savoy, ascended the throne in 1645 and for the next century and a half Turin expanded and prospered, despite French ingressions. Napoleon drove out the House of Savoy, but it returned all the stronger in 1814, with an empire which soon joined an enlarged Piedmont to Sardinia. The power of Piedmont mounted in the next decades, accompanied by the rise of Turin as the centre of the Italian patriotic movement. The Prime Minister from 1852, Count Camillo Cavour, pushed Piedmont's expansion still further. Through bloody battles and a tradeoff to the French in the form of Nice and Savoy, he won Lombardy, after which successive Italian states sought union with powerful Piedmont. In 1861 the first Italian parliament met in Turin and declared Piedmont's sovereign, Victor Emmanuel II, first King of Italy. By then it was one of the finest cities in the whole peninsula.

Gibbon recoiled with horror at the sight of 'palaces which have been cemented with the blood of the people' but Nietzsche loved Turin's seventeenth-century architecture because those sober, solid, central buildings, pure and unified, gave off a sense of aesthetic stability. If absolute Savoy rule was responsible for their existence then military absolutism be praised! Nietzsche's instincts were profoundly undemocratic in almost every respect, but I think it is worth remembering his greatest reason for opposing democracy and praising the architectural consequences of absolutism was cultural. Europe for him had been in political and aesthetic decline since the Renaissance. The Renaissance, against a background of rampant bloodshed and soaring humanism, from Dante to Raphael, had glorified war as a work of art and given a central cultivated place to the soldier. Turin was not a Renaissance city, but, apart from preferring its palaces to Renaissance castles, Nietzsche seemed to wish it so with his fond attribution of the word 'noble'.[20]

He was a writer of *virtù*, with sword in one hand, pen in the other. He had to defend style from decay, as he had to defend full-bodied life from being attacked by illness. What a battle he fought constantly inside himself! It was as if the cosmopolitan and 'southern' Renaissance Nietzsche, bold of heart, fine-minded, and with an exquisitely trained physique enabling him if not to dance or fence, then certainly to ride, as the high style of the *Übermensch* demanded, were constantly threatened by a German-inspired 'northern' Reformation which would replace those outgoing pleasures with an inward concentration on the things of the mind, a reformation which could only make him sick. The cultural and the personal physical battle intermingled. He told Brandes, referring to his worst winter, 1879–80, when he nearly died: 'My speciality was to endure extreme pain neat and raw with complete clarity two or three days running . . . it was only in that terrible time that my mind grew to maturity.' His virtue, as man and writer, as a *uomo singolare*, was true grit.[21]

Burckhardt wrote of those 'singular' Renaissance men:

Despotism . . . fostered the utmost individuality not only in the tyrant or *condottiere*, but also in the men he protected or used as his tools – the secretary, minister, poet and companion. These people were forced to know all the inward resources of their own nature, the momentary as well as the permanent; and their enjoyment of life was enhanced and concentrated by the desire to obtain the greatest satisfaction from a period of power and influence that might be very brief.[22]

In Nietzsche's case the twin despots were not political patrons but illness and Christian idealism, and he was determined to flourish despite them.

When he transferred his personal battle to that historical canvas, therefore, he made one of those giant leaps from style to opinion, and from subjective to objective, so characteristic of him. Thus for a moment it might seem as if he came to Turin to protect Renaissance individualism against modern forces of democracy and social fragmentation. Once arrived he sought allies everywhere: in art, architecture and music.

But whatever campaign he had to wage he needed to be strong in himself, and finally that is what Turin did: boosted him, made him all the fitter for his cause. Nietzsche felt himself ennobled in the presence of this grand and dignified person called Turin. Its 'aristocratic', 'tranquil' and 'not at all modern' identity helped him remember his passionate calling to restore Renaissance values. That identity, pieced together in symbols, justified the seriousness, took away the guilt, and allowed Professor Nietzsche to wander under the porticoes plunged in thought. There are words in *Beyond Good and Evil* which the first letter to Köselitz from Turin clearly echoes. They emphasize the role of the aristocratic in Nietzsche's self-justification and continual self-defence:

What is noble? . . . What beneath this heavy, overcast sky of the beginning rule of the rabble which makes everything leaden and opaque, betrays and makes evident the noble human being? – It is not his actions . . . neither is it his works . . . it is the faith . . . *The noble soul has reverence for itself.*

The guilt of the lonely and serious thinker, out of tune with his time and place, was easier to overcome in Turin than in most places he knew.

There are some curious details involved in Nietzsche's assimilation of Turin to his inmost cause which I must tack on because they support that idea of the struggle taking place in his soul between Renaissance and Reformation. He singled out the general cleanliness and the smooth pavements, for instance, where Burckhardt had once generally contrasted the pavements in Renaissance cities with German cobbles and filth, and seen in them tokens of Renaissance wealth and progress against Reformation backwardness and decline. Did Nietzsche remember that? Subconsciously perhaps. He was certainly consciously happy to be abroad in a non-German place whose 'nobility' sheltered him from the 'heavy' northern intellectual world imposed by the Reformation.[24]

Now Nietzsche's foremost Turin critic, being himself a near-native and long-time resident of the city, argues that most of what Nietzsche says about Turin comes secondhand or, in the case of its having 'no squalid suburbs', was wrong. Had he walked far enough he would have seen for himself. But it is not a sensible criticism of Nietzsche in Turin to say that his reactions were unoriginal.[25] Something much more important, mediating between the man and his experience and the philosophy, was taking place. By attributing such qualities to Turin as he did, Nietzsche was raising it to the level he required, as if the level of ideas outside him had to equal the level within for his being to feel light and fulfilled. The moment inner and outer levels matched each other he heaped the greatest praise on Turin, saying it was the first place where he was possible.

> Turin, my dear friend, is a capital discovery. I'll say a bit about it, bearing in mind that under certain circumstances you too could get something out of it. I'm in a good mood, and working from morning to evening – a little pamphlet about music is keeping my fingers busy. I'm eating like a demigod, I can sleep, despite the carriages rattling past at night. All these are signs of the eminent adaptation of Nietzsche to Turin. It's the air that does it – dry, energizing, jolly. There have been days with the most beautiful air of all, like in the Engadine. When I think of my Springs elsewhere, e.g. in your comparable magic shell [Venice], how great is the contrast: the first place where I am possible! . . . And at the same time everything comes to meet me, the people are likeable and good-humoured.

This was the second letter from Turin to Köselitz, on 20 April. Nietzsche had been in place a fortnight and his personal stage was set for production. The energizing air made him feel like the King of Italy. A third letter on 1 May established that the Turin air put him in that divine mood otherwise only inspired by Bizet's *Carmen* or the music of Köselitz himself. 'A charming, light, frivolous wind in which the heaviest thoughts take wing blows [here] on good days . . .'

Nietzsche in the first uncertain Turin days half-attempted to lure Köselitz from Venice with the words 'you too could get something out of it'. But essentially he preferred to be alone. In the end he had settled in so very easily, and now at last his real work could begin.

3

AN INDESCRIBABLY CLOSE INTIMACY

The most famous prompt for a rash of Nietzsche thoughts in Turin was a production of Bizet's *Carmen* at the Carignano Music Theatre. Those reflections, being marshalled into shape for an essay he would call *The Wagner Case*, were what 'busied his fingers' as he reported in the 20 April letter to Köselitz. The essay said something about Nietzsche's love of *Carmen* but primarily it concerned Wagner. Wagner was a composer whose music Nietzsche never ceased to love. This was despite his enormous reservations concerning the man who had been dead for more than five years now. Only one book of Nietzsche's, *The Antichristian*, fails either to mention directly or to allude to Wagner. The relationship to R., or R.W. or even Magner, as he enjoyed punning on his name, was a fixation of love and of love deteriorated into constant antagonism. 'That was a man I very much loved,' he called out from his madness.[1]

Many of the memories of the Nietzsche–Wagner friendship were erased when Cosima burnt the letters, but enough remain in Nietzsche's own work and correspondence to suggest a tumultuous intellectual romance. Their first meeting in Leipzig is so momentous the twenty-four-year-old Nietzsche recounts it in the present tense:

We arrive in the very well-appointed Brockhaus drawing room; there is no one else present but his closest family,

46

Richard and the two of us. I am introduced to Richard and speak a few words of reverence: he makes very exact inquiries as to how intimately I know his music, furiously castigates all productions of his operas with the exception of the most famous in Munich and makes fun of the conductors, who exhort their orchestras in such cosy tones: 'Come on now, lads, a bit more passion!' W. is very fond of imitating the Leipzig dialect . . . Before and after dinner Wagner played, including all the important passages from *The Mastersingers*. He imitated all the voices and was very forthcoming. You see he is a fantastically lively and fiery man, who speaks very quickly, is very amusing and is the heart and soul of a private party like this. In between I had a fairly long conversation with him about Schopenhauer: ah, you can imagine what a pleasure it was for me to hear him spoken about with quite indescribable warmth, what he owed him, how he was the only philosopher who understood the nature of music; he asked me how the professors felt about him these days, laughed a lot about the Philosophers' Congress in Prague and spoke of 'philosophical time-servers'. . . . At the end . . . he squeezed my hand very warmly and invited me in a most friendly way to visit him to make music and philosophy . . .[2]

Wagner, who showed genuine concern for Nietzsche over the next ten years, and in a poem invited him to take from the musical and theoretical work what he could, loved the idolization. Nietzsche loved the stimulation of being close to a man whose music never ceased to evoke in him wonder, though also eventually vehement anger and disbelief.[3]

Nietzsche, at twenty-four newly appointed in Basel, from 1869 regularly crossed Switzerland to visit Wagner and Cosima at their country house near Lucerne. At the Tribschen villa beside Lake Vierwaldstätt paradisaical days and weeks passed. The welcome visitor described the atmosphere as sunlit and cheerful; Wagner himself was fresh and tireless and gave Nietzsche the impression of divinity; he had never had such a sublime experience. Thirteen years later he remembered: 'We loved each other and hoped for everything on each other's behalf – it was a really deep love without ulterior thoughts.' Nietzsche used the first person plural pronoun rarely; here he did so with rare genuine feeling and some accuracy. Wagner said Nietzsche was with one exception the only living person 'who has provided me with a positive enrichment of my outlook'.[4]

His enthusiasm however was already slowly waning when the Wagners moved to Bayreuth in April 1872. Nietzsche who always advocated humour as a way of minimizing life's un-happinesses, though he achieved it less in life than in theory, made a pun out of that personal tragedy in *The Wagner Case*. He imagined a disillusioned young Wagner acolyte sending a telegram: *Bayreuth – bereits bereut!* ('Reached Bayreuth and already really regretting it.') Regret was a bathetic understatement. No sooner was Wagner's dream in place, than Nietzsche became disillusioned, and felt the enormous folly of having allowed himself to be seduced by the Wagnerian idea.[5] When it appeared in 1875 his encomium 'Richard Wagner in Bayreuth' was already an anachronism. The notebooks overspilt with criticism. Yet he was still fascinated by Wagner's personality. Cosima, who watched him shrewdly at Tribschen and spent many hours in his company when Richard was working, noticed the unnaturalness that seized Nietzsche in her husband's presence, as if he were struggling to affect more detachment from an overwhelming personality than he felt. At the same time the gifted young professor seemed to drain the composer with his needs and to provide little in return.[6]

What Nietzsche also lost when the Wagners moved from Tribschen was a warm, bustling life in which he had a place. Richard and Cosima, devoted to literature and music, and both highly talented, offered unlimited intellectual and artistic dis-cussion. They were also amusing, daring, bohemian and relaxed, always surrounded by children, animals and visitors. They were numerous at table and they were fond of treats. (One of the most famous birthday treats in history was Richard's present to Cosima of the *Siegfried Idyll*, performed in Nietzsche's presence, on her birthday on Christmas Day 1870.)

That the end of this 'indescribably close intimacy', as he was still calling it in 1888, caused Nietzsche catastrophic heartache he leaves his readers in no doubt in a passage written six years earlier:

> *Star friendship* – We were friends and have become estranged. But this was right, and we do not want to conceal and obscure it from ourselves as if we had reason to feel ashamed. We are two ships each of which has its goal and course; our paths may cross and we may celebrate a feast together, as we did – and then the good ships rested so quietly in one harbour and one sunshine that it may have looked as if they had reached their goal and as if they had one goal. But then the almighty force of our tasks drove us apart again into different seas and sunny zones, and perhaps we shall never see each other again; perhaps we shall meet again but fail to recognize each other; our exposure to different seas and suns has changed us. That we have to become estranged is the law *above* us; by the same token we should also become more venerable for each other – and the memory of our former friendship more sacred. There is probably a tremendous but invisible stellar orbit in which our different ways and goals may be *included* as small parts of this path; let us rise up to this thought. But our life is too short and our power of vision too small for us to be more than friends in the sense of this sublime possibility. – Let us then *believe* in our star friendship even if we should be compelled to be earth enemies.[7]

This epitaph on the friendship with Wagner is remarkable for its beauty. It also seems to me an unusually unmasked manifestation of that Idealism Nietzsche never quite quashed in himself and perhaps here, in *The Science of Joy*, was willing to reveal through the stylistic music of his words. The style here tells the reader that compared with his activity as a philosopher,

Nietzsche's emotional self was more vulnerable, tempted for all his intellectual 'nihilism' still to believe that a higher scheme of things existed where opposites were united.

Clearly he was also still steeped in Wagner's music in 1882, for 'star friendship' refers directly to the triumphal sacerdotal awakening by Siegfried of Brunnhilde, the goddess whose readiness to welcome love over power ushers in a new human era at the end of *The Ring*. Nietzsche, who missed his father, loved Wagner, passionately and asexually, and felt bereft without him. With Brunnhilde he could cry: 'He who has awakened me has done me harm.'[8]

What kind of harm? The layered, boxed-in, bracketed and much qualified *Wagner Case*, with its preface and two afterwords and an epilogue, suggests something of his difficulty in unravelling the finely interwoven strands of an epoch-making human bond. He had to sort out his feelings towards the man, his music, and, generally, where art, especially musical art, after Wagner and after Romanticism, was moving in the future. On the level of feeling in Wagner was everything Nietzsche feared and hated: uncontrolled sensuality, German chauvinism – Bayreuth was intolerably vulgar – and an emotional scenario dominated by manipulation and deceit. Yet Wagner also contained all that Nietzsche's high intellect revered in terms of an art which captured the finest nuances of human emotion. Wagner's art penetrated to a psychological underworld, revealing an inchoate, irreligious, suprapersonal life-force both thoroughly disturbing and dazzlingly beautiful. The dark depths once mined gave forth a power which was life-enhancing beyond comparison. As Nietzsche said of *Twilight of the Gods*, the experience was of 'heaven on earth'.[9]

Possibly no critic of Wagner has ever felt these contradictions so keenly as did Nietzsche, who came to associate Wagner's music with his own experience of illness. Wagner took him to the brink and threatened his spirit with annihilation. Tempted by Wagner's unprecedentedly rich harmonies and awe-inspiringly delicate lyricism to lose control, Nietzsche rebelled and retreated

50

inside himself at the same time as he felt the deep desire to submit. One might compare the rage he felt when Wagner's surging music threatened to dissolve his willpower with his rage at losing control over himself while travelling to Turin. Yet the traveller's problem was just the wretchedness of a lonely half-blind invalid, whereas the problem of the troubled Wagner-lover seemed to confront the future of mankind.

Nietzsche's launch theme was 'healing' – *Genesung* – in that twofold sense which makes all his work both deeply subjective and universally relevant. On the most intimate level, *The Wagner Case* represented the problem of Nietzsche's striving for happiness after the loss of Wagner's friendship. He dreamt of him often. He wept. He had never laughed so much with anyone. This was the hardest sacrifice life had demanded of him, and he sometimes doubted it was worth it, just to be 'right'. Those around him said Nietzsche was never the same man again, neither mentally nor physically after the break.[10]

Nietzsche faced the problem of any man or woman who has lost faith in the ideal or the divine or the true; a problem of personal and also of post-modern psychology. The greater interest of his plight though arises, once again, through his projection of his own conflicts into cultural history. The problem now was the nature of modernity, which he had been discussing with Brandes all winter, and the place within it of 'decadent' Romanticism. Nietzsche avowed he was a decadent himself, because he was of his time; and also to Brandes that he loved music too much not to be a Romantic. In 1888, though he had been battling Romanticism and decadence for more than ten years, it was still as if he were caught up in a doomed love affair, which only the cerebral part of him could criticize, while the heart pursued its own reasons for loving Schumann, Mendelssohn, Weber, Liszt, Wagner – and even Brahms. In *The Wagner Case* explicitly he turned his philosophical mind to an examination of these captive, complex feelings, using the grand example of Wagner, and looked for solutions, or as he put it characteristically, 'ways out of the labyrinth'. Romanticism is delivery for the soul through the imagined transcendence of real limitations. It may have a god, or an art form, or a national soul at its core. When I say Nietzsche was a closet metaphysician I mean he never overcame the attraction of a belief in such transcendence, though he did his best to stop it diminishing the quality of immediate life. His philosophy was not a source of encouragement for dreamers, though paradoxically that has made it all the more potent for those who believe art actively redeems life.[11]

How did Romantic magic work? *The Wagner Case* traced how the great Wagner operas exercised a revolutionary attraction through their subject matter, the instinctual life. The nominal setting was a mythical world of gods in decline, or one of medieval history spiced with magic, but the passions plotted were the deepest feelings and darkest thoughts of modern human beings, and that was their immense appeal and frightfulness. As Freud would suggest, and Eliot would say, man cannot bear too much reality. Nietzsche was in love with passion, but feared its expression. Some of the finest passages in the whole of Nietzsche occur in 'Richard Wagner in Bayreuth' where he first did valedictory justice to the Wagner phenomenon. Wagner's long, seamless music dramas expressed incestuous and adulterous desire; the will to conquer and the wish to be delivered through love or death. The orchestra functioned like a chorus of voices, and the human voice flowered out of that living whirlpool of sound. This music seeped into the being of its listeners and transformed them from within. Nothing in the history of music was so daring in composition and so seeringly accurate and dangerously effective in conveying the power and nature of the human *Machtgefühl*.[12]

Wagner's music was an extraordinary elemental embodiment of will. Both the action and the score showed strongly individualized wills being swept along towards fulfilment of the composer's symphonic goal. Such a power to restate the world reminded the young Nietzsche of Greek tragedy with its unflinching capacity to confront an absurd and chaotic world and simultaneously rejoice. At twenty-seven he was overjoyed to have this experience in contemporary music:

> I wouldn't know in what way I could ever have partaken of the *purest* sun-bright happiness except through Wagner's music; and this even though his music by no means always speaks about happiness, but about the dreadful and uncanny subterranean forces of human action, the sorrows in all happiness and the finite nature of our happiness; hence the happiness which that music radiates must lie in the manner in which it speaks.

With *The Birth of Tragedy* in progress, Nietzsche embarked on a long and personally fruitful analysis of that manner of speaking, Wagner's musical style, and cherished thoughts of a renewed European culture inspired by the new German music.[13]

But the notebooks which betray his disenchantment with Bayreuth speak of Wagner's addiction to luxury and glitter, his misuse of the musical medium, the false liberation his music brings, its author's desire to submit the audience to his will, and his vanity. By 1878 Nietzsche's private thoughts were already framing a critique of Wagner alongside Schopenhauer on a much broader scale. Out of it his own world view was taking shape. With their embodiment of the relentless 'will', 'the creaturely life which enjoys wildly, gluts itself on excess and longs for metamorphosis', these truth-seekers and overthrowers of convention and morality offered an intoxicating vision of life which might entrance but would never lead to a this-wordly, healthy, Greek kind of happiness. Nietzsche appropriately called the book in which he took his mentors to task *Human, All Too Human*. It attacked them and his earlier self. The task of a more mature Nietzsche had meanwhile become clearer:

> Neither to suffer so intensely from life, nor to live in such a flat and emotionally deficient way, that Wagner's art would be needed as medicine.[14]

Nietzsche was aware of the personal motivation in his post-Wagner cultural vision, and it made him value his opposition to Wagner all the more highly. A sense of the over-fullness of life – his own intensity – first led him to the composer, of whom he said no man better embodied the fullness of life. Equally the emotional uneventfulness of his life drove him towards Wagner's music. But once he became aware of 'what had here become creative' – an addiction to emotional excess, some might say – he didn't want to solve his problems this way, by administering the Wagnerian drug.[15] Nietzsche was already hampered by illness and Wagner undermined his efforts to grasp life firmly. So he removed himself from his orbit, defying the ambitions of most of musical Europe which wanted an introduction to the master. The social wrench cost him pain but he never feared harbouring 'untimely reflections'. On the deepest level there was a component in Nietzsche's psychosexual nature which dreamt of wide-awake unfettered physical celebration of life yet always demanded that the real Nietzsche live soberly on well-disciplined nerves. To make that contradiction productive in intellectual and artistic terms he had to step back.

This is the theory, and the projection of a self beyond Wagner, that Nietzsche envisaged. But in personal terms the whole Romantic tradition remained then, after Wagner had gone, a kind of personal tragedy, powering him on to imagine a less vulnerable, less inward kind of art and life, and needing to invent a suitable new music.

A good part of *The Wagner Case* is funny, deriding the postures of the Wagnerian stage in a rather pure, unvengeful way, so that Nietzsche was right later to comment that his attack was not shabbily motivated. Nietzsche shows rather his own acute desire not to be manipulated and a fierce intellectual honesty in settling accounts with himself. But he was concerned at Wagner's immense popularity because Wagner was a pseudo-saviour. He hated to feel that the one he knew from their Tribschen days to be egotistical and manipulative equally tried to dominate his audiences through hypnosis, intoxication and nervous excitement. It disgusted Nietzsche's individualism and his aesthetic purity, the way Wagner created a religious following for himself, playing on a mixture of romantic and German patriotic sentiment. Not 'Redemption for the Redeemer', Nietzsche now corrected Wagner's graveside mourners in *The Wagner Case*, but 'Redemption from the Redeemer' was what was required.[16]

Yet, oh gods in heaven protect him, he still fell at Wagner's feet with barely qualified admiration H have bracketed one word here in the first line and removed a sentence about audience manipulation to make this passage read as the highest praise:

> To repeat, Wagner is admirable and lovable [only] in his invention of the smallest things, in his poeticization of detail here one is thoroughly justified in proclaiming him a master of the first rank and as our greatest miniaturist in music, who packs the smallest space with an infinity of sensuality and sweetness. His wealth of colours, of semi-tones, of the secrets of fading light is so tempting that afterwards almost all other musicians appear too robust [...] Wagner [...] sets aside small rare delights; [he is] our great musical melancholic, full of glances, caresses, and words of comfort which no one ever produced before him, the master in musical sound of a heavyhearted and somnolent happiness . . . A lexicon of Wagner's most intimate words, nothing more than short phrases of five to fifteen bars, pure music that no one knows . . . Wagner has the virtue of the decadent, compassion [*das Mitleilen*] —

The final omissions in this passage are Nietzsche's, signalling his emotion.[17]

Nietzsche's last meeting with Wagner took place in Sorrento and there he wrote the first book of *Human, All Too Human*. Always with Nietzsche one has a sense of urgent emotional need driving him to creativity. It was like writing himself a set of resolutions. He would never again pursue first and last things, but rather be a free spirit; he would throw off the great deception of religion, would spurn great deceivers among men who pretend to bring answers, would accept the absence of a benevolent divinity. The outlook for art under these conditions, however, was poor; it might even disappear.[18]

In Sorrento in the autumn of 1876 Wagner, working on the libretto of *Parsifal*, had told Nietzsche of his growing Catholicism and desire to preach compassion. Nietzsche was left speechless. Wagner disdained to read *Human, All Too Human*, while Nietzsche retired, saying he wished the world to leave him alone. Each proud genius went away grumbling over the insult of the other's creativity.

Eight years later in a new Preface to *Human, All Too Human* Nietzsche conceded how hard he struggled to overcome the Wagner influence. It helped to imagine himself like Siegfried leaving the wicked guardian Mime, who would have killed him and the hope he signified of a regenerated humanity. Nietzsche had Siegfried's need to forge himself a new sword and an 'anvil-beating desire to wander into the wide and unknown world'. Nietzsche's prose in this passage is particularly strong and lyrical, its music conveying the dominant theme in the Nietzsche drama, both on stage in his books and off stage in his heart. His need to overcome Wagner transcended his own plight and needed to be put on show, like a Dionysian or a Wagnerian spectacle, that was, in the finest mythological terms, the best the modern stage could offer. *Thus Spake Zarathustra* was the opera in prose intended to do that job. Though I still think our most immediate sense of Nietzsche's personal tragedy comes from juxtaposing fragments of his solitary, suffering life with fragments of ecstatic Wagner.[19]

4

THE SPIRIT OF MUSIC AND THE
MAKING OF NIETZSCHE

Having read the reviews and declared Turin *tutto Carmenizzato*,
Nietzsche began writing *The Wagner Case* more than a week
before he finally went to hear the <u>other</u> opera himself for the
twentieth time. The sudden triumph of having found a form for
his long-standing Wagner thoughts meant there was no great
hurry actually to hear Bizet's work again.[1]

As for the writing, after completing *The Genealogy of Morals* the
previous July he had waited patiently for the impulse to begin
something new. Short of money and without friends in Turin, he
had little to do except wander and think and eat and monitor his
bodily and mental states. On the other hand being sure of himself
he did not find patience and even emptiness hard to bear. As he
said in *The Science of Joy*, unlike most people he did not work for
money, but for pleasure, therefore he was less afraid of boredom
than of work without interest: 'For the thinker and all sensitive
spirits boredom is that unpleasant lull in the soul which precedes a
successful voyage with cheerful winds; he must bear it, he must
wait within himself for it to take effect – this is just what lesser
natures cannot demand of themselves!'

Nietzsche the epicurean was proud of the control he had over
the plainest of days. Maximum unhappiness might be regarded as
positively bearable provided it allowed that rarity, the maximum
of happiness, occasionally to come by; from which conviction
came his deep pessimism against prevailing scientific positivism

and his dislike of theories of material progress. He made the political comparison to illuminate all the ramifications of his chosen way of life. Socialists were latter-day stoics who wished to avoid extremes, he declared. By contrast Nietzsche, bringing the passionate troubadour spirit back into the modern world, invited science and philosophy to inflict real wounds. Only then would follow, out of pain, the highest quality of human experience. So, from the depths of his philosophical and artistic convictions, he was content to wait, to be bored, to endure his solitude: an example, one might say, to all those tempted to look for solutions to happiness outside themselves.[2]

In Turin the proximity of the Alps brought cooling currents to temper the already growing heat of the sun. Letters from Brandes about the progress of his Copenhagen lectures suggested that a favourable wind from the north was also making Nietzsche feel well. That breeze became positively African for him with the reported success of *Carmen*, such a thoroughly unWagnerian work. So fond of fresh air as reality and as a metaphor, he sat at his desk and plunged into his most productive spring in memory.

He set a photograph of the musicologist and Wagner-admirer Carl Fuchs on his desk, just I suppose to remind himself that he had other gods now than Wagner, and in other ways too he set about trying to deceive himself. *The Wagner Case* on one level concerns how he couldn't get away from an old love, and derives its strength from thwarted effort, the subconscious viciously undermining consciousness's bold, ego-led campaign.

It was part of that absurd effort at self-deception, and therefore seems like an elaborate joke that Ariadne's role in heading Nietzsche out of the Wagner maze fell in the first instance to so popular, lightweight and charming a work as Bizet's *Carmen*. Nevertheless Nietzsche, who admitted his essay was 'a relief', 'an operetta' and 'something very amusing', felt it that way.[3] *Carmen* made him happy. Bizet's depiction of love, unlike Wagner's, was natural, naturally violent, painful but not requiring higher explanation. The effect of this buoyant music was liberating, not enslaving. Thus Bizet provided the perfect relief from his obsession and at the same time suggested a possible way forward for the human spirit. The French composer whose final opera had failed in Paris but taken Vienna by storm offered a different kind of music, a different vision of love. The whole cultural future of mankind indeed looked different if one contrasted Bizet with Wagner.

This music strikes me as perfect. It moves lightly, with suppleness and politeness. It is lovable, it doesn't sweat. 'What is good is light, everything divine runs on delicate feet' – this is the first proposition of my aesthetics. This music is wicked, clever, fatalistic [. . .], it is rich, precise. It builds, organizes and is finished; thereby it contrasts with that polyp of music, the 'unending melody' [. . .] Its cheerfulness is African [. . .] I envy Bizet his courage for this way of being, for which the cultivated music of Europe has as yet no language – for something more southern, browner, a more sunburnt outlook [. . .] Finally comes love, love which has been put back in its place in nature . . .[4]

Bizet's south suggested the renewed beauty, self-assurance and resilience Nietzsche the neo-Greek craved. He had already invented it as an aesthetic ideal for himself in *The Science of Joy* and Bizet at last brought an echo. The willed lightness of being offered a better way of coping with the dreadful human condition than the heavy Nordic pessimism of Wagner. He put it like this towards the end of *The Wagner Case*:

What we Halcyons miss in Wagner – *la gaya scienza*; light feet; humour, fire and grace; bold logic; the dance of the stars; an exuberant spirituality; the tremor of southern light; the smooth sea – perfection.[5]

This was Nietzsche's credo, to be found variously voiced in all the later books. 'Dance' expressed that vision of light, sunshine, mountain altitude, pleasure in nature, intellectual flexibility and serenity, endless calm joy, which Wagner's music failed now to give him. Nietzsche wanted sunshine, the south, the Mediterranean. There was a constant desire in him for the clarity of a summer's day, away from the fog and mist of northern weather and thoughts. He loved the south, music which would sustain him and give him the light of the Riviera and the gaiety of troubadour Provence.[6]

The pursuit of an aesthetic to match this vision became the dominant theme of his post-Wagnerian work, sounding out in major chords and bold dissonances of the kind Richard Strauss used to set *Thus Spake Zarathustra* to music. He never produced his own music to match this vision, but achieved a fine parallel in the *Zarathustra* books written in the wake of Wagner's death.

It's important to understand why Nietzsche chose to express his philosophical ideas by writing so much about music and about Wagner. Like Schopenhauer he regarded it as the summit of artistic expression. It was absolute art, and though it could have a real content, the nature of that content was open to dispute. One of his main complaints against Wagner was that the creator of *The Ring*, the story of a once rich and glamorous family in crisis, introduced too much that was theatrical and novelettish into music. Equally *Tristan* could take its legitimate place among the great nineteenth-century novels of adultery. Music should be pure. Or should it? Nietzsche, who even found an extraneous content in Brahms (music for frustrated women) and heaped a symbolic content upon Bizet, was no more consistent and consequential than the entire German nineteenth-century debate into what was or wasn't absolute music. Wagner himself, at least in the period Nietzsche knew him, did one thing (wrote supreme music) whilst saying he did another (gave the words it set equal moment). There was therefore a demanding topical reason why a writer and philosopher should concern himself with music and musical literature.[7]

The other reason was deeply personal. Music had been a joy in Nietzsche's life since he was a boy, and it was natural for him to see his own development and enthusiasms reflected in musical terms and in the history of music. Until his late teens, having inherited his father's skills at the piano and won a little local fame for his virtuoso improvisations, he still thought of making music his career. There had been family renderings of Haydn in the parlour, when his father played, and after Carl Ludwig's death the tradition was well enough continued by the rest of the musical family. His aunt Rosalie gave her nephew piano reductions of twelve Haydn symphonies for his twelfth birthday. He attended concerts in Naumberg and by the time he was fourteen had formed a club at school for the appreciation of the arts, foremost among them music. In this setting he first encountered Wagner's music, in the form of the piano transcription of *Tristan*. Here ended a curious period when he had limited his taste to music his father had liked and refused to countenance anything new, namely, at the time, Berlioz and Liszt. Wagner was the first of his adult tastes.[8]

To bring both strands of Nietzsche's mature musical life together again then: he both loved music and as soon as he began to read philosophy knew why he did: it was so very close to the essence of his being, the Schopenhauerian will. Consequently music gives us our greatest insight into Nietzsche's nature. Freud saw too few clues extant to Nietzsche's sexuality partly because he was afraid to read him, partly because the founding father of psychoanalysis was notoriously indifferent to music.

Giving music up for a year to concentrate on philology as a first-year student in Bonn, Nietzsche conducted an unwitting experiment on the form that Schopenhauerian will took in him. The deprivation of music was powerfully physical, no doubt intensified by his arrival at sexual maturity. He took to redoubled long walks to dissipate his surplus energy, when he surely recognized in music the power to express not only romantic and sexual love, but also love of the world. Fifty years later in *Das Unbehagen in der Kultur* (a more intimate title suggesting 'What makes us uncomfortable about culture' than the familiar English *Civilization and its Discontents* conveys) Freud would write that we unconsciously redirect or sublimate the immediate satisfaction of our physical being, the libidinous drive, to create the higher satisfactions of culture. It is as humanly important to understand the broad and creative nature of our sexuality as it is to grasp that neither Freud, nor Nietzsche saw anything undesirable about the power of 'sublimation' which became apparent to Nietzsche in his early Schopenhauerian student days. It's a simple idea, that if you want to lead a cultivated existence, flowers are better than weeds, flowers encouraged to grow in some order, rather than weeds growing at random. Only some people are extreme when they discover that choice, like Nietzsche, hence his year of self-deprivation.[9]

Paul Deussen recounted, in a story Nietzsche told him when they were fellow students in Bonn, how at the end of that year Nietzsche visited a brothel in Cologne. The story has since fascinated many Nietzsche interpreters, though to my mind they have failed to see Nietzsche's creative imagination at work in its telling. In an unfamiliar town, he had asked a local guide to take him to a restaurant and found himself elsewhere. 'I suddenly saw myself surrounded by half a dozen apparitions in sequins and gauze, who looked at me expectantly. I stood there for a while speechless. Then I went instinctively to the piano as the only soulful being in this company and played a few chords. They unlocked the paralysis and I got out into the open.'[10]

I suggest Nietzsche told this story perfectly to illustrate Schopenhauer's theory that art and above all music compensated a man for the base instinctual life in which he was caught up by virtue of his individual will. Whether the young Nietzsche had sexual intercourse or not on this occasion (later association with prostitutes was certainly his only experience of women), he couldn't cope emotionally and fled back to music. His behaviour and/or his story masking it reinforce my impression that he was in love with passion but afraid of its physical expression. This was the whole problem of his relationship to Wagner's music, turning on his fear of loss of control.[11]

Through his very love of music then becomes visible to us a cultivated and civilized young man, too restrained and uncomfortable with women for his future good, and yet also intellectually and physically passionate. The way moral imperatives crowded in on him as a young man he resembles those extreme near-virginal protagonists in Tolstoy, Pierre Bezukhov in *War and Peace* and Konstantin Levin in *Anna Karenina*. Nietzsche also reminds me of the intense Russian literary critic Vissarion Belinsky, who spent much of his time reading German Idealism a generation before. Belinsky told how for several years Schiller's moral idealism addicted him to graceful abstinence for the body and dignity for the soul. He also related how, when for compelling ideological reasons he gave up Schiller for Hegel, he went straight to a brothel. With Nietzsche we are talking about a man hugely influenced in all aspects of his life by ideas on the page. The degree to which his frustrated sexuality was caught up and expressed through his love of music can also only emphasize the torment Wagner caused him, because – the very opposite of what Elisabeth contended – his sexuality was hardly weak. Underscoring the intensity, Wagner spoke of music conducting Nietzsche, and Nietzsche concurred.[12]

He liked to play the piano, though he did so less when his health and particularly his eyesight worsened in the early 1870s. When he played for Wagner, Wagner paid him the dubious compliment of saying he was too good. Schoolfriend Gersdorff believed Beethoven could not have played more movingly.[13] Nietzsche also composed intermittently throughout his life, though increasingly with a sense of inferiority he would not admit to himself. Still in 1888 he was pursuing success for his compositions. Brahms offered no comment on 'The Hymn to Life'. Hans von Bülow called the early 'Manfred Meditation' a crime. Wagner even told Nietzsche he was a failed musician, to which Nietzsche, wounded, replied: 'And you are a failed philologist!' Most tellingly both Wagner and the otherwise blindly loyal Köselitz found Nietzsche's music too ecclesiastical, '*kirchlich*'. Once again surfaced unconsciously that religious–idealistic background he struggled to overcome.[14]

He couldn't accept musical failure. From Turin there he was

still sending off the uncharming score of *The Hymn to Life* to Brandes, his latest saviour, in the hope of a Copenhagen premiere. Yet he did realize. He was embarrassed to succumb to temptation. His letter of 4 May to the Danish professor contained a disingenuous little rider: 'We philosophers are grateful for nothing more than when we are confused with artists.' Two weeks later he offered a new variation to Köselitz of his old admission of folly: he lacked a sufficiently powerful musical idiom in which to express himself.

What he had instead of course was a wonderful musical way with words. In that sense he was a musician. In that sense he did fulfill his desire to make music the fundament of his creative life.

What, one can ask at any point in any of his books, would life be without its music, without music as a metaphor for the beyond-rational, and without music in itself as sublime tune-fulness? As with so much in Nietzsche the metaphysical value and the function of the thing in daily life are so intertwined that they sometimes leave the mind in a maze, while the heart knows exactly what he means. Music betokens the fullest and the most fearless life. It is the form towards which all the arts, and science and philosophy too, should tend in spirit, to capture but not to kill the life-force. Nietzsche found many ways of conveying this message, by calling on philosophy to study the shapes and colours and the appetites of the world at hand, rather than indulge in abstract and unvarying conjecture. One of his means was to doubt any pretensions to one truth. There was after all a kind of music of the personality which attracted perceptions into a particular key, let's say, here materialist, there Christian, all of which went under the grand title of 'thinking' but in truth was not at all objective or scientific. Nietzsche's greatest wish, as an artist, was that his written style should convey that kind of simultaneous 'musical' possibility. He wished through the musicality of his prose to convey the idea of a meaning that was open-ended and unfixed and many-fold. He hoped his style was a kind of dance, moving like Bizet's music on light feet, and leaping over the conceptual limits of words. In practice it is an uneven and often difficult style, and in the expressly poetic *Zarathustra* it can become almost too exaggerated and densely clotted. But its richness, its susceptibility to interpretation, is one of the reasons why we go on reading Nietzsche with so much pleasure a hundred years after his death. As the singer and conductor Dietrich Fischer-Dieskau pioneeringly observed, Wagner released in Nietzsche the verbal instrumentalist.[15]

Nietzsche drew from a great and revolutionary artist the clue to a new musical expression in words. In his later writing, particularly in *Zarathustra*, but also in *The Science of Joy* and *Beyond Good and Evil*, he was just what in *The Wagner Case* he perceived Wagner to be, a kind of miniaturist, deepening, backgrounding, opening up new dimensions behind a small surface experience, or name, or word. The style is evident in *Zarathustra* which like Wagner's operas introduces themes from the author's own life and reanimates friends in quasi-mythical situations. Its mass of life, to misconstrue the title of Delius's musical setting, is a mass of imagery, enriched with alliteration. It is the same Stabreim which Wagner imitated from German medieval poetry. The sound patterns of the prose poems are carefully worked. Leitmotifs link the various parts of the text. The whole book may be conceived like a Wagnerian music drama as a delicately woven orchestral carpet with a raised heroic pattern of action. In imagery too, *Zarathustra* is as richly endowed as *The Ring* in bird song, forest voices, caves, animals, dwarves, wanderers and sorcerers. Only the flesh-and-blood lovers are absent.[16]

Book I of *Zarathustra*, with its opening crowd scenes and its wandering lyrical hero, who passes from adventure to adventure singing of his heart's joys and losses as he goes, Nietzsche classified as a symphony. But he had elsewhere argued that symphonic form should underlie each opera act. The whole of the four-book *Zarathustra* has the feel of an opera. It is not Wagnerian, admittedly. Nietzsche made his point about the symphony against Wagner and clung to the aria and chorus form in preference to Wagnerian 'unending melody'. But so much of the musical background is drawn from Wagner and so much seems intended as an answer. Nietzsche's 'drama' has four parts corresponding to the four parts of *The Ring*. Wagner's *Ring* is about the death of the gods, Nietzsche's work is about the death of God. In Wagner love overcomes the inhuman greed of the gods, in Nietzsche self-love will help men overcome their human limitations. Proposition and response are spectacular: *Zarathustra* as an answer to *The Ring Cycle* or as an answer to Wagner *tout court*.[17]

Cosima narrowed the field. She saw in Zarathustra a direct challenge to the symbolic figure of Parsifal, whose barely disguised Christian message enraged Nietzsche. She understood the element of competition, but read too narrowly. *Zarathustra* was more broadly aimed.

It needs to be stated quite plainly: as much as Bizet, Nietzsche set *himself* up as Wagner's competitor, and in more ways than he could control. Wagner and his music became the principle leitmotifs in the score of Nietzsche's life while the prose came closer and closer to music.[18] The idea was to write philosophy which through its internal music never lost contact with the irrational in man, whilst trying to make some order out of life. Later Nietzsche agreed with Rohde that he could have written *The Birth of Tragedy*, which first announced this message, in a more poetic form, better suited to his 'inner music and philosophy'.[19] All he needed was time. In *The Science of Joy* and *Zarathustra*, where the new stylist broke through in triumph, he consciously worked on the sounds and the phrasing beside the meaning, and finally called himself a poet.

Of course there were sources for Nietzsche's musical prose besides Wagner. Some lay deep in his own musical being. From his youth came that family music-making, concerts, church songs and the Lutheran Bible. Nor did he ever forget the pulpit oratory which was the aesthetic legacy of being born to three generations of churchmen. Later, as a student, he began to read classical poetry aloud, which made him appreciate the importance of correct breathing. 'Wagner once said I write Latin, not German,' he told the Wagner acolyte Heinrich von Stein in 1882. The comparison was another point in favour of the Latin Renaissance against the German Reformation, but Nietzsche was not just making a point. He loved the classical literary languages, having written his thesis on the elegaic poet Theognis.

To Nietzsche himself by 1884, when the last book of *Zarathustra* was completed, the style was dance and dance had the philosophical advantage of being plodding reason's chief opponent:

> My style is a dance; it plays with all kinds of symmetries then leaps over them and mocks them! That is true right down to the choice of vowels [. . .] I have incidentally remained a poet to the end whichever way the term is defined . . .[20]

The musicality of Nietzsche's prose is confirmed by the musical attention writers and composers have brought to it, as a mystery, as a source of fascination and as something they wish to understand and translate into their own musical medium. Fischer-Dieskau, because 'the Dionysian was . . . closer to their creative aims than the conceptual world of the philologist, moralist and biologist', holds that it was musicians who first properly understood Nietzsche's work.[21]

5

THE FUTURE OF ART: THE CASE
AGAINST WAGNER

The case *against* Wagner is a summit meeting on aesthetics with only one party, Nietzsche, present to argue. Wagner's music and its issue for posterity are coerced passively to represent the other side. On one level, as two men of genius, or one and a ghost, sup in an atmosphere of dependence, pride and lost love, a contest takes place between two types of music, as if Nietzsche were staging his own *Meistersinger*. On another, through Nietzsche's interpretation of these two 'songs', the whole future of European art is called to account. The essay has often been scantily or wrongly read, as if it were a paeon to Bizet in the years his popular music took Europe by storm, and audiences were recoiling from the Wagner onslaught. The main philosophical point about *The Wagner Case* was that Wagner represented a modernity – decadence – which Nietzsche believed the whole of Western mankind had to overcome. To what end? Where were art and civilization moving? Those questions, in the words of the subtitle, formed 'A Musician's Problem'. Nietzsche could see a battle of great general ideas taking place in contemporary music. And if one believes that music after Wagner mirrored the whole fate of Western culture, with the collapse of benevolent certainties, the emergence of an edgy, rootless spirit in the artistic post-Wagnerian inheritance of Mahler and Schoenberg, and the eventual emergence of a hypnotic and instinctual popular music, then clearly Nietzsche was right.[1]

68

The debate on aesthetics, and following from it the debate on morality and on happiness, took shape in Nietzsche's mind with the genesis of *The Birth of Tragedy*. It continued through the Tribschen-Bayreuth years and lasted for Nietzsche's creative lifetime. Nietzsche, the lesser creator, was the more perspicacious critic. He knew the importance of his relationship with Wagner: that it was a piece of cultural history in the making, because of the way, out of their two giant personalities, emerged two distinctly antagonistic approaches to art and quite different roles for the artist. When it came to the middle of his life the need to set down that relationship for posterity took precedence over all other tasks. It wasn't a conscious, premeditated wish to write a particular work, and in 1887 what Nietzsche had to say about Wagner became part of *The Genealogy of Morals*. *Beyond Good and Evil* the previous year had spelt out an ideal for the music of the future, that it should be beyond-European, beyond-good-and-evil and beyond-German. *Genealogy* explored the sexual psychology of Wagner's art in the context of a politically sinister German fascination with asceticism and mystical delivery from its tortures. But only Bizet and *Carmen* gave Nietzsche the contrapuntal form he needed to write an essay generally on music and culture, interweaving all those threads spun before, and all his personal feelings about Wagner.[2]

Nietzsche understood more about tragedy – the problem of the irrational and endlessly painful in human life – and more about self-reliance because of his broken ideal friendship with Wagner. But how could the world benefit equally? How could it be made to understand that Wagner's art was weakening and actually led away from the tragic outlook the decadent modern age so desperately lacked? The answer was for Nietzsche to define modern insufficiency. So the Foreword to *The Wagner Case* began:

To turn my back on Wagner was my fate; ever to love anything again afterwards was my victory. No one had become more dangerously entangled with the Wagner business, no one defended himself harder against it, no one was happier to be free of it. A long story! – Is there one word for it? – Were I a moralist, who knows what I would call it! Perhaps self-mastery. But a philosopher doesn't like moralists [. . .] I am as much as Wagner [. . .] a decadent: only I understood that and defended myself against it. The philosopher in me defended himself against it.

Nietzsche's thoughts on modern culture, on the need to move out of the nineteenth century with gravity and energy, and not into new deceptions and weakness, framed the topical pro-Bizet, anti-Wagner polemic, with the intention *ridendo dicere severum*.

Extrapolating from his duel with Wagner, his thoughts on Greek life and modernity, and his comparison of the Renaissance with the Reformation, Nietzsche suggested the history of mankind oscillated between poles of health and decadence. Either life was in the ascendant, with art saying yes to the material world and the present moment, or it was declining, concentrating on God and Beyond and Selflessness and rejecting the world of instinct. One of his philosophical objections to Wagner was that the one he called a magician and a rattlesnake and a theatre-monger fudged the two, tricking his audience with old decadence dressed up as a new salvation. To Nietzsche's mind the opposite was true. Cultivated humanity would probably only survive if in future art reflected and encouraged healthier feelings of independence, strength and well-being in its audience, rather than those emotions to be found in late Wagner, where the element of extreme sublimation resulted in self-torture and enslavement.[3] Nietzsche did not state the argument directly in political terms, but there were obvious implications for the politics of culture and political life itself. We might think of Goebbels' love of such film music as would inspire love for the Fatherland and the whole phenomenon of art pressed into the service of twentieth-century totalitarian regimes. No thinker could have been more alive to the danger of mass intoxication and the collapse of individual responsibility than that Nietzsche who was once absurdly taken for a Nazi.[4]

Health, a healthy society, a healthy psyche, healthy art: because of precisely that Nazi corruption of ideas we have come to regard these terms as suspect, being the cover for a scheme to level and control society. But Nietzsche's concern with purity: purity of artistic intent, purity of artistic response was of an ancient and more solid order.

The question of purity deeply concerned Plato, as it has concerned artists suspicious of art, musicians suspicious of music, philosophers suspicious of words, ever since. It is one of the most interesting and appealing aspects of Nietzsche, linked to his own desire that his writing should not be misunderstood or misappropriated.[5]

Everything that has ever grown out of the soil of impoverished life, the whole counterfeit industry of transcendence and the Beyond, has found its most sublime spokesman in Wagner's art − not in formulae: Wagner is too clever for formulae − but in the persuasiveness of sensuality, which for its part makes the mind rotten and tired. Music as Circe . . . His last work was in this respect his greatest achievement. *Parsifal* will maintain its rank eternally in the art of seduction, as a work of genius in its seductiveness . . . I admire this work; I would like to have written it myself, in the absence of which I understand it . . .[6]

What is behind Nietzsche's ostensible puritanism here? It seems the rebel country pastor's son baulked at Wagner's pretensions to Christian religion. Wagner trivialized the idea of redemption by staging it thus for the modern world, with a whiff of quasi-Catholic incense and a lot of humbug about emasculated purity. Nietzsche staked his own notion of purity against Wagner's, in other words. This was the same Nietzsche who fourteen years earlier had taken to task the popular Christian apologist, David Strauss, for denying the Resurrection and, with his relentless anthropomorphizing, denying the Christian mysteries. Nietzsche, the Anti-Christian, about to write a book

71

with that title, was at heart deeply concerned at any travesty he perceived of the faith he knew as a child.[7]

Another far-reaching example *The Wagner Case* provides of Nietzsche's pursuit comes with the quest for a future art form which will be the psychological antithesis of Romanticism. Nietzsche envisaged a form of art which would encourage non-decadent feelings and not manipulate its audience. In a healthy psyche deep cravings were neither repressed nor disguised unknowingly. Most desirable were an art and culture which supported such insight and self-mastery. Nietzsche encouraged the kind of psychic health which would guard against political despotisms and religious manias for ever: resilience and individuality. These qualities of the *Übermensch* were required in the wake of the death of God. What else would protect the best in mankind? Nietzsche advocated neither the crass positivism, nor the simple-minded materialism which were seizing the public imagination of his day in the forms of popular Darwinism and Marxist dialectics. Human beings could be spiritual without worshipping either God or progress.[8]

Actually Nietzsche did not get far, saying or showing what that art might be. Bizet's *Carmen* was more a token than an example, corresponding to the psychologically healthier world of *Übermenschen*. There was the rub. Could the summit meeting on aesthetics downgrade the whole business of art? Nietzsche's burning concern with self-transcendence for all men, like Plato's for the secure state and the non–contamination of reason, drove him to deal with art itself as a secondary matter. In preferring a lesser artist over a great one, for psychological reasons, he made a philosophical decision which tormented him as an artist. That torment is a subcurrent of *The Wagner Case* and a remarkable sign of the crisis to come in Western cultural history.

Nietzsche declared in *The Science of Joy* that a careless mankind had murdered God. That was the nature of the modern. In the operatic creation that was *Zarathustra*, a wandering madman was to tell this epic event to the people. After the death of God men had to be stronger, more self-reliant, less self-destructive than

Christian idealism had left them. They had to accept the fact that God was dead as a tragedy, which acceptance in the Greek sense would be a meaningful and strengthening social rite. Zarathustra told them so. Nietzsche produced a beautiful argument in pictures, but as a work of art *Thus Spake Zarathustra* did not live like Wagner's music. Its tone was critical, non-involving.

Plato was wont to say tragedy in real life is not necessary, if only people will listen to me. Nietzsche by the middle of his career came to say in a more strident, less confident modern key: 'Live dangerously! Love fate! It's true we don't have the confidence of the tragic Greeks, but we can still strive in their direction and reject what we are. Man is the creature who must constantly overcome himself to live fully.' In the end Nietzsche's writing points, even occasionally explicitly, to only one way out, the gradual withering away of grand high art, the Romantics' ultimate repository of meaning, in tandem with the growing practice by individuals, artists or not, of the art of life.[9]

The artistically reshaped man would finally achieve that blend of the Apollonian and Dionysian elements in himself, the merger of individual dream and collective frenzy, of proud form and acknowledged chaos, which Wagner's young friend had first seen to be the way forward, and which he was still searching in vain to find reflected in an ideal art form. The problem of that form was that, as raw material, only man himself would do, creating his own life out of his imaginative resources. With Nietzsche not only philosophy but also aesthetics were passing over into psychology.

The impulse might be seen as an aesthetic formulation of Feuerbach's social vision. For centuries men had worshipped art to the extent that they had allowed it control over their emotions. Now man was taking back into himself that energy of aesthetic and emotional attentiveness given to a power outside. As for the withering away of art when all men become creators of their own lives, I have deliberately construed Nietzsche's ideal of the *Übermensch* here in terms reminiscent of early Marxism: the idea that as men matured *politically* the state would wither away.

Nietzsche's concern was for aesthetics and psychology. Nevertheless this was the ideological climate in which Nietzsche grew up, of 1840s Young Hegelianism and after.

Over Nietzsche the warrior philosopher who decried Wagner and over Plato the despotic philosopher who 'banished the artists' there has been so much misunderstanding. Both comprehended with exceptional clarity the power of imagination and art. But what they wanted as philosophers for the people lay beyond art; and they were prepared in theory at least to sacrifice art to that goal. *They* remained artists. Who was there to censure them? But as philosophers they preferred to encourage men in the direction of the art of life: that people might know how, out of the inner struggles that are human, all too human, out of inchoate, unreliable emotion, they could fashion a good and satisfying life.[10]

Socrates expressed for Nietzsche the ambivalence of the Platonic position. Nietzsche's own contradictoriness welled up every time he heard Wagner.[11] That was the *personal* problem, the one he wanted us to laugh over while he talked on, of serious things. Nietzsche disapproved of Wagner's apparently pseudo-Christian goal of Redemption, because he did not want art to make its audience feel the easy delivery of the passions was possible; art should not leave its connoisseurs in a stupor of emotional and physical satisfaction. But he was deeply moved by the emotional intensity of Wagner's suffering men and women. He attacked the moral influences of Wagner's art, and its power to move masses through an appeal to instinct, but he hallowed the deep substance of the dramas embodied in the most delicate music. Just as Socrates, who had spent his whole life defending rationality, parted from it as if finally throwing off a sickness he had been compelled to disguise, so Nietzsche pretended or hoped music could be not 'sick', while Wagner kept persuading him to give up the ghost and admit with his dying breath what he really knew.

We tend not to take art's responsibilities so seriously today, but more recently we have been alive to the moral problems of science. In his condemnation of Wagner and of decadence generally Nietzsche was like a scientist refusing to extend or apply his research, out of concern for the moral consequences to mankind. This was the sense in which he attacked the compassion for human nature of which Wagner was a master, and used the word decadent to describe the whole Romantic–Nationalist age which culminated in Wagner. Decadent culture could be magnificent, the term did not signify lack of quality. But the problem was that under its leadership mankind would simply run out of energy and individuals would fail to find their own tragic strength. Nietzsche was generalizing from his own experience, as he made clear in *The Wagner Case*, but he believed that experience to be typical. He felt his vitality drained when he listened to Wagner. Indeed he felt drunk. If he was to survive and create, the philosopher in him had to achieve supremacy over the wounded, erring human creature, so immobilized by the music of the heart. So the *Übermensch* arose. The *Übermensch* was proof of the great ingenuity Nietzsche mustered to heave himself and Europe out of the nineteenth century. He was a kind of Platonic guardian whose duty was only to educate himself, and certainly not to pity others.

As early as 1884 Nietzsche grasped the ramifications of his Wagner criticism. He pointed out to Carl Fuchs in a long musical letter that decadence described the age they lived in and included himself. It was not in itself a negative phenomenon. But compared with earlier ages it meant a radical shift of cultural emphasis onto the individual at the expense of the whole; it precluded classical simplicity and openly invited the modern obsession with ambiguity.

The decadent Nietzsche hated his own ambiguity. He hated being stuck in himself. He also longed for his problems to have a communal form, where he could share them publicly. As more and more communal celebrations disappear today we can surely sympathize with his message. Without the church we lack ceremonies for birth, marriage and death; without marriage we lack ceremonies for love. The communality of the electronic media, of global entertainment and of fashion are no more than a passive togetherness.

Forgive me; what I think I am apprehending is a change in perspective: the individual is seen hr too sharply, the whole is far too undefined, moreover the will to this view in music exists, and above all the talent exists to bring it off. But it is decadence, a word which of course, as we understand it, is intended to describe, not to condemn [. . .], I mean, even decadence has inumerable things about it which are highly attractive, valuable, new and worthy of respect – our modern music for example [. . .] Forgive me if I add something else though: what the taste for decadence is furthest removed from is the grand style: this is the style to which, for example, the Pitti Palace [in Florence] belongs, but not the Ninth Symphony [of Beethoven].[12]

Nietzsche here anticipated the view that seems clear to us today of 'the fall of public man ' from the late eighteenth century, of the loss of a Roman concern with *res publica* after the advent of the French Revolution, and of a corresponding rise in preoccupations with the sincerity of the heart. It is curious to hear an echo of this thesis in his branding Wagner 'the most impolite of composers' in *The Wagner Case*, in contrast to his endorsement in *The Science of Joy* of Stendhal's view of Mozart as 'the most polite'. With the Palazzo Pitti and Beethoven's Ninth he went on to refer to Wagner's 1870 essay on Beethoven in which the 'Cagliostro of modernity' saw himself as Beethoven's direct successor, leading mankind into a new democratic and liberated golden age. Nietzsche saw Wagner as more likely presaging a future cultural vacuum. Without a more socially galvanizing notion of beauty and a more invigorating ideal of happiness than Romantic art, the cultural world would simply collapse.

As a spearhead for cultural renewal Nietzsche might have invented Bizet, but lo! he already existed. With the assumed 'Spanishness' of his highly successful opera he represented one way in which European music was already trying to free itself from Wagner by looking to the Latin and Slav and Scandinavian worlds for new inspiration. Yet strategically Bizet could have been replaced by any composer Nietzsche enjoyed who was untouched by Wagner. Nietzsche wanted only some kind of music to lead the modern heart back, or on, to a sunnier, more open ideal for art and humanity, and to give him the chance to restate his goal. The pagan, neo-Renaissance art of the future would shine with a bright light. It would be musical, but not hypnotic; it would be metaphorical rather than theatrical; it would strengthen not sap its audience's grip on life.

Nietzsche's physiology played its part in determining this vision because *Carmen* made him feel 'cheerful'. His tight physical make-up demanded from art a release from tension not an excitation of it.[13] Haydn, and Rossini, to whom in *The Wagner Case* he attributed 'overflowing animality', had provided such a joyful outlet in the past, and now Bizet joined their ranks. Curiously Nietzsche detected in his own taste an explicit craving for the popular, the non-inward, the ordinary, and perhaps that most encouraged him to believe the way forward led away from intellectual complexity. He did respond to Bizet with genuine enthusiasm, of course, but on what level? The analogy may be too trivial for some tastes, but I suggest he loved Bizet the same way as Wittgenstein loved cinema Westerns. There are so many pointers in *The Wagner Case* making clear that to compare Wagner and Bizet was not to compare equals; that Nietzsche's adoption of Bizet was strategic and rather amusing, given the deep seriousness of his quarrel with Wagner. On the comparison with Wittgenstein then: here in both cases was a simple, active, temporary way out of the self for the highly strung modern genius obsessed with the problem of expression. Except, heaven knows, it was confusing for Nietzsche to write the way he did, rather as if Wittgenstein had suggested all philosophers should become cinema ushers instead.

To see one's own case as universal is either genius or madness. In Nietzsche's it seems to have been genius contained in a brilliant grasp of what the nineteenth century lacked. We can see now how much late nineteenth-century music was with him in his struggle to wrest himself free of Wagner's over-abundant, shocking harmonies. Western music had been pushed to the brink of traditional possibility. All the imminent leading composers from Bruckner to Mahler, Richard Strauss to Schoenberg to Debussy had to confront Wagner's unprecedented lush chromaticism before they could find a language of their own. It was too overwhelming, too exhaustive of the possibilities of the major-minor system for new composers not to fall initially into helpless imitation, but they were determined to escape the straitjacket. The effect of Wagner's music was also felt, particularly in France, as of a piece with the dominance of the Prussian Empire. Hence, three cheers for Bizet, a Frenchman with a quite different style!

Yet perhaps Wagner's dominance too would have to have been invented had it not existed, for all the arts were freeing themselves in pursuit of a new expressiveness. Nietzsche, whose Dionysian goals and poor health made him dream of Mexico and Spain, made much of the contrasting visual correlatives of Wagner and Bizet. *Carmen* brought on African skies, whereas Wotan was the god of bad weather, the deity of those rain-sodden clouds or swirling mists which hung over Bayreuth on Nietzsche's few unhappy visits. He made it sound amusingly personal, but we can see with hindsight Nietzsche was not alone in his time, searching to lose urban nervous tension and northern formality in a glorious blaze of colour and light and the simple life. We need look only at the history of painting. The same spring of 1888, when Nietzsche moved to Turin, Van Gogh arrived in Provence, having come south in search of the colour and light which would transform European art. Gauguin joined him a month later to live in the same aesthetic ambience as Nietzsche had enjoyed in Nice.

The questions would be asked in the two decades after Nietzsche's demise: how to move out of the nineteenth century. A great critic, he foresaw them. Where was music moving without the traditional major–minor system which had bound it to Christianity since the medieval era? Where was philosophy headed after the death of God? Concealed in the body of Nietzsche's work was the even more powerful suggestion that the cogitating subject, the infallible 'I' of Descartes, was probably not the key to understanding the truth of the world, a truth which would not be understood until philosophers could somehow elude the grammar of language. Meanwhile where should the poetry of love direct itself without the notion of the Holy Grail? Could it survive the language and insights of Freud, who took so many of his insights into the psychosexual life from Nietzsche himself?

Nietzsche foresaw that music at least would try to resolve these questions with stylization, secularism and a new deliberately narrowing rigour. Its projects would be small-scale. Intellect would dominate over the inevitable fragmentation of religious feeling and insist on cool objectivity and formal precision. Small-scale cerebral projects, however much emotion they still contain, are the mark of the atonal Schoenberg. Schoenberg's pupil Anton Webern used the 12 tone system to create the most condensed, ascetic music in history up to his day. Stravinsky's aesthetic was radically different from that of the Second Viennese School. But it was all the more a rejection of that Austro-German tradition in music, which, with Beethoven as its great inspiration, understood both life and music as a spiritual journey, whereby the individual would finally become himself. Nietzsche foresaw that if art failed to find a new language and new goals post-Wagner, then the danger was that art would give way to entertainment. It is roughly where music has arrived today, with relatively inaccessible modern forms on the one hand, and a mass of popular forms, the most extreme glorifying the brutal, on the other. All the arts are threatened by the values of mass entertainment.[14]

Occasionally musicologists have been tempted to see in Nietzsche's own Lieder a foretaste of modern music's rawness and despair in riding out the cusp between the centuries. Fischer-Dieskau detects features that anticipate Mahler and Webern and 'the coming discords' of the soon-to-be-shattered European world. Moods of defiance, seriousness, irony and caricature follow in quick succession. I remain unconvinced by the musical examples I have heard. But Nietzsche's mature philosophical style is undoubtedly related to modernist music and painting.

As in Schoenberg's atonal music, the highly condensed, aphoristic style makes no concession to the reader/listener who would skip through. From *The Science of Joy* onwards Nietzsche's writing is glancing, discontinuous, crammed with a diversity of swiftly changing moods, worthy of long consideration; it calls on intellect and imagination and ear but it never manipulates the nerves. It has the almost static quality to be found in some of Schoenberg's atonal orchestral pieces. Eliot's words in 'East Coker' come to mind: 'Neither from nor towards; at the still point, there the dance is,/But neither arrest nor movement.' Or one might compare Nietzsche's style to the experimental novel of the mid-twentieth century, for that same static quality, combined with a high degree of self-consciousness about the nature of reading and writing. The style also dips back to the seventeenth century and forward into the early twentieth with a pronounced neo-classicism. The stilted, intense quality of the prose in *Zarathustra* exists because Nietzsche is writing within the stylized, exaggerated province of classical tragedy. The prose is literally on stilts. The protagonist is without illusion, shies from nothing, is uncomforted, alone and self-reliant; he is noble and superior and never base; his heart is the action, while his language and the various masks he tries on are the chorus. Nietzsche sought a grand, high vision, far removed from the world of the common man which had begun to dominate literature in his day and would expand its realm unstoppably in the twentieth century. His language was as far removed from that of the novel as it is possible for artistic prose to be. Again in his fastidiousness Nietzsche recalls the short-form perfectionist in Schoenberg. And one final link between the two unhappy geniuses. Both longed against the odds to be understood. Schoenberg wanted nothing so much as to have people whistling his tunes. Both he and Nietzsche after a hundred years remain minority, so-called 'élitist', interests. Still they represent a landmark in modern sensibility. 'Some imagination, a certain measure of asceticism, a bit of intelligence, and finally a sensibility that will not blow away at the first breeze.'

When Pierre Boulez described it thus he surely had Nietzsche's ideas in mind.[15]

Eduard Munch painted Nietzsche in 1905–06 as a monumental troubled figure, drawing into his high knitted brow and deep, dark, hooded eyes all the tension from the surrounding landscape. The human body is simplified, the landscape dynamic, the colours vibrant. Munch used the same dynamic form and colour and almost identical background in the Nietzsche portrait as he did in his iconic modern canvas, *The Scream*. At the same time he laid mesmerizing emphasis on the hands of this village priest figure to remind us of Nietzsche's function as one who cared for other men's souls. A Seelsorger was the traditional Lutheran term Freud would use. It is a marvellous portrait because it tells us instantly what was the visual world into which Nietzsche's prose translated and how what was happening in fine art at the turn of the century was one with his cultural vision. Munch shows graphically how Nietzsche dwelt on the cusp of two ages, as Reformation idealism gave way to modern Godlessness, and what were the aesthetic compensations.[16]

Thus the same forces of southern colour and primitivism and dance as we find in Nietzsche's Dionysian *Heiterkeit* are graphically present in a painting such as Matisse's *The Dance*. They emphasize resonant nature and primitive life, singing and dancing. We can see them in the whole movement of painting from Degas's Spartan youths through Gauguin's stylized natives to the invitingly frenzied jungle life of Henri Douanier Rousseau. (Nietzsche himself used jungle imagery in *Zarathustra*.) By the same token as the most serious music of Mahler, explicitly prompted by Nietzsche, was courting the folksongs of *Des Knaben Wunderhorn*, painting was becoming 'simpler' by drawing its inspiration from non-Western, non-urban, non-Christian peoples, and by bypassing the traditions of the Academy; and this would seem to be very much what Nietzsche had in mind with his own going 'back to the Greeks'.[17]

The new Primitivism of Gauguin reflected an urban European longing for pagan unsophistication. Art disliked life seen in the moderate and undistinguished northern light of Paris and Amsterdam, Brussels and Berlin. The Fauves brought a radiant southern palate to bear on their interior subjects. Raoul Dufy transformed Paris, while Hodler did for Switzerland what only Nietzsche with a brush and rival painterly genius might have done. Freud's Unconscious played its part in creating this expressive climate. But for the Unconscious read what Nietzsche meant by the tragic irrational.

The vibrant, expressive, revelatory, sun-drenched art of the early twentieth century seems to me best to capture the collective pleasure dream which Nietzsche thirsted after in *The Science of Joy* and elsewhere. He longed for that sharpness and colour which would make Romanticism seem tired and insipid. A painterly correlative for Nietzsche is so often sought in Caspar David Friedrich, that master of the reflective individual dwarfed by a magnificent Super-Nature. But the ethereal northern palate of pinks and greys and lilacs, as well as the mood of sublime absorption into the universe, like a combination of the Lakeland poets and Walter Scott, belong to another Europe and a previous century – to Bayreuth one might say. Nietzsche, as a painter in words and a philosophical conjuror of images, is a Primitivist and an Expressionist. It is only we outsiders, later commentators, who might care to see him as a Friedrich-like dreamer and victim.

Nietzsche turned to colour and music because of the absence of a suitable response to the death of God. Colour replaced sense and meaning. Colour and music were what life had to offer. They were the original tragic vision. Life was a goat-dance performed to the accompaniment of pan-pipes. The actors wore masks and walked on stilts. All life was like that, a 'serious joke', or ought to be seen as such; yet most people took it with a seriousness Nietzsche could only laugh at; seriousness which was without foundation and sapped energy. That energy might be better directed into celebrating the rite of existence.[18]

What Nietzsche feared was the growth of a civilization in which individuals lacked the strength to convert the fear and the threat of the irrational into a force for positive living. What he wanted to see was joyous human self-affirmation despite and in the face of an absence of absolute values and fixed answers.

Nietzsche had a poetic ally in W.B. Yeats, born in 1865, who sailed in his mind to a more colourful Byzantium, durable through its shimmering pagan artefacts. In Eliot, born in the September of Nietzsche's crux year, 1888, he had a formidable equal and adversary. Perhaps Nietzsche's want of tragedy in the modern world was best expressed by Pound, born in 1885, the same year Nietzsche wrote *Beyond Good and Evil*. Against Pound's 'tawdry cheapness' which 'shall outlast our days', against an over-democratized world which had lost religion and made a commodity out of beauty, and which had been taken over by the values of newspapers, Nietzsche hoped for his 'pessimism of strength'. It would arise out of a society in which aesthetic values were rated most highly because they could transform the harshnesses of human life into a cause for celebration. There is in Nietzsche always this readiness to let art inherit the place of the Olympian gods, until men became gods themselves.'[19]

Nietzsche's hopes for the modern world were aristocratic or noble aims, as Brandes acknowledged. Late in 1887 Brandes spoke of Nietzsche's 'aristocratic radicalism' and his correspondent was delighted. 'The expression [. . .] which you employ is very good. It is, permit me to say, the cleverest thing I have yet read about myself.[20]

In *The Genealogy of Morals*, Nietzsche gave the Pagan/Renaissance tradition the name 'aristocratic morality', 'master morality' and 'the will to power' because it instinctively said yes to life, beautified it and made sense of it, out of a natural plenitude of being; whereas the decadent opposite struggled to find meaning, despite the world, in a thin, morbid, sickly symbolism. To point up the difference, Nietzsche contrasted Goethe, 'the last of the aristocratic Germans', with the downtrodden and physically abject characters in Dostoevsky's novels. He referred again to these two contrasting forces for civilization in *The Wagner Case*. Had Nietzsche known Tolstoy better he might, like Thomas Mann and like Dmitri Merezhkovsky in subsequent decades, have accepted the symbolic comparison of those two authors on similar grounds and specifically asked with them which was to be the way forward.[21]

Wagner unforgivably mixed the two, the this-wordly plenitude and the other-worldly symbolism. He dressed up paganism as Christian modesty. He muddled optimism and pessimism. *The Ring*, having grown with its creator, in the end expressed both a hopeful Socialist view of the perfectability of man and Schopenhauerian resignation at man's impurity. Nietzsche was unforgiving. Wagner's art was irresponsible in that sense he and Plato would not tolerate.

It is another strand of modernism, linking Nietzsche to the artistic future after his death: the future of art would exclude self-indulgence in both audience and creator. The communist modernist Brecht took up this stance, pioneering a theatre which in terms redolent of Plato would exclude all *Kulinarismus* and deliberately tried to prevent the audience's emotional identification with the actors by means of alienation effects. There would be no manipulation and purging of private emotion here. Rather, just as Nietzsche counselled, theatregoers would go away stronger in their thoughts, clearer in their minds about the social forces and issues on which the quality of their moral lives depended. Or, with Pirandello, they would be made to think about the nature of theatre itself, about the way an author manipulated his characters, and how it might be if the action on stage were presented as only one version of many possibilities. By this token the dramatist could be a spectator of human behaviour down to the tiniest Wagnerian detail, without being a magician and forefeiting our trust.[22]

Brandes was astute with his aristocratic radicalism because it is very difficult to stick labels on Nietzsche. It is typical of his barely definable position as an artist and critic that he shared territory and ideals with groups as far opposed as symbolists and communists.

I not so much want to label him aristocratic, radical or modern in any of the foregoing senses but rather to suggest that he solved the problems of *The Wagner Case* in one small but vital area on the cultural canvas: in his written style. What he achieved is finely put in the comparison between 'two speakers' in the second book of *The Science of Joy*. The first 'can only show the full rationality of his cause when he abandons himself to passion; this alone pumps enough blood and heat into his brain to force his high spirituality to reveal itself'. The second has less confidence in his own passion, 'makes sudden leaps into the coldest and most repugnant tones' and inspires distrust in his audience. The second is the Nietzsche of 1888:

> He is at the height of his powers when he resists the flood of his emotions and virtually derides it; only then does his spirit emerge fully from its hiding place – a logical, mocking, playful and yet awesome spirit.[23]

Here finally is decided the question Nietzsche first asked in *The Birth of Tragedy* and only resolved there because at the time he believed with too much young man's ardour in the genius of Wagner. What was the fate of Dionysian spirit in the modern world? Then it had seemed possible to propose 'a fraternal union of Apollo and Dionysus' in a music at once concrete and pictorial and transcendent. 'We regarded the drama and penetrated the tumultuous world of its motives and yet felt as though what was passing before us was merely a symbolic image, whose deepest meaning we almost divined and which we longed to tear away in order to reveal the original image behind it.' Through a glass darkly. Then Nietzsche's imagery was at once Platonic, Christian, Gnostic and Hegelian. On the question of the art of the future he brought the whole weight of his schooling in Idealism to bear. But the Idealism proved only so much hocus-pocus. In Nietzsche that 'logical, mocking, playful and yet awesome spirit' was born to take its place. In his case we might say what succeeded the classical tragedy he once saw reborn in Wagner was neither drama nor novel but a hybrid discursive form, part lyrical, part philosophical, part musical, part symbolic, with excursions into politics and satire, couched in a prose in which poetry and philosophy compete in the classic Greek spirit for dominance. He defined, through its desired life-enhancing effect upon its audience, a style, though not a structure or even a genre. Perhaps truly both these possibilities were no longer available to art.[24]

6

NEW DEPARTURES AND
HIGH MOUNTAINS

The Wagner Case, 'funny but at base almost too serious', had pressed upon him, but by the end of May Nietzsche was ready to resume his main task: to draw a line under the past, sum up his achievements, and consummate their message with a new work or works 'transvaluing all values'.[1] To Resa von Schirnhofer he asked without further elucidation: 'Do you understand the trope?'[2] Perhaps they had talked over these long-standing ideas of his in Nice. To Brandes, having already explained he was making a mission out of his disbelief in culture, and 'circling round this paramount problem of values, very much from above and in the manner of a bird, and with the best intention of looking down upon the modern world with as unmodern an eye as possible',[3] he preferred to elaborate.

> My problem this time is rather a curious one: I have asked myself what hitherto has been best hated, feared, despised by mankind – and of that and nothing else I have made my *gold* . . .[4]

However he might put it though, it wasn't a new task, nor even a new formulation, just a point whereon Nietzsche, always full of plans and titles, had decided to concentrate for the summer.[5]

He sought 'values' he believed would be more helpful to humanity than the Christian teaching concerning the universal afflictions, loneliness and suffering, which were so much his own. But 'values' is a difficult word to use when Nietzsche regarded them all as only relative. It is probably better to say he scanned the psychological horizon for a vantage point, and point of stability, 'beyond'. A man enlightened by seeing life from above, 'from beyond good and evil', could one day redescend to a full and excellent existence. *Zarathustra* showed the way. But again enlightened, *aufgeklärt* is a word in the wrong tradition. *Verklärt*, the experience of Schoenberg's *Verklärte Nacht*, 'Transfigured Night', seems closer to Nietzsche's transvalued world.[6]

The fullness and excellence of a transfigured existence was the goal of Nietzsche's art of life. It was his only positive teaching that individual strength emanated from self-knowledge and self-management. He spoke of *Herrenmoral* and meant 'self-mastery morality'. It mattered how a man ate, how he lived, how he organized his day. It mattered for the sake not of his image but his soul. Between Nietzsche's view of the artistically shaped life and the popular notion of lifestyle today a qualitative gulf seems to yawn. On the other hand Nietzsche at least *maintained* that 'image' was the only reality there was, and he might well be called a lifestyle guru today. The pitch of his thought is what makes him hardest of all to know. In all events it was gratifying to hear from Brandes that in Copenhagen the lecture audience seemed to understand him at last:

> I believe I may sum up the impression of my audience in the feeling of a young painter, who said to me: 'What makes this so interesting is that it has not to do with books, *but with life.*'[7]

Nietzsche wrote knowingly about the joy of living to the point of utter satisfaction. Zarathustra's favourite metaphor is of the inner life overflowing its confines like honey from a jar. There is poise, there is invigoration, happiness, sexual fulfilment, intoxication, sadness, pious love, hurt silences and deep quiet in Nietzsche's writing, and many other emotions and sensations besides.

Yet how did he know, when his life was outwardly so barren? Through love of music, through critical dedication to philosophy, and through self-knowledge is the astonishing answer. To distil the *Übermensch* out of his weaknesses as a mortal and Christian soul was his life's task and to accomplish it he had to learn to love and feel and enjoy.

The odds were stacked high against him. He took one of his first glimpses at his self-appointed task in a letter to Heinrich von Stein in December 1882. He had been talking of 'the hero' as 'the most acceptable form of human existence, namely when one has no other choice'. But Nietzsche's philosophy always began, in every personal and impersonal instance he gave of it, in a *post-certain* world:

> One comes to love something and hardly has it become thoroughly lovable than says the tyrant in us (which all too readily we are happy to call 'our higher self'): 'That's just what I want you to give me in sacrifice.' We give it too, though there's much animal torture and burning on a slow fire in the process. You are dealing with nothing but problems of horror and cruelty: do you feel well on it? I will tell you sincerely, I have myself too much of this tragic make-up in me not to curse it often; my experiences great and small always take the same course. Then I mostly need a high spot, from which vantage point the tragic problem lies beneath me. I would like to relieve human existence of some of its heartbreaking, horrific and cruel character. But to go on I would have to reveal to you what I have not yet revealed to anyone – the task I stand before, my life's task.[8]

The talk here is of a 'horrific' vision of humanity and what the philosopher can do about it. If he were Christ, if he had the psychology of a Redeemer, he would want to rid or spare humanity of *all* pain, out of an excessive sensitivity to it. This long-held thought he would soon express in *The Antichristian*.[9] But Nietzsche was not a Redeemer and in any case the human predicament he now construed as pain meted out not by an external God, but rather by malevolent gods within, encouraging self-sacrifice. The individual thus had to find a way of delivering himself from *self*-enslavement.

Thus originated the transvaluation task. Its beginnings in a critique of self-inflicted human pain explain the title of the next book he would write in 1888, *Twilight of the Idols*. The 'idols' were concepts hitherto cherished by humanity, such as love and benevolence, selflessness and truth, which Nietzsche would now show had long since been turned into weapons against the full development of humane individuals.

Destroying the idols, which would become Freud's totems, was the work of the psychologist in Nietzsche. The first Existentialist we might also call him. The psychologist's role – to change the metaphor to another of Nietzsche's favourites from the classical world – was to point ways out of the labyrinth for souls who had lost faith in received moral guidance. It was the same job of emotional reinforcement Dionysus had been doing in all Nietzsche's works since *The Birth of Tragedy*, supplying an alternative to Christian faith and Schopenhauerian pessimism without resort to a too simple materialism.

Now came a third metaphor of transvaluation, the one with which we began. Nietzsche in his latest variant saw the Dionysian task, in the parting letter to Brandes from Turin, as a kind of alchemy. 'Basically [the alchemist is] the most worthwhile kind of man that exists. I mean the man who out of something slight and despicable makes something valuable, even gold itself. This man alone enriches, other men only give change.'[10]

If we were Resa von Schirnhofer perhaps we could say now, yes, we understand this trope with reference to its close relatives. The instinctual life, that jungle of good and bad impulses, propelling us towards pleasure and pain, the whole equatorial furnace of the inner life so despised by Christianity because so unruly, Nietzsche would reassess as mankind's best hope for the future.

Nietzsche was inclined to duplicate himself. Restless in

obscurity, he could never be sure his message was getting through. The most complete statement of his philosophy, *Beyond Good and Evil*, had been published two years now and still he had only a handful of readers worldwide and so few people understood. *Twilight of the Idols* was yet another attempt to explain his whole outlook in one short excursion, and only after it could he sit down to *The Antichristian*. This post-Christian send-off for readers still actively seeking the meaning of life he designated the first 'transvaluation' volume. Into it he would put all his sympathy for human pain and all his hatred of the Christian church for exploiting that pain as a means of 'herd' control – the opposite of 'self-mastery morality'. *Twilight* would form, as Nietzsche's books so often did, one to another, once again a kind of prelude, an introduction. A magnificent recapitulation of the Dionysian, sweeping across the millennia from Aristotle on tragedy to what would become Freud on Eros and Thanatos, the life urge and the death wish, ends *Twilight*. Nowhere better does Nietzsche set out the finely modulated psychology of inner plenitude, that keen sense of joy he had despite a wretched life.

Nietzsche always claimed incidentally, and would soon reiterate to an American professor whose letter reached him in Switzerland, that he was a bad publicist. At the same time, since 1885 he had been continually reframing his work, writing new prefaces, offering new ways into it, in the hope of being better understood. This phenomenon is much commented on by scholars of his 'perspectivism' but in the biographical context it seems simple enough; only faintly obsessive. He was also becoming a practised hand at writing the kind of short autobiographical sketches which, ironically, his slowly growing fame now necessitated. Like Brandes in Copenhagen, Karl Knortz in Indiana faced the problem in 1888 of describing Nietzsche for the first time to an American public. 'To give a picture of me whether as a poet or a writer seems to me extraordinarily difficult,' Nietzsche accepted, before appending this peerless description:

Because of their wealth of psychological experience, their

fearlessness in the face of the greatest dangers and their sublime intellectual free-spiritedness, I consider my books first-rate. Nor do I accept any comparison in terms of artistic presentation, aims and refinement. Long love, close and intimate knowledge and deep respect bind me to the German language.[11]

This then was Nietzsche's own view: if he was to be understood as a philosopher his art and his language and his psychology had to be seen to matter above all.

But before we can watch Nietzsche resume work as poet and philosopher, German writer, psychologist and artist, we have to get him up into the Swiss Alps from Turin for the summer. He left on 6 June and was still complaining about the dislocation in mid-July. Only this time, after the personal trauma of the journey, the reasons for his misery were shared by all the early season visitors to the Upper Engadine village of Sils Maria. The weather played such cruel tricks that some guests went home, not seeing, as Nietzsche observed, why they should pay to freeze in a snow-enveloped hotel in July when they could be more comfortable at home in Hamburg. He took another moment of unwonted worldliness to wonder how the hotels would survive the loss of income, before allowing his own problems once again to close in. Until the weather improved he would go through a debilitating period of depressed introspection, to which he gently attached the label melancholy. No work would be done until August.

How wretchedly those intervening weeks compared to Turin! Every letter Nietzsche wrote from Sils for the next six weeks would stress the loss of that paradisaical location.

The journey into the Alps from Turin, with the train running northwest through Milan, is splendid from Lecco onwards. The railway line to Colico skirts the entire eastern side of Lake Como and the sparkling water, bordered by tall cypresses, palm trees, spruces and firs, is a spectacular sight at the foot of sheer mountains. The water side of the pretty single track is humanly busier, with people courting, bathing, boating, fishing and congregating. The rail terminus lies in the low Alpine foothills in Chiavenna. The journey thus far takes about six hours today, though it required several more in Nietzsche's day. Changing trains once or twice is still inevitable.

Nietzsche didn't look forward to a journey again so soon, as he feared any journey, but the summer heat had already come to the Po plain. Moreover the Alps were a proven productive habitat for him. He had been coming to Sils and round about for more than eight years, and there had written parts of *The Science of Joy*, *Zarathustra*, *Beyond Good and Evil* and *The Genealogy of Morals*. So he set off in a good heart, with a new suitcase and some lean continental sausage – *Lachsschinkenwurst* for those who know it – supplied by his mother to provide his evening meals. Grocery supplies in Sils were very limited, he knew from experience, and to eat in a hotel twice a day was beyond his meagre budget. The correspondence with his mother over the next month would be dominated by the need for more sausage from Naumburg, of a higher quality than the first batch which was too dry and the second which was too salty. He also requested and received a tablecloth so that he might eat his solitary suppers in an orderly and pleasing fashion, and some *Zwiebeck* (French toast) for his breakfast, equally impossible to buy in Sils. As always mindful of that delicate balance of life in himself, which required artistic attention, he set out.[12]

After Chiavenna begins the mountain scenery. This pretty little town with a central statue of Charlemagne lies belittled by immense, almost vertical peaks, where even in high summer streaks of snow seem to form half-letters across a giant slate in the sky. But by this stage Nietzsche was already feeling terrible. Of his journey he noted only to his mother that he spent the night of 5 June miserable in 'that stifling hole'. Beyond Chiavenna the road crosses the Italian-Swiss frontier and twists and turns up to the Maloja Pass at 5,500 feet. Then the steep gradient suddenly gives way to level ground revealing the broad, light, open space of the Sils valley and the adjacent lakes Sils and Silvaplana. The impression is of emerging from a long dark cave. But Nietzsche had no eyes for it. By now he had been six hours in the post-chaise and was vomiting bile.

There had been better journeys. In an Alpine stagecoach the young Nietzsche once met the Italian patriot Mazzini, which not only diverted him for the moment but inspired after-thoughts about one of his most familiar topics, heroism. He formed the view that here indeed was a hero and a kind of poet, whose actions in the world entirely expressed his inner life. As Malvida von Meysenbug, an old friend from his Wagner days, noted: 'Nietzsche said that of all lives he most envied Mazzini's, this complete concentration on a single idea, which became, as it were, a mighty flame consuming every individual trait. The poet frees himself from the violence of deeds, which is in him, by incarnating it in forms and extrapolating deeds and suffering outside himself.' But the problem in 1888 was that sickly Nietzsche was quite the opposite of his own ideal. In 1888 he only sat in the post-chaise, queasy, locked into himself, and thinking. The landscape passed him by. In Sils moreover he began a bout of migraine.[13]

But at least he could collapse in familiar lodgings. An austere wood-pannelled upstairs room with a small window facing south, furnished with a bed, a table and a washstand, he had made his own for several years now. He rented it from the Durisch family and left 'a basket of books' each year for his return. The village was small and Nietzsche lived right in the centre. The Durisches, whose head of household was sometime *Bürgermeister* of the small permanent community, kept the private house and grocer's next door to the Hotel Edelweiss. Actually Nietzsche often shivered in that room and several times resolved to find another warmer one, but for such troublesome things as moving he didn't really have the will. Some degree of familiarity was anyway essential for a wanderer, and the little energy of revolt he mustered over what he did not like was easily spent in petty complaining. So he pottered on, taking a very ordinary midday meal occasionally at the Edelweiss next door, but mainly at the Hotel Alpenrose across the bridge towards Sils Baselgia, and ceremoniously eating alone in the evening. He unpacked new shirts from his mother to replace those fallen into holes over the years of penury and self-neglect. The routine was good enough for him by 10 June to be writing letters again.

Not so the weather. For the first week of Nietzsche's stay it was so disappointing – warm and humid – that he wished himself back in Turin where temperatures as high as 31C had been unusually bearable throughout May. He told all his correspondents about it in pedantic meteorological detail. Weather, because of its apparent bearing on his health, was another of his obsessions, and made even the devoted Köselitz sigh. Yet when the atmosphere lifted Sils was once again Nietzsche's *perla perlissima*, 'with a definite Latin quality' and 'a wealth of colours, in which it is a hundred times more southerly than Turin.' The colours were in June the brilliant deep pink of the alpine rose and intense blue hues of gentian. He put on the new horsehair hat bought for the purpose in Turin and walked out to inspect the damage of recent avalanches.[14]

With those unseasonal high temperatures, the snow had melted all at once. The slopes above Sils, which has the highest tree-line in Europe, were strewn with broken trees. Walking up the Fex Valley behind the hotel towards the glacier, he noticed the economic consequences of this disaster, with its curious legalities. Ownership of logs was determined by where they came to rest. One man was 5,000 Swiss francs richer overnight thanks to the whim of nature. That sum would have paid Nietzsche's rent in Turin for the next sixteen years, so no wonder it impressed him, already wondering about the budget for printing *The Wagner Case*. Striking out in different directions from the hotel he resumed his other old walks too, to the far end of the Silvaplana lake where the locally famous Surlej monolith stands, and out to the wooded Chasté peninsula on Lake Sils. This was land he once described as the meeting point of Italy and Finland, the home of all the silver tones nature possessed, a place where he recognized

95

himself with pleasant dread. Not that he had ever been to Finland. The symbol was what counted.

Tourist brochures now quote him. Thanks to the activities of the century-old local beautification society, now the tourist office, Sils Maria, to distinguish it from adjacent Sils Baselgia, has barely changed in a hundred years, so that it is possible to experience today just what Nietzsche wanted, and loved. It is an unassuming village, quite unlike its glamorous neighbour St Moritz, quite undramatic except for its natural location, but with a regular summer clientele. That clientele in 1992 struck this visitor as people of reserved manners, unsensational requirements and apparent deep conservatism in their private lives. Nietzsche, despite his explosive freethinking, in practice would have been quite at home among them. They wouldn't have interfered, and he would have been free to indulge his main pleasure, walking.

He would have walked anywhere, though he did love Sils. He had a childlike joy in motion and that same vitality was reflected in his hardy pleasure in cold water, a quality he passed on to his 'son' Zarasthustra. Nietzsche plunged into pools when others found them icily forbidding, and sluiced himself from a cold jug every morning. Such a constitution gave him a natural kinship with Epicurus, which is to say his highly reactive body prompted him to enjoy the world, not reject it, and to admire in all ages thoughtful connoisseurs of happiness. His physical vitality, despite his sickness, was one of his chief instinctive weapons against Christianity.[15]

Many writers and artists are ambulatory. Nietzsche shared his habit with Rousseau and Beethoven and Mahler and with all those Victorian Englishmen like J.L. Symonds and Leslie Stephen who came to Switzerland to write, though it is interesting to contrast him with Wagner, for here was the quintessential indoor man, a man made for twentieth-century comforts, creating at his decadent best in a study furnished and perfumed like a boudoir. In defining his physiology against Wagner's, Nietzsche arrived at so many of his original and important thoughts.[16]

Nietzsche walked, concerned with his inner state, yet he did notice many specific things about Sils, a place to which he felt so close he once expressed the wish to die there. So what was it opened his ailing eyes? I think probably no one, not even a thinker preoccupied with man's disproportionate efforts to elevate himself above the status of God's ape, could ignore those moody, transparent lakes which are Sils's centrepiece. Perhaps the very power of nature in Sils reinforced Nietzsche's sense that man's pride in his conscious achievements and his status in the universe was overweening and immodest.

The wind around the lakes is sudden and very strong, the play of light and shadow dramatic. The weather changes often and quickly, a dangerous and temperamental force locally acknowledged. A large public barometer inscribed with routine advice and warnings to visitors on local meteorological behaviour stands in the centre of the village, in front of the Hotel Edelweiss. With the wind the water changes colour from turquoise to emerald to black, and now silver; it seethes and eddies round the Chasté headland, where Nietzsche as a newcomer to the resort dreamed of building a hut and staying for ever. Yet at certain moments the breathtaking clarity of the water reveals the sandy bottom. Lake Silvaplana has an even, undramatic perimeter, but above the Surlej rock the near-perpendicular Surlej waterfall crashes down with a force and beauty which make it seem like water tumbling sheer from heaven. The sound is deafening, blotting out the bird song and cowbells and voices which normally relieve the silence of the valley. At the same time spray fills the air like billowing smoke. The experience looking up into the fall is dizzying. Looking back towards Sils it becomes clear how much the conifers give the lake water its mysterious palette of green and blue and pink. There is an experience of *Urnatur* here akin to Goethe's at the Rhine Falls in Schaffhausen, yet it is never to the service of Romantic nature worship that Nietzsche puts his borrowed metaphors of raw energy and forcefulness, rather to the will to power – the *Machtgefühl* – of the triumphant individual man.

High mountain metaphors, especially in *Zarathustra*, show

Nietzsche straining after an energy, grandeur and resource-fulness, which, palpable in the material world, would also express human spiritual strengths and give inspiration for the *Übermensch*, a creature undoubtedly born of the view from 'high up' rather than the idea of dominating his fellow men. As if to reinforce the connection for posterity between his human ideal and his ideal landscape Nietzsche said of Sils: 'I know nothing so suited to my nature as this piece of Over-Earth [*Ober-Erde*].'[17]

He loved this landscape so much as nature that transfigured by that love it became art. High mountains corresponded to that 'middle world' which classical tragedy in its Apollonian aspect occupied. Nietzsche had already created for it a mythical parallel in the *Zarathustra* arena. Nietzsche also knew well the stylized world of the seventeenth-century artist Claude and I think his transfigured landscape merged with Claude's in his mind's eye. Claude's heroic canvases – and they are heroic, to use that concept so favoured by Nietzsche – weave biblical and semi-mythical stories around greatness in nature and great buildings, invoking an imaginary distant classical civilization where culti-vated men and women sing and dance and make music as if it were second nature. The nature surrounding is powerful, serene, and most astonishing for the quality of the light. The power of light to transform, and especially the moment of transformation, fasci-nated Claude, as it did Nietzsche.[18]

Mountain altitude elicited his praise because he felt he could get on with his work more efficiently in elevated climes; that he could see further; that it really was a place where his mind had an extra vantage point and was better able to carry out its ambitious resolutions. In other words high mountains were a metaphor for understanding. From a mountain height Nietzsche felt he could see his whole philosophical achievement in relief, and his contribution to the history of philosophy. The height could be reimagined, once he had experienced it. The strongest statement of this accordingly came from flatland Turin where recently 'almost every day I have mustered enough energy for one or two hours to be able to see my whole conception [*meine Gesammt-*

Conception] from top to bottom: the enormous multiplicity of problems lay spread out before me as though in relief and clear in its lines . . . It all fits together . . .'[19]

Three things, then, high mountains signified for Nietzsche: aesthetic beauty, moral courage and intellectual clarity. It is quite striking that, thus distilled, they gratified the trinity of Kantian faculties and heightened them. The *Übermensch* was the one who could get, as far as is possible for a human being, 'beyond' the world which his humanity obliged him to contemplate. Whether Nietzsche's message is metaphysical here, suggesting some possibility of conscious transcendence, is very difficult to determine. It was less a two-tier value system he sought to compensate for the apparent limitations of human existence, rather a better way of seeing that that existence was indeed limited. The high vantage point gave him not a sense of the world below being inferior to some higher realm, but a sense of the sheer relativity of its judgements. The paradox was that the realization of limitation was liberating. The Upper Engadine's 5,500 feet above sea level stood for the most desirable capacity in human beings to see far and over the heads of individual nations and people and creeds, the ability to survive by rising above the fray, and the need to go beyond the familiar world in order to see the arbitrariness of its values. In *Twilight*, Nietzsche wrote of this extreme standpoint:

One would have to be situated *outside* life, and on the other hand to know it as thoroughly as any, as many, as all who have experienced it, to be permitted to touch on the problem of the *value* of life at all . . .[20]

It is a beautiful problem, the moment human beings realize they belong to no other realm but the present and have no God to whom they can pray.

One thing for which we can thank the mountains is that they helped Nietzsche to express this philosophical world so graphically. Whatever the metaphysical nuances, it was in the end surprisingly visual for a man with impaired sight. The basic geography of *Zarathustra* contrasted the mountains of discernment with the uncritical, utilitarian 'flatland' (which in turn would inspire Thomas Mann's novel *The Magic Mountain*). *Zarathustra* was a hilltop survey of the resentful spirit and the impoverished spirituality of the modern world, with its unthinking mass movements, its vengeful class antagonisms, its insensitivity to nature and poetry, its hidden and institutionalized brutalities, insipidness, false righteousness and cultural feebleness. Nietzsche's other books exuded the spirit of the mountains too, whenever they were saying a Yes to the Over-Life, and a No to the subordinate, enslaved one. By mountain air the 'Science of Joy' lived and breathed, moving swiftly because of the cold. As the musical metaphor for the 'Science of Joy', of wisdom running on light feet, shaded into a physical one, Nietzsche's fanciful disdain for gravity took him again and again onto high ground. Mountains existed in the spirit of dance.

On the other hand not all this obsession with mountains in the books was the product of the Alps – Nietzsche had spoken of the intellectually clarifying role of the *Hochwald*, the high forests of Saxony, when he was still a student. (This was where Munch's portrait was set, with Munch having himself photographed as a model in place of Nietzsche.)[21] Nor was the mountain *idée fixe* entirely derived from observation. Nietzsche was a child of the ancient world and the Bible. Moses received his revelation from God on Mount Sinai and Christ preached his Sermon on the Mount. Also one of the most cherished poems in the German language, Goethe's *Über allen Gipfeln ist Ruh'* ('Beyond all mountain peaks is peace'), conveys the humanist experience of Weimar classicism, shaped by the ancient world and shot through in Goethe's mature case with the wisdom of the East. The power of this literary tradition Nietzsche never denied or ignored, no matter how much he chipped away at its moral certainties. Indeed he was a great admirer of Weimar classicism, with its love of Greece and its felicities of language. Only he could *not* say, as Goethe did at the end of *Faust*, Part II: 'Alles Vergängliche/ist nur ein Gleichnis' ('Everything mortal is only an image'). Rather he retorted through Zarasthustra: *'Alles Unvergängliche – das ist nur ein Gleichnis! Und die Dichter lügen zuviel'* ('All that is immortal – it's that which is only the image, and the poets lie too much'). Nietzsche's high mountains then did not suggest an unknowable, unchanging ideal world beyond, like Plato's realm of Ideas, but only the best vantage point available in this real world – a world which is only the sum of its images.[22]

Zarathustra, only nominally based on the historical Zoroaster, lived ten years in the mountains. Then he descended, at the beginning of Nietzsche's four *Zarasthustra* gospels, to teach the people in parables or images (*Gleichnisse*) the consequences of God's death, the relativity of all values, a condition which therefore required each individual to work out his own. His 'going down' was a form of 'going out of himself' like Nietzsche's in overcoming pain and gloom in Genoa to address the people in *Daybreak*. Zarathustra compared the going down to love and even to a *Liebestod*, while his 'going over' was a return to the mountains, to a collected state of selfhood in the beyond. Beyond all peaks there *was* peace. Nietzsche was greatly touched by Goethe, who veered towards mysticism in later life. Only Goethe was yet another Nietzschean hero, whereas Nietzsche himself was not. The spiritual to-ing and fro-ing, between self-objectivization, or will to power, and a nirvanic state of being whole within himself, racked him, except occasionally, when he was writing and thinking at his most productive, as he hoped to be doing in Sils.[23]

A precondition of that productiveness was not necessarily a clear overview of his purpose. He compiled his books almost scrap by scrap, or 'tunnelling like a beaver'. At the same time, there was an aerial map inside his head of targets already hit and targets yet to be blasted. Specifically dynamite was another image Nietzsche associated with the Alps and which he delightedly borrowed from a Swiss reviewer of *Beyond Good and Evil*, Karl Widmann, to describe his own work. Like the dynamite destined in 1886 to blast open the St Gottard pass for the railway,

Beyond Good and Evil should have black warning flags set round it, Widmann suggested. A marvellous image from a positive reviewer with unusual contemporary insight into Nietzsche, it was also an alternative to Nietzsche's own metaphor of philosophizing with a hammer, the subtitle to *Twilight of the Idols*, and more modern publicity. Though there was a difference. The older idea incorporated a tuning-fork. It also I believe referred back to Siegfried's hammering the anvil, forging the sword that would rescue humanity from the power-mongering gods. It stood for a complexity of self-empowering and self-justifying motives in Nietzsche's mind of which he himself was not wholly conscious. By contrast the new idea was simple: bang! Probably we have to bear both attacking Nietzsches in mind. In *Twilight* he stressed the need to glorify force, as the antidote to centuries of Christian repression and disguise. Now he did his work subtly, via the Renaissance ideal of *virtù*, and the need to stymie the gods of Valhalla. Now he carried it out with untempered, bad-tempered force.[24]

To demolish religion and philosophy as if they were rickety old buildings, he swung a lump of iron through the air, knocking through the venerated outer walls and exposing the insides as empty. In *Twilight*, under the heading 'What I Owe to the Ancients', Nietzsche seemed to see his own explosiveness even emerging from within the Greek midst, that is, from wherever reason was breaking down:

I saw their strongest instinct, the will to power, I saw them trembling at the intractable force of this drive, I saw all their institutions evolve out of protective measures designed for mutual security against the *explosive material* within them . . . The Socratic virtues were preached *because* the Greeks had lost them . . .

I cannot doubt, given the fascination most of us feel watching buildings crumble, that Nietzsche found his huge philosophical project exciting.

Still philosophies aren't buildings, and cannot just have their bricks knocked out. More effective battering rams may be counter-reasoning, and in Nietzsche's case scorn. In modern times he poured especial scorn on the German soul, which had flowered in philosophies of 'becoming'. These were monumental rationalizations of the inner life, construed in poetic and religious systems which matched that spiritual life to the outer world. 'Foreigners are astonished and drawn by the enigmas which the contradictory nature at the bottom of the German soul propounds to them (which Hegel reduced to a system and Richard Wagner finally set to music),' he marvelled disingenuously.[25] He had heard of an Italian poet in love with German philosophy. He remembered how Hippolyte Taine, the French philosopher with, as it happened, a quasi-Nietzschean interest in how psychology and the body affected thinking, had declared the discovery of Hegel the high point of his life. Nietzsche was truly amused. How could intelligent people be taken in by such self-deceiving fabrications of the mind? This gentle scorn is to be found in his first letter from Sils, to Pasquale d'Ercole, along with his guilty apology for having slipped away anti-socially from Turin.[26]

So far the demolition of reason. As a self-proclaimed immoralist Nietzsche hammered away at moral philosophy too, abjuring selflessness and compassion and a fixed notion of the good. Here too there is a kind of brutal toughness at work which repels, while a sensitive spirit sets out a cogent case behind the combative façade. Nietzsche's famous rejection of pity (*Mitleid*), for instance, demonstrates how pity diminishes the integrity of the other.[27] If I flood another person with pity I may dull his or her ability to find strength within, for pity is a crippling kind of sympathy which confirms misfortune and woe, expressing the idea: 'Yes, hasn't life treated you badly, you deserve to feel sorry for yourself.' At issue for Nietzsche the psychologist is the way people manipulate each other, often making others feel weak in order to enhance their own power. It is the manipulativeness that Zarathustra and Nietzsche reject as being beneath love. Nietzsche also rejects the cowardice and lack of self-love which lurk when the dispenser of pity confirms a secret desire to shrink from life, and to hide from challenges and competition. There is no pity in the world of Dionysus. Dionysian life positively celebrates human capacity by looking absurd existence in the eye. In all this it is difficult not to side with Nietzsche. To reject pity is not unloving, rather the contrary: it is the only way to treat the other as an equal and whole person.

Moreover, I bring myself in here as the lingering friend because at last with the transvaluation of pity we come very close to Nietzsche as philosopher and man. Menacing was not only the self-pity which obviously threatened him as he lay vomiting in strange, dark rooms about Europe, without friends and without success, but also the legacy from his Pietist childhood. We only have to remember that morally stuffy German front room in which he grew up, a devout lad at the mercy of a disappointed mother, two unmarried aunts and a grandmother, to feel with him the desire to open all the windows and eventually blow up the vicarage. No doubt those relatives all showered him with pity for having lost his father at the age of four. No doubt slowly he became aware of his vital, pretty mother, so young widowed, refusing to marry again, and turning all her love of life into piety, all her libido into good works. He inherited from his mother the physical vitality he most cherished in himself, and he saw her waste it. Franziska Oehler-Nietzsche's son, until he came to his independent adult senses, was pious and obedient to the point of ridicule. But, lord, how he then burst out, released by Wagner and by philosophy! That was the explosion, the dynamite in his own life and having experienced it he knew what kind of good he wanted to bring to humanity.[28]

It was good. Nietzsche's detractors overreact to the mere idea of a person not feeling pity as being somehow monstrous. Nietzsche's new moral alchemy was more subtle, converting pity into a value which might be called 'the integrity of the personality'. In the 'flatland' Nietzsche confronts us with social problems as fresh today as they seemed to him over a hundred years ago.

Of the several versions of God's death in *Zarathustra* we read in Book 4 that God died of excessive sympathy for men. Forcing Himself to face their disharmonious, muddled, muddied souls, he mixed with them and the ugliest among them axed him out of shame. The same ugliest man, who is no fool, and may well be Dostoevsky, offers God's murder as a warning to Zarathustra.[29] God and Zarathustra stand to have their energy drained in the same way as a drowning man will pull down his rescuer, in the same way as a man full of doubt latches on to one who seems certain. To show pity is not the way God and Zarathustra can do most good. They are likely to be destroyed in the process.

Here are the plots of our daily newspapers. Here is the moral underside of life, in which the good are destroyed by their own goodness: an excess of sympathy. Nietzsche did require Zarathustra to descend and wander in the world below. That much is clearly loving and essentially Christian, though it must also remind us of the descent of classical heroes into Hades. Odysseus and Aeneas both resurface to lead stronger lives on earth, Zarathustra returns to live with the dumb creatures who are his ultimate companions, in a high-up cave. He descends for his own sake and having learned the nature of the human soul retreats again.[30]

'Man is something that must be overcome' was Zarathustra's teaching. Nietzsche's position was founded on such compassion for the suffering human race, such a strong vision of the misery human beings faced, that he required them to be strong in themselves.

We have moved on heedlessly since his day. An over-abundant or perhaps a misplaced sympathy: is it not on this that the prevalent cure-all belief in social psychotherapy is founded? Psychotherapy *as an attitude to life* encourages many people to assume that forces outside their doing are to blame for disturbances within. Does it thereby create strong, responsible individuals?

Psychotherapy has become incorporated into the Welfare State. How Nietzsche, with his sensitivity to language, would have baulked even at that name, which might be translated back into German as *der Mitleidsstaat*, and given a Nietzschean reading as the state which killed God. He retaliated eloquently in advance, in *Twilight*, only flipping over into excess with a manic statement open to gross misinterpretation out of context: 'The sick man is the parasite of society.'[31]

Arrogance is built into Nietzsche's mission and his style, and you may think after that attack on psychotherapy *as an attitude to life* that it is built into mine. But if Nietzsche at least were only an arrogant genius he would be far more unpleasant to read. He has compassion and he is passionately interested in philosophy, both as a heuristic history of error and a repository of the greatest personal confessions. For, as he said, all great philosophies are disguised personal confessions.[32] If all he had done was to hammer home that untruth was a condition of life, as he did in the first pages of *Beyond Good and Evil*, he would remain infinitely valuable.[33] His critiques of past philosophers from Plato to Kant helped him define his own identity more closely and create new and varying perspectives. These two were most important to him. Less passionately, having read Kuno Fischer's monograph in his first Sils summer in 1881, he felt a philosophical affinity with Spinoza in their mutual desire to show how much of knowledge comprises emotion, imagination and other impurities. For reasons more to do with the battle against pessimism, he felt close to Epicurus and loved Montaigne.

What comes over from a reading of Nietzsche's works of demolition is therefore actually a great love of philosophy and a fine sense of irony. He took the whip to cant and its purveyors, but only like Christ to the erring children of God. Nietzsche's position was a radical modesty, quite new to a philosophical tradition dominated by the self-centred 'I think therefore I am' and 'therefore the world is'. 'What do I matter!' stands over the door of Nietzsche's thinker of the future in *Daybreak*. Nietzsche's radical modesty meant philosophy would never be the same again. It could barely trust its own words.[34]

In Sils, having settled down, he would work on *Twilight*

towards the end of July, pointing out the error of assuming there even existed a determining 'I', supported by something called the individual will, which then caused events to happen in the world. The so-called inner life was murkier or perhaps simply empty:

> The 'inner world' is full of phantoms and false lights; the will is one of them. The will no longer moves anything, consequently no longer explains anything – it merely accompanies events, it can also be absent [. . .] And as for the ego! It has become a fable, a fiction, a play on words: it has totally ceased to think, to feel and to will! . . . What follows from this? There are no spiritual causes at all![35]

'Willing seems to me to be above all something *complicated*, something that is a unity only as a word,' he had written in *Beyond Good and Evil*.[36]

Try telling that to the hundreds of thousands of readers who have appropriated 'will to power' as the exercise of blunt, brute force.

7

HEREDITY AND BORROWED TIME

Thick cloud followed the week of snow. Fourteen early season guests, mostly from Hamburg, having fled from the tropical summer forecast for the continental lowland, were now stuck in the Hotel Alpenrose. Nietzsche shared their grumbles at mealtimes and the prevailing atmosphere of boredom. Not that he was bored, but the physical life which he could enjoy to a point where he felt cheerfully himself was particularly lacking because of the weather, and, for as long as he did not come to trust individual acquaintances, bourgeois company, which naturally doubted his unusual qualities, intensified his restlessness.

He compiled and sent to the long-suffering Köselitz a table showing precipitation, bright and overcast days in Turin, Florence, Rome, Naples and Palermo, and observed that Turin, the furthest north, paradoxically enjoyed the best weather. The calculation was part of his regret that he had moved on from that centre of almost Renaissance epicureanism at all. He fussed about his diet, holding on as ever to the notion of an ideal psycho-physical regime that was nourishing, gracious and productive. Conveniently the Durisch house was partly given over to a grocery, though Nietzsche had long grown tired of its range: 'English biscuits, tea and soap'. The Lachsschinken by post from his mother was his mainstay, to be eaten with bread, fruit and nuts and a glass of milk. It was calculated to last into August, supplemented by boiled eggs. Deussen, curious about his bachelor friend, noticed eggshells on the desk, a boot still in a boot jack and an unmade bed when he visited the previous year.[1]

Apart from Knortz the post brought nothing unusual. The letters he received generally, except from Brandes, were strikingly banal, in content and in style, compared with his own. Overbeck was pedestrian and professorial, with a poor grasp of syntax, Köselitz of limited spirit and expressiveness. But warm banality with a measure of admiration and concern for himself was all Nietzsche needed. From his sister arrived 'the best' news of the inauguration ceremony of the new residence for the founders of the Aryan German colony in Nueva Germania. She and Förster were prototypes for the leaders of a cult sect, to judge from a late twentieth-century standpoint. They ascribed uncommon privileges to themselves, not least superior food and lodgings in an extreme climate.[2] Nietzsche had his forebodings, though it is clear he wanted the best for his sister and was prepared to put a positive construction on a way of life he knew nothing about. He read now of shots in the air, beribboned horses, people lined up outside their houses giving flowers and cigars and asking Elisabeth to bless their children. There were speeches, poems and a procession under a triumphal arch. A breakfast feast followed. He told both Köselitz and Meta von Salis the Nueva Germania inauguration sounded magical.[3] It was a word easily used, and often used by him to criticize Wagner. But Nietzsche loved pomp, inspired perhaps by his early experience of the church. It chimed oddly with his fastidious intellectual hatred of theatre. That internal division gave a particular colour to the solitude we are considering throughout 1888. In Sils Maria, as everywhere after Wagner, this intense man was underestimated by life but endured by finding rich companionship with himself. The Dionysian had begun as a communal ideal, a way to new myth and ritual. When it became possible only as an individual, artistic vision Nietzsche internalized the ritual joy, seeking 'superabundant substitutes' for the life he was not leading. Not to understand the constant pregnancy of his inner life in the continuum of infertile ordinariness would be to misunderstand him entirely.[4]

Another snowbound day Nietzsche found Nohl's biography of Wagner in the hotel library and looked himself up. He found the description 'brilliant friend and patron' and conveyed it with a touch of sarcasm to Köselitz.[5] Nohl reported the homosexual King Ludwig of Bavaria jumping to the conclusion that Wagner also 'did not like' women, but Nietzsche, having long ago proofread parts of *My Life*, knew the question of Wagner's sexuality, which had also caused Cosima to be jealous of Ludwig, was not so simply stated. Wagner loved women and, effectively separated from Minna Planer, the actress he married at twenty-three, had numerous affairs. The liaison with the married Cosima, daughter of Franz Liszt, brought lasting happiness to both. She, balancing guilty pain against a sense of calling, left her husband Hans von Bülow for him.[6]

Whatever its orientation, Nietzsche found Wagner's personal sexuality, as well as that of his music, vulgar. Even in the idyllic Tribschen days the older man had embarrassed Nietzsche with his bedroom braggadocio. The famous exhortation: 'Either write an opera, Fritz, or get married', reflected a no doubt true perception of Nietzsche's frustration at the age of twenty-eight, but any counsel Wagner delivered would have seemed all the more tactless to the extent that Nietzsche, for all his adoration of Wagner, in those days longed himself for Cosima.[7] At the same time Nietzsche was aware of Wagner's sublimated homosexuality. He alluded in *The Wagner Case* to his 'femininity'. More than a year ago he had written in his notebook, anticipating Gutman's judgement that 'an air of homosexuality hangs heavy over Monsalvat', that *Parsifal* was a parting tribute to the Catholic wife Wagner 'let down'. Of the sexuality portrayed here and in *Lohengrin* (though not in *Tristan*) Nietzsche instinctively felt the asceticism was false. Some commentators such as Schmidt-Löbbecke have asked whether Nietzsche ever received any homoerotic overture from Wagner. Nietzsche was so moved by a performance of the *Parsifal* Prelude in Monte Carlo in January

1887 she wonders if its melancholy love did not bring back real memories.[8] We will never know, only that Nietzsche had no conscious sexual desire for another man.

Nohl's volume yet found Nietzsche in a balanced frame of mind, such that he could write to Knortz on 21 June: 'With Richard Wagner and Mrs Cosima Wagner I was for several years which count amongst the most valuable of my life linked in the deepest trust and intimate understanding. If I now belong among the opponents of the Wagner movement it must be evident no squalid motives lie behind it.' The writing of *The Wagner Case* had for the present purged him of his fiercest resentments.

Calmly he wrote letters, and considered the typography and layout of *The Wagner Case*. Having dispatched the manuscript to his publisher Naumann on 26 June he followed it with numerous insertions, only to receive the whole back on grounds of illegibility a week or so later. He wrote out a new fair copy, to which by turns through July and into August he added the two Afterwords and the Epilogue, and the whole was published in September. It is curious to see him deliberating over whether to order Latin or German lettering. It seems in the last analysis everything for Nietzsche was symbolic. Latin was his preference, in typography as in culture, and yet passingly he was swayed by the cynical thought that Germans took most seriously what was printed in Gothic script.

At the Alpenrose, that now decayed and disused hotel on the edge of Sils, whose name is fading into the weather-beaten façade, Nietzsche liked lunch to be quiet, and would go early to avoid the children in the dining room. Nevertheless, as Carol Diethe has suggested, his attendances there, surrounded by a curious public, and especially once his old friends and admirers arrived later in the season, had the character of a *levée*.[9] Disused as Herr Professor Doktor Nietzsche was, and decaying inwardly, he was a fascinating man to talk to. In his communion with himself the two great preoccupations of his summer were Germany and Christianity, and some of those thoughts seeped out. Out of tact he would not have raised the religious question, but Germany was another matter, and obvious common ground between him and the Hamburg guests. In June the Kaiser Friedrich III died only eleven weeks after succeeding his ninety-one-year-old father, Wilhelm. The news gave a fresh fillip to Nietzsche's fears for German culture in spiralling decline under Bismarck's reign of philistinism. Friedrich had been 'a small flickering light of free thought, the last hope for Germany'. 'Now begins the Stöcker regime: – I draw the consequences and know already that from now on my *Will to Power* will be confiscated in Germany.'[10] Pastor Adolf Stöcker was a covetously ambitious Evangelical keen to save Germany from Socialism. Not that Socialism was a cause dear to Nietzsche's heart either, but what he abhorred was the demagogic style of an orator who stirred the mass of Germans into an anti-Semitism not previously felt in the Reich. In this 'Christian' who came to prominence after carrying the day for Bismarck in the 1881 elections we might see a model of the type of ascetic priest Nietzsche decried in *The Genealogy of Morals*. The name Stöcker stuck doggedly in Nietzsche's mind, as a cause of disgust, to the end.

It stuck there (how easy it would be to make a pun out of Stöcker's name: Stocker means just that) because Nietzsche's main project in 1888 was to incorporate his antipathy towards the Reich and his exposure of Christianity as a despotism in one conclusive artistic statement. Considering the opposition he was likely to meet, he still called this project 'The Will to Power', though already it had the subtitle 'Transvaluation of All Values'. In the event only Elisabeth would ever compile a 'book' called *The Will to Power* from notes not meant for publication and in some cases discarded. Nietzsche extracted *Twilight* from the greater 'Will to Power' plan, while *The Antichristian* became the first book of an intended four-part Transvaluation, then the whole project:

And one calculates time from the *dies nefastus* on which this fatality arose – from the first day of Christianity! – Why not rather from its last? From today? – Revaluation of all values![11]

112

The last words of *The Antichristian* proclaimed the beginning and end of Nietzsche's summary work.

His provisional title for *Twilight* – A Philosopher's Leisure Hours (*Mussiggang eines Philosophen*) – bore directly on the days he spent wandering about Turin and Sils Maria. It reflected exactly how Nietzsche worked, in conversation with himself out walking by day, jotting down his thoughts, adding to them in the evening. Yet the final title is yet one more piece of evidence for Wagner's continuing dominance of Nietzsche's imagination. Köselitz doubted *Mussiggang* would grab attention, so in mid-September Nietzsche came up with this replacement, a mischievous allusion to *Twilight of the Gods*. It certainly won him publicity. In posthumous years the title would be misconstrued to make Nietzsche into a crude iconoclast.

We can talk titles and plans here since for the time being nothing was moving forward. When Naumann sent back the illegible manuscript of *The Wagner Case*, Nietzsche claimed the handwriting was the result of constant poor health since he arrived in Sils: nervous exhaustion, headaches, vomiting. He remained under the influence of his negative planet (*mein Unstern*) until mid-July. He really did miss his rarely happy days in Turin. It was his way out of decadence and hypochondria to choose his environment, right down to the selection of books, food, music and walks. This was his pharmacopoeia. To have the choice so narrowed by the bizarre inclemency of the 1888 season was intolerable.[12]

He told his mother on 25 June he felt his strength waning for life generally. A few days later hearing the local priest swear at his dog and call him the devil was a rare light moment – and, one might add, a rare example of genuine humour on Nietzsche's part.[13] The low point came on 4 July when he wrote to Overbeck: 'I lack not only health but the predisposition to get healthy. My life-force is no longer intact. The losses of at least the last ten years can no longer be made good . . .' It is sometimes said of Nietzsche that the alternating euphoria and sickness evident in 1888 were characteristic of the overarching illness closing in on him. Yet it was a common enough rhythm of his life since that terrible first winter in Genoa, and it certainly did not convince him syphilis was gradually propelling him towards paralysis. Instead he sat in his wood-panelled room in Sils, reading the English founding father of genetics, Francis Galton, and imagining he would soon pay the ultimate price for being his father's son.

Galton published *Hereditary Genius* in 1869. Nietzsche had a copy of the first, 1883, edition of *Inquiries into Human Faculty and its Development* which continued this pioneering work, establishing the overriding debt children owed their parents and grandparents for physical and mental character traits. The scientist was talking about infant illnesses affecting people's whole lives. Nietzsche read enough English to understand:

> The development had been arrested by something, and was not made up for by after growth . . . There remained no doubt in my mind that if these illnesses had been warded off, the development of the children would have been increased by almost the precise amount lost in these halts. In other words, the disease had drawn largely upon the capital, and not only on the income, of their constitutions. (*Inquiries* 'History of Twins')

Janz suggests that in *Hereditary Genius* Nietzsche found scientific support for his idea that the *Übermensch* could be bred. But what Nietzsche found in Galton was rather solace for his own case. He was thinking about the sickness which he told Brandes in April had no local cause. If he thought back, he could remember the headaches that kept him away from school. Elisabeth too shared the family tendency to migraine and short-sightedness, though not as severely as her brother. The father who died of brain disease is not mentioned here, but Nietzsche had long made the connection and was afraid it destined him to madness.[14] From Sils now he addressed first his mother, then Overbeck in the 4 July letter, using Galton's metaphor:

You know it seems to me that I don't only lack health but the basis by which I might become healthy – my vital strength is so weak I can never again make good the losses of more than ten years, during which I was only ever living off 'capital' and earned nothing, absolutely nothing to supplement it –

I've been thinking very clearly although not to my advantage over my general position. Not only is health lacking, but also the predisposition to get healthy – the life force [Lebenskraft] is no longer intact. The losses of at least ten years can no longer be made good; during that time I have lived entirely off 'capital' and added nothing to it, nothing at all. That way though one gets poor . . . In psychological matters one can't catch up, each bad day counts: I have learnt this from the Englishman Galton. I can under favourable conditions, with extreme care and cunning, achieve an unstable equilibrium; if these favourable conditions are absent, then any amount of care and cunning will do nothing for me. The first case was Turin; the second is, unfortunately this time, Sils.

To adapt Thomas Mann's description of Dostoevsky's world, Nietzsche believed himself 'metaphysically abject' and Galton's research particularly encouraged him to believe his future was short. The issue was all the more poignant to consider in July 1888, thirty-nine years to the month since his father died on 30 July 1849. Nietzsche's relationship with his father, whose death had given him occasional nightmares ever since, hangs like the darkest of clouds over this month, compared to the Turin sunshine when he had tried even to throw off that father substitute, Wagner. In Sils he sat trying to come to terms with the quality of *Geist* he had from his father, compared with his vitality from his mother. He had recently told Brandes he came closest to dying at the same age his father died. A Greek sense of hereditary curse hung over him, encouraged by his reading of Theognis and Aeschylus.[15]

In *Ecce Homo* he toyed with the metaphor that the father from whom he received his spiritual and intellectual gifts was long dead within him. This association of reflective activity with death confirmed Nietzsche's intellectual remove from the world at hand and reinforced that sense of guilt which hung over his isolation – both those sentiments powerfully alive in him when he first arrived in Turin. At the same time the dead father idea underscored that equally continuing loyalty to an inner calling no one else could know or touch. Altogether the association of his greatest gifts with his dead father and his own death adds a dimension of inward poetic coherence to Nietzsche's *über-menschlich* desire to be above the world, to be outside it, in order to see it. It also reilluminates his well-known claim to being a 'posthumous thinker'. We assume Nietzsche meant his greatness would only be recognized when he was dead. But besides this rather routine thought for genius he may also have meant that he was the thinker he was because of something already dead within him. If Nietzsche were for a moment dropping his disingenuous guard it might also allude to the nature of syphilis, engendering a lifetime spent dying and occasionally a simultaneous efflorescence of genius.[16]

Actually the poetic story he told himself of the paternal inheritance sounds a little as if it was inspired by Goethe's well-known poem on *his* parental inheritance, *'Vom Vater habe ich die Statur'*. But whatever the origin, this powerful fiction gave Nietzsche a myth to live by. To believe the best part of himself dead shored up his sense of isolation and allowed him to feel superior even as he sat in Sils Maria:

> I need only to talk with any of the 'cultured people' who come to the Ober-Engadin in the summer to convince myself that I am *not* alive.[17]

Moreover, as-my-father-I-am-dead ran like a red thread through much of his life's work, because Nietzsche associated with Carl Ludwig the quality of compassion.[18] This was Christ's original virtue, conveyed in *The Antichristian* in the sweetest language in the whole of Nietzsche, and a quality Nietzsche normally perceived mainly in women (where he feared it would be applied smotheringly to him). It seems he allowed himself to accept pity in the male. Certainly when we consider Nietzsche on his father and on God/Jesus, alongside his constant exhortations to himself to reject pity, not to be weakened by it, we find a moving contradiction. (The Pietist tradition in which Nietzsche grew up identified Jesus with God.) It is tinged with the pathos of the bereft child and vulnerable fatherless teenager he saw himself to be.[19] From the deprivations of Nietzsche's fatherless childhood we can see straight to the frantic and incoherent letter of November 1882, probably to Lou Salomé, where, trying to deal with this momentous personal disappointment, he lists among the most significant events of his life being 'without father and adviser'.[20] The rejection of pity, the becoming hard, the 'Dionysian' direct confrontation of pain as themes for his writing, were an elaborate way of both mourning the loss and making it good. After the trauma of failure with Lou, to sing the 'hardness' of Zarathustra was apt and no doubt consoling. When he claimed not to want his works really to be understood he also extended his rejection of pity to an indefinite audience. This was the boy of seven, 'whom already no human word would ever reach', become a writer and a wretchedly defensive man.[21]

The full drama of pity in Nietzsche's life was played out in *Zarathustra*, whose protagonist he called his son, and whose God resembled Carl Ludwig. Zarathustra had to learn to live without him. The capacity for pity killed this compassionate God. *Thus Spake Zarathustra*, Nietzsche's extraordinary musical new testament of 1883–4, contains the nightmare vision of a dying shepherd choked by a dark snake entering his mouth, but surviving to laugh and inspire Zarathustra.[22] The dog howling beside the fallen man has been said to allude to the death of Carl Ludwig. 'Did I ever hear a dog howl like that? My thoughts ran back. Yes! When I was a child, in most distant childhood.' This kind of imagery is straight out of the nursery picture-book of religion. It is like a child's dream about evil, into which we can read of a devilish threat to the Word of God.[23]

Now it seems to me the idealized picture of the father is one of the few real clues we have to Nietzsche's interior life. Freud did not come to it because he did not delve deeply enough into Nietzsche's life and work.[24] It was as if with his physical debility, symbol of the paternal inheritance which was death-in-life, Nietzsche bore the stigma of one cast out of the kingdom of love. In an early poem, later set to music by Schoenberg, he writes of wandering through a forest, hearing an enchanting bird sing, only to be told by the bird that the song is not for him.[25] The genetic inheritance was a form of inherited burden, classical though not Christian guilt. Against the church he raged, because it urged men to believe affliction was their natural desert. He rejected God the law-giver, God who demanded sacrifices of man, God who declared so much human life a sin. None of that cruel paternalism was to be found in the loving fatherly example of Jesus, who only set an example of goodness, not virtue. The emotional drama of Nietzsche's life was thus played out between seeing his father as Jesus but inheriting only his distorted legacy in a punitive church.

The attack against the church though is complicated by the boy Nietzsche's reverence for the pious life in the immediate years after Carl Ludwig's death. He had been all too ready to obey and sacrifice himself and believe in sin. Even in a rainstorm he refused to run home from school because a school rule required boys to walk, Elisabeth later recounted. His schoolfriends remembered his deliberately burning his hand to prove his self-control.[26] To understand this connection, between love of the father and excessive early obedience, and later violent rebellion against those values, we may well want to consult Freud on Dostoevsky. But we may also follow the train of thought of Brandes, who immediately in 1888 was struck by Nietzsche's closeness in spirit to the highly inward and rebellious Danish religious thinker, Søren Kierkegaard. The religious burden so weighed down the early lives of these spiritual men, Nietzsche and Kierkegaard,

118

born a generation apart, that looking back from adulthood they saw Christianity as cruel and inhuman.[27]

Neither was a simple rebel. Kierkegaard, who both feared and revered his disciplinarian and devout father, was the devout son who accused the established church of obscuring true religion. His piety and his reaction were intensified by his being another 'metaphysically abject' character, a hunchback. Nietzsche accused Christianity of travestying the message of the life of Jesus. As a sick man he denounced a religion which profited, as he saw it, from the weak to retain its power. Intense inwardness, distrust of religious institutions and, most poignantly, a ferocious reaction to lost faith, defined these thinkers' role in an increasingly rationalistic nineteenth century. Both showed an almost equal frustration with the Hegelian legacy of their day, because they still cared passionately about the transcendent dimension which had disappointed them.[28] When they called for attention to psychology, they not only benefited our culture to this day, but also unconsciously highlighted their *own* needs as sons in an age which doubted God the father and overestimated science. They wrestled with a desire for metaphysical goodness which neither they alone nor the world could fulfil. Nietzsche's self-overcoming was an attempt at a surrogate. Kierkegaard encouraged an extreme form of taking the self to account.

Freud drew parallels from Sophocles through Shakespeare's *Hamlet* to Dostoevsky's *The Brothers Karamazov* to establish that complex web of emotion, the Oedipus complex. Without considering the validity of the claim that these feelings are fundamentally sexual, I think we are bound to accept the powerful effect on a son of his father's death, whether natural, desired or resented, willed by imagination, or actually brought about by murder. At stake is the son's sense of the moral order in tandem with the drive to assert his own needs. 'Without God everything is permitted', the most overquoted line in Dostoevsky, retains its potency to remind us of filial guilt or hurt as the greatest source of metaphysical despair. Nietzsche felt a great affinity with Dostoevsky. He also felt it for Stendhal and his shiftless moral world illuminated by the challenge of power and artistic beauty; and Stendhal was, or at least believed himself, another victim of a vicious-tempered father who tried to thwart his ambitions. Meanwhile, yet to express his despair was Kafka, who in 1888 was five years old, and already stuck in a frightening paternally dominated world where obedience was required but made no sense.[29]

Out of the maze of father–son relations emerged these famous sons, with their creative threads to guide them to freedom. Nietzsche in spinning that creative thread was in fact inclined more to worship than rebel, the celebratory poetic impulse and the love of language and music being so strong in him. That is the meaning of his Dionysian cultural vision, that despite the loss of the highest authority nihilism had little purchase on the dancing, excited soul.[30]

In Nietzsche's case though there is an additional dimension to the complex of religious feeling, and that is provided by his mother. His father stood for a religious ideal, for which he could not be questioned, and therefore remained ideal in Nietzsche's mind, whereas his mother, whose extreme piety seemed actually to have created the religious burden, was still there in the form of the Naumburg virtue Nietzsche decried. To survive the pressure from Christianity, which he hated, the adult Nietzsche had to fight his father's church, which he loved. Köselitz knew not what profundity he touched on, surely, when he pointed out that *The Antichristian* was fine propaganda for the church. When Nietzsche writes poignantly in *Human, All Too Human* that the 'unresolved dissonances in the relation of character and cast of mind of the parents resound in the children and delineate the story of their inner pain', we can only speculate that he had a conflict of his own in mind, which he imagined was due to a fundamental difference between his parents.[31] Such speculation is unsatisfyingly inconclusive; nevertheless we have somehow to understand Nietzsche, in relation to the father who *was* his illness, as born fighting and born having to compensate. The church his mother gave him didn't make good the pain, but rather increased it by making him feel guilty.

In life Nietzsche unconsciously sought father substitutes, who were then associated with his delivery. The most powerful and notorious of these of course was Wagner, born in the same year as Carl Ludwig, and possessed of remarkably similar Saxon speech intonations and outward appearance. But Professor Ritschl in Leipzig and Professor Burckhardt in Basel also played their part.

There is also that interesting evidence in 'Schopenhauer as Educator' of how much importance Nietzsche aged thirty-one still attached to fathers. His admiration for Schopenhauer's father, who set *his* son on a secure worldly path, is penned almost in envy, coupled with an all too brief dismissal of Schopenhauer's mother as trivial. Johanna Schopenhauer was worth more.[32]

Nietzsche's good association with his father was music. That his vision of the fatherless universe aspired to be happy surely stems from that early implanted lyricism. It does also seem plausible that the young Nietzsche found a discipline in music the dead father could not supply, though the net result was, thankfully, less good behaviour than joy.[33] From the death of the father came this glorious remission, running through the son's morbidly infected life.

'Singing is for those who are getting better,' he wrote in *Zarathustra*.[34] Singing, dancing, dithyrambic poeticizing: those music elements Nietzsche identified as fundamental to his creative work were both a tribute to the father and a way of overcoming the grief of his death. Music at least was alive; and here was the bridge from death to life Nietzsche leapt over to find his contribution to philosophy.

I suggest it was Nietzsche's view that his patrimony in the philosophical respect, German Idealism, was as much a mistake without music as he declared his own life was. The mass of abstraction needed a new injection of real vitality, that could be felt on the page. Schopenhauer saw the power of music even as a form of perception, and pointed the way for Nietzsche to revivify the life of the mind. In philosophy with his 'music' Nietzsche the dancing thinker was undoing all claims to absolute truth. On the other hand Schopenhauer, and Nietzsche, parallel with Wagner, at the same time forged a concept of *absolute* music which dominated nineteenth-century musical thinking. There was a contradiction there and that is one reason why by the time of *The Wagner Case* he was attacking a tradition he had helped to create. Wagner had set German Idealism to music. Over the quality of that achievement Nietzsche the philosopher and Nietzsche the music lover were at odds.[35]

No one was more aware than Nietzsche of the ecclesiastical roots of German Idealism through the lives of its thinkers, and not least in the seminarist Hegel. Nietzsche himself came from three generations of Lutheran pastors, and had begun in Bonn as a theology student. 'The protestant priest is the grandfather of German Idealism,' he wrote now in *The Antichristian*.[36] Men of the church were not the paternal forebears Nietzsche wanted. Each time he attacked German Idealism, each time he attacked the organized church he expressed resentment that they did not offer him a lovely enough vision of sublimity. For that he would have to turn to the fatherless church of Buddhism. But oh! the Buddhist ideal was also there in what for him was Wagner's greatest work, *Tristan*.

The emotion of early loss, after which he was always restless and homeless, dramatized Nietzsche's later sense of the loss of his fatherland. What began as a young man's ire and critical disappointment deepened into a sense of personal rejection reaching its apogee in 1888. He told Brandes Germans treated him as 'something odd and absurd'. (The word he used for 'odd' – *absonderlich* – had the biological meaning of a secretion of pus.)[37] Only towards the Germans was Nietzsche, so falsely accused of envisaging a German master race, racist. When Brandes pointed out to him how German he yet was, Nietzsche countered that German mind (*Geist*) was a *contradictio in adjecto*; logically he could not be his German father's son, only ever an exile. He fondly associated his fate with that of Heine, the German Jewish poet who fled to France. Heine debunked the excesses of German

Idealism yet was mournful for the old country. The two poets cherished the German language, loved colour, celebrated physical exuberance and hated establishment pomposity.

Or Nietzsche saw himself as Polish. When Resa von Schirnhofer told him he looked like the Polish *szlachta* she had seen in a Jan Matejko canvas in Vienna, he was so delighted he included that 'fact' in his April '88 *curriculum vitae* for Brandes. It wasn't true, genealogists have since proved, but Nietzsche stuck to the family myth. Indeed he was additionally delighted in 1888 when Carl Fuchs, well placed in Danzig to know Polish, told him that the name Nietzsche could mean 'man of nothing'.[38] That theatrical capacity for assuming other, more desirable identities gave him strength against the world which rejected him.

It reached a particularly refined form in his identification with Wagner's orphaned creation Siegfried, whose role in *The Ring* begins in early manhood when, realizing the dwarf Mime is only his guardian, he sets out, inspired by love of life, to discover who his father was. Through Nietzsche's many notebook jottings on Wagner and allusions in the published works the fearless Siegfried is one hero on whom he does not pour scorn, but rather hails as a free spirit. To break from the false tie to Mime, Siegfried forges the sword with which in Wagner's penultimate plan he was to rid the gods of the Nibelung curse and deliver humanity. Nietzsche's association appears to be a twin one. Memory of the day he first arrived at Tribschen and heard Wagner working on Siegfried's Rhine Journey became bound up with admiration for the saviour character. Nietzsche gave himself Siegfried's weapons to break free of Wagner – Mime in *Human, All Too Human*. He cut his sword in Vulcan's workshop and went out into the world. Thus when Wagner modified Siegfried's role, having him die ahead of the death of the gods, it was a symbolic blow for Nietzsche too.[39]

It is a point both about this association with Wagner's heroic tenor and Nietzsche's search for masculine role models and quasi-father figures that scattered in celebration throughout his writing are powerful individuals, breakers of moulds and laws. From

Mazzini to Shakespeare's Brutus and the great criminal Cesare Borgia these battling, disciplined, concentrated, utterly purposeful men of power helped Nietzsche attack the moral smallness of the age in which he lived, and the pettiness of a culture which craved stasis. At times it seems anything was better than the staidness of provincial Saxony and the obtuse, increasingly militaristic conventions of Wilhelmine Germany.[40]

But I think we should remember what Nietzsche was trying to do, shaping these tropes into the work of a lifetime, and trying in parallel to make sense of his own emotional genealogy. With all the will he brought to overcome his inheritance he strove for psychic health. That goal was less a search for perfection, paradise or peace than for an equilibrium or an accommodation with pain. And it was just that accommodation he could not see in Sils in 1888. The possibility of an improvement in the condition of the wretched *physis* seemed rather to recede. Nietzsche's whole thinking life had been spent seeking an alternative account of suffering with reference to the Greek world, but in the end he turned involuntarily to Christian ideals of steadfastness because they ennobled suffering:

The most spiritual human beings, assuming they are the most courageous, also experience by far the most painful tragedies: but it is precisely for that reason they honour life, because it brings against them its most formidable weapons.[41]

Nietzsche the insufficient *Übermensch* couldn't escape the Christian bind. Yet out of that tradition he created a unique post-Christian artistic vision.[42]

His efforts to climb out of his depression in Sils involved a state of mind he had known before and needed to summon up now more than ever:

One must test oneself to see whether one is destined for independence and command . . . One should not avoid one's tests, although they are perhaps the most dangerous game one

124

could play ... Not to cleave to another person ... not to cleave to a fatherland ... not to cleave to a feeling of pity ... not to cleave to a science ... not to cleave to one's own detachment ... not to cleave to our own virtues ... One must know how *to conserve oneself*: the sternest test of independence.[43]

Nietzsche, whose only absolute criterion was his sense of loss, envisaged fulfilling his emptiness with the help of so much self-discipline and training that the result amounted to an art of life.

'To conserve oneself', to hold one's energy in check, through training: the images here are strikingly physical. They remind us of the would-be military Nietzsche, and also of the animals in his life and *Zarathustra*: the wild cat waiting to pounce, the eagle waiting to swoop, and the dressage horse, with its muscular resources refined to execute the most delicate movements. Nietzsche's metaphors of energy lead constantly to self-collection and will to power. Those two depicted states relate to each other as implicit strength relates to explicit power.[44]

The self is held in check rapturously in 'The Night Song' of *Zarathustra*:

It is night: now do all leaping fountains speak louder. And my soul too is a leaping fountain.

It is night; now do all songs of lovers awaken. And my soul too is the song of a lover.

Something unquenched, unquenchable, is in me, that wants to speak out. A craving for love is in me, that itself speaks the language of love.

Light am I: ah that I were night! But this is my solitude, that I am girded round with light.

Ah that I were dark and obscure! How I would suck at the breasts of light!

And I should bless you, little sparkling stars and glow-worms above! – and be happy in your gifts of light.

But I live in my own light, I drink back into myself the flames that break from me ...

A beautiful self-sufficiency is poised here to disavow itself at any moment. Yet when Nietzsche's lines of energy uncurl and spring forward the result is inevitably conflict and collision with the world. Will to power is required, not to survive (which is actually unlikely) but to preserve spiritual grace. A famous maxim from *Twilight*: 'What does not kill me makes me strong', is reminiscent of that old piece of playground self-defence in the spirit of *Pilgrim's Progress*: 'Sticks and stones may break my bones but words will never hurt me.' To avoid conflict with the world Nietzsche kept lifting his sights: better than to attack other men's convictions is to attack one's own is a principle of *The Science of Joy*.[45] Better than the self-destruction of energetic, creative, exceptional humanity in pursuit of one truth is to accept the absence of truths. The human proclivity to self-deception, that is to a kind of inevitable perceptual embroidery, might indeed be celebrated in a world that could get beyond good and evil. There all men would function as artists of life.[46]

A subtle and widely overlooked aspect of Nietzsche's thought is that he eschewed self-conflict as something which weakened men, in which sense the run of reflective, religious, idealistic, thoughtful men and women put themselves at a terrible disadvantage because of the constantly debilitating effects of having to wrestle with their consciences. The *Übermensch* was someone way past this kind of inner self-doubt. Questions of 'spirit' no longer troubled him.[47] For doubt was a kind of sickness, as was ambivalence, as was idealism. The way out or beyond was *amor fati*.

On one of his walks around Sils in 1883, beside the Surlej rock, Nietzsche claimed to have formulated his notion of Eternal Recurrence. He had the sense that not only he but the whole world was not going anywhere; that man was not getting better; and that the future was so little to be coveted that it was hardly worth considering as a concept. The most important aspect of Eternal Recurrence, after the acceptance of a kind of cosmological monotony, is the notion that there can be no end or goal or final purpose for mankind. Life is an endlessly self-repeating process, in which the individual can only wait for a release from consciousness. Such a death in life Nietzsche envisaged quasi-mystically in the poem 'From High Mountains' which closes *Beyond Good and Evil*.

A window-pane of consciousness distances the real, familiar world of friends and renders it ghostly. But it is not unattractive and here behind the pane man lives in the eternal, while what he has left behind grows old in time, and will do until the dread curtain is rent and the wedding day comes of light and darkness. (From here surely Rohde took his criticism of Nietzsche living in a land where no one else lives: how often in life do we supply to our critics their most potent words.) My belief is that the high, flinty Fex Valley, relic of an Ice Age, inspired this poem with its persistent references to glaciers. It helped consolidate in Nietzsche the notion of an eternity without a Second Coming or Another Life or a Day of Judgement.

An interesting passage in Nietzsche's 23 May letter to Brandes shows him spontaneously interpreting his own life after the Turin happiness in this quasi-Oriental light:

> . . . Now and again I forget I am alive. A coincidence . . . made me aware recently that one of the main ideas of life has been extinguished in me, the idea of the future. I haven't a wish, not the tiniest cloud of a wish before me. A smooth expanse. Why shouldn't a day out of my seventieth year not be exactly the same as my present day? Have I lived too long in the nearness of death to be able to open my eyes to beautiful possibilities? What is certain is that I limit myself to thinking from one day to the next, that I decide today what will happen tomorrow and on more days ahead. That may not be rational, it may be impractical and even unChristian – that Sermonizer on the Mount forebade even this concern with the morrow – but it seems to me in the highest degree philosophical . . .
>
> I understood that I had lost the habit of wishing, without even wanting to lose it.

In fact, the future had not been a temporal concept in Nietzsche since the days of *The Birth of Tragedy* when he assimilated Wagner's 'Music of the Future'. He spoke in 1884 to Rohde of 'My Zarathustra [being] . . . a kind of abyss of the future'. The subtitle to *Beyond Good and Evil*, 'Prelude to a Philosophy of the Future', is manifestly ironic. Periodically writing to his friends of the likely shortness of his life, of his own lack of a future, in the winter of 1887-8 he became obsessed with drawing a line under his achievements and summing up. (Thomas Mann would take this as a motif prefiguring the artistic dissolution of the declining patrician family in *Buddenbrooks*.)

We remember again that the obsession with death derived from Nietzsche's thoughts of the dead father within and what he supposed was his fatal genetic inheritance. Measured against these deep preoccupations his philosophy is a reaching into the fatherless beyond, and a speaking out of it, quasi-unintelligibly, to a world dominated by mundane rational time. To the kind of time which Hegel systematized into a deification of success, and upon which Socialism built its hopes for a secular golden age, there could be no greater contrast than Nietzsche.[48]

Nietzsche was always 'out of time' – *unzeitgemäss*. Like the expectation of posthumous recognition of genius, it is a common enough feeling for writers. But again the dead father within made Nietzsche out of time in his own unique sense. *Ecce Homo* would present his discovery of his true self as a slow retreat from life. This paragraph from that last book, yet to be written, follows thoughts on the breach with Wagner, the publication of *Human, All Too Human*, and the declaration of a cultural war against narcotic art. Nietzsche gives up even the salutary habits of fantasy. He won't even pretend to be someone else, in which sense he has never been closer to death:

Then my instinct decided irrevocably to oppose any further conceding, any further playing along with, any further taking of myself for someone else . . . Here the bad inheritance from my father's side came to my rescue in a way I cannot wonder at enough and just at the right time – the predestiny to an early death. Illness slowly unravelled my being; it spared me the forging of any upheaval, the taking of any violent and conflictual step . . . I was never so happy in my being as I was in the sickliest and most painful times of my life: one only has to look at 'Daybreak' or perhaps 'The Wanderer and His Shadow' to grasp what this 'retreat back into myself' was: the highest form of cure![49]

The Buddhist–Schopenhauerian tone of that 'retreat' is as unmistakable as the parallel with the death of Socrates, with which he would open the main body of *Twilight*. Reason was a cunning trick, persuading men that life was not an aberration. The greatest man of reason on his deathbed only expressed relief that he was casting off sickness.

But there is of course a double paradox about Nietzsche by comparison: that he spent his short life writing against the misleading and constraining rational tradition and that, writing for so many years against the ticking clock of poor health, he desperately needed to hold on to reason to finish his work.

8

THE BRAHMIN OF SUPERABUNDANCE
AND THE MAD PROFESSOR

Theodor Adorno, visiting in the 1960s the Durisches' pension, met a nonagenarian, Mr Zuan, who remembered Nietzsche. The local children, of whom Zuan was one, used to torment the visitor who signed his name in the guest book 'University Professor'. Rain or shine, Nietzsche never went out without a red umbrella to shield his afflicted eyes from the light. Over the years other witnesses recalled a grey umbrella and a yellow one. Lou Salomé remembered his putting a red shade over the interior light in the Thuringen Forest resort of Tautenburg, near Jena. Zuan and his friends, in their insensitivity, put a handful of stones in the folded umbrella so that when the absorbed thinker opened it the pebbles showered down on his head. The way the all-too-young Lou never did, Adorno felt for Nietzsche in the moment of humiliation and rage. Should Nietzsche chase after the children who represented the Life he courted so fiercely in words? He could never hope to catch up. Did the experience of real pitilessness stoke his rage or encourage his passive admiration and conciliatory retreat? Well, who knows, but certainly the problem of being effective in a life which rejected him hurt Nietzsche greatly.[1]

The personality which resulted, morbid, melodramatic, full of inverted rage and useless exaltation, was his greatest handicap. In the midst of his unhappiness over Lou he called himself a worldly saint. His trust abused, his integrity maligned, he had been treated as a man of lesser moral stature than he was. Later, in madness, he sat dressed by others in a white robe, half-alive and vegetating, but appearing with that high smooth brow and the deep, dark, pinched eyes to think thoughts beyond the reach of ordinary mortals. Rudolph Steiner and Ernst Bertram, who worked with Elisabeth in the first years of the archive after Nietzsche's death, have long stood accused of trying with this picture, preserved in Hans Olde's photographs of 1889, to turn Nietzsche into a mystical figure. Indeed there is nothing holy about mindlessness.[2]

But in life there was surely something holy about Nietzsche, in the sense of vulnerable and *unworldly*, since his life was devoted in poverty and solitude to the highest thought. His *esprit de finesse*, in Pascal's sense, his judicious weighing of judgements, his intellectual conscience, combined with an almost exaggerated courtesy and concern, particularly impressed the thoughtful women he knew. Clothed in Indian robes instead of the shabby propriety of his German apparel he might have resembled a yoga mystic, and the speculation is not idle, because the Indian religions fascinated and influenced him, strengthening his ideas on the importance of the body and 'the things near at hand' over and against the dominance of abstractions and principles, and the tyranny of institutions. His schoolfriend Paul Deussen wrote a book on the *Vedanta* in 1883, which Lou Salome regarded as highly influential on Nietzsche. In May 1888 he became fascinated by a book he bought in Turin, *The Laws of Manu.* When in a subsequent letter to Köselitz he called Plato a Brahmin he might equally have referred to himself (as so often with his allusions to Plato the man, not his philosophy). Nietzsche believed in a superior quality of soul which men and women could cultivate in themselves, whence that aristocratic radicalism Brandes named. The nobility wasn't innate, but the *Übermensch* acquired it through the disciplined inner life. The so-called Superman, one of an invisible, timeless caste, was grand, refined, and materially and demogogically powerless. He was the Indo-European idea of a spiritual leader.[3]

It is curious to see the gloss Adorno, a Marxist, put on Nietzsche's social position. He observed that in Nietzsche's day it was possible to be poor with dignity; that with a modest life it was possible to buy intellectual freedom and still not be 'socially declassified by the bourgeoisie'. With that romantic view of nineteenth-century society Adorno resisted seeing Nietzsche himself romantically. Nietzsche was simply 'free'. By contrast, Adorno implied the mid-twentieth-century economic order made such spirituality impossible for a writer who wanted to be productive without losing his social place and roots.

The end of the century is a better vantage point from which to judge. My view is that all Nietzsche's experience, of being Godless, jobless, wifeless and homeless, gave him direct, first-hand knowledge of the pathology of the outsider whatever the age; that writers tend to be outsiders whatever the economic order but that Nietzsche experienced the outsideness with an almost wilful intensity. On the other hand his fellow *Kurgäste* in Sils found him unassuming and personable, ready to talk and keep company, even to break his routine to see off departees.[4]

It's also true that he stuck outwardly to the social routine of a professor, from which he derived a framework, a European itinerary and that cultivated company he leant on in correspondence. Meta von Salis-Marschlins, to use her full high-born title, observed how much Nietzsche appreciated the narrow confines of social rules and expectations, responding to them, we might add, in the manner of Goethe at the court of Weimar, the Goethe who was critical of the wilder kind of writer exemplified by Tasso. Von Salis added that Nietzsche's views were more tolerated in conservative and religious circles because those apparent adversaries of his were sure enough of themselves to follow him with deep interest. But, all the while, this was the man writing *Twilight* and *The Antichristian* in the solitude of his head and complaining of the emptiness of his life. The great problem for the biographer is to understand the gaps between Nietzsche's experience and his reflection, and between both of those and his writing for publication, and thus to reconstruct, however approximately, the process of self-overcoming.[5]

Women were his best company. Nietzsche liked talented, intelligent, articulate members of the opposite sex and was fortunate to have received the most significant introductions from his old Wagnerian friend Malvida von Meysenbug. Resa von Schirnhofer, one of the rare European New Women seeking higher education and independence in unpromising social circumstances, was one. Having enjoyed her company in Nice and once before in Sils he had written to Resa in April that he hoped their summer plans would intertwine, and even that she might make a special effort to coincide with him. The coy tone fits with Nietzsche's manifest unease among women. He knew how to be chivalrous but not how to be intimate, and that perhaps was one of his great problems when he was rarely sexually attracted to a woman. Given the near-purposelessness of his letter to Resa it is remarkable that six years before he wrote in similar terms to Lou, yet *meaning* to convey incomparable endearment and tenderness. The invitation to Lou to join him in Tautenburg was a unique and disastrous experiment in intimacy.[6]

In that relationship there were incapacities on both sides. Lou Salomé, of Baltic German origin and brilliant and beautiful at twenty, loved and sought out the company of clever men. She had radical views on women's social freedom and had in prospect a book on her loss of religious faith when she met Nietzsche. What distinguished the non-intellectual aspect of her relationships with the many men who loved her was her avoidance of sexual contact. Confusion over her own feelings for the married religious teacher of her adolescence in St Petersburg contributed to an inhibition which lasted until, at thirty-six, she met the poet Rilke. Nietzsche, who fell in love with Lou as with no other woman in his life, failed to notice until it was too late that she declined to be sexually attracted to him. He became jealous of their mutual friend Paul Rée, whom Lou preferred, though again, unbeknown to Nietzsche, only 'as a brother'. Nietzsche's disappointment over Lou dealt the fiercest blow to his pride because he had confided in her; explained that his character and illness had isolated him for so long he would need time to relearn human intimacy. A true radical of his day in not regarding marriage as his goal, he still probably took the wrong tack. He wanted Lou to be his intimate companion, yet he wooed her to be his intellectual disciple and heir. During one of their summer discussions did he attempt to embrace her? If so his humble advance met with astonishment and horror. Lou was terrified of her own womanliness. The relationship cooled, fanned into a painful memory on both sides by Elisabeth's monumentally vituperative interventions. Yet before the descent into crude hostilities, Lou was perceptive about Nietzsche's wanting talent for love. He was too precise in word and feeling and his mind oppressed others ('Nietzsche's weakness – supersensitivity'); he couldn't bear the difference between himself and those others; also it seemed he was trying less to be true to himself than to adhere to a deliberately created model. I suggest this last inauthenticity is one a young woman, even had she wanted to be close to him, would have found particularly alienating. For his part, failure with Lou exhausted Nietzsche emotionally. He never tried to court a woman again and none of his books was ever again as sexually vivid as *Zarathustra* which followed their non-affair.[7]

In 1888 from the end of July he had the admiring, go-ahead company of von Salis, though not the interesting Englishwomen of previous years, Mrs Emily Fynn and her daughter and Miss Helen Zimmern, nor Resa, nor the elderly woman who had retired from the Russian court, 'Fräulein' Mansuroff. Von Salis, rich and eleven years his junior, might well have married him, but Nietzsche, who in theory had this formula in mind for a suitable wife, never considered her, and deprecated her appearance. ('Even a bit paler and thinner than before,' he told his mother this year.) With Resa he emphatically declared she was 'too ugly', all of which was surely a pose, since with defensive hindsight he had taken to calling even the beautiful Lou so repulsive he had barely been able to hide his repugnance in her presence. Well, whatever the device, distance was the thing, supported by routine. Emily

Fynn, who missed him and Sils, wrote twice in August from Geneva. He sent a long friendly missive in reply.

The Engadine weather was still variable, though greatly improved since the middle of July. Paraguay would have been better, he joked, but with philosophy on his conscience he needed to live in the culture museum of Europe. 'I need so much time to reflect deeply on my own that nowhere is quiet enough, nowhere antimodern enough.' He thought he would go to Corsica for the winter. Mrs Fynn earned his respect for her kindness and Catholic faith. He once burst into tears at the idea of how much his anti-Christian thoughts would hurt her and evidently that memory touched her greatly. Teasing him for his feigned indifference to the fame stealing upon him in 1888, she suggested that though he had forbidden her to read his books she could not believe anything ignoble could flow from his pen.[8]

The women the forty-three-year-old Nietzsche mixed with became mothers to his good reputation, in contrast to his own mother and sister, who could not understand. Helen Zimmern, two years younger, and who had the splendid qualification of having translated Schopenhauer into English, prized his personality and work and bemoaned the gap between the man and his public image.

Nietzsche was reserved and almost awkwardly shy, when he came together with people with whom he had nothing in common. But once the ice was broken, then one immediately became aware of being in the presence of a man who was completely conscious of his value . . . he was not even eccentric, as are so many artists and authors.

'The clever Jewish woman,' as he called her, born in Germany, brought up in England, and resident in Italy, was one of Nietzsche's good Europeans. The translation of *Beyond Good and Evil* for Dr Oscar Levy's first collected Nietzsche in English was hers.[9]

These women missed Nietzsche as much as he them. They liked

him, they supported him, and also they realized he was a highly distinguished man. Resa, who accompanied him out walking in previous years, and heard him talk about his work, and even compose on the spot, used the word genius. Meta, a poet and an advocate of women's rights, would one day write a book about Nietzsche, while von Meysenbug, who had long supported him in spirit and tried to find him a wife, assured him that very July that he had a place in many hearts.[10]

Resa said that when Nietzsche *spoke* of his writing there was not a trace of pathological megalomania nor even of quasi-normal boastfulness.[11]

Yet I am sure that what Nietzsche lacked, in conversation with himself, was a realistic way of assessing his social situation. When he told his mother of his social pre-eminence at the beginning of August – to endorse which he had only a few days before received a gift of money from admirers in Kiel, via his friend Deussen – there was something characteristically odd about the way he did so:

> The company in the hotel is not bad: anyone who is anyone tries to get themselves introduced to me . . . even the pretty girls pay court to me quite openly. People have the approximate idea that I am 'a beast'. The cook is cooking for me this year with particular finesse. Letters have arrived which are in part crazy with enthusiasm for my books . . . Yet I keep very cool . . .

Lou, in a temper over Elisabeth's onslaught on her character in the summer of 1882, accused her friend of vanity and *Grossenwahn*, that affliction for which 'delusions of grandeur' and 'megalomania' are both customary English translations, despite their difference in pitch.[12]

Nietzsche defended himself by *admitting* these vices, yet in a characteristic way that suggested they were not his essential character. Some say in that case he had no character and in Goethe's sense of a personality made in the flow of the world, his character probably was slight, compared with his talent. He had no great experience to furnish anecdotes nor was humour his strong card. Lack of personality made him exaggerate his importance and justify his failings with constant recourse to a world and a terminology of his own making. Yet to identify this in English as megalomania seems too strong.[13]

In anguish he wrote to Lou who by December 1882 was with Rée in Berlin:

> Don't worry yourselves too much over my outbreaks of 'megalomania' and 'wounded vanity' – and if by chance some feeling drove me to take my life, there wouldn't be much to mourn over there either. What business of yours are my fantasies! (Not even my 'truths' have been your concern up to now.) Only you might care together to dwell on the fact that ultimately I am a semi-lunatic with head trouble, one whom long loneliness has completely distracted.

This letter shows exactly how Nietzsche retreated emotionally from the world, turning difficult emotions into 'words', which might then be treated as masks. He felt he was playing a fantastic game with the world, that he was in control, that his 'truth' was elsewhere. He had an inflated sense of his inner power over that world. He *imagined* greatness and strength and desirability to protect himself. Thus, just as transvaluation defined his philosophical agenda, so it dominated his emotional needs: he transvalued his vulnerability in order to survive. The psychology was troubled but undoubtedly he retained great self-control on the surface, where his mind was powerful and lucid.

The late 1880s brought no emotional crises, and less and less did Nietzsche need to *imagine* success. Yet the habits of a lonely life were too firmly in place for the psychological mechanisms not to come routinely into play. So he made silly claims such as that the pretty girls were admiring him in Sils, that he inspired the Alpenrose cook to produce particularly fine dishes, just as he did in Turin, with the waitress at his favourite trattoria, believing she kept back those sweet grapes for him.

Nietzsche lacked the ability to observe others objectively, being so absorbed in his own thoughts and feelings. When he did cherish friendships, especially earlier in his life, with men, he always needed to dominate. At the same time with people he loved, like Burckhardt, he could be overwhelmingly intense.[14] Lou said he couldn't accept the difference between himself and others. I think he couldn't see it and the greater his need the greater his blindness. It is, for example, striking that in his early letters to her he worries about her health the same way he worries about his own, and decides she will not live long; also the form his love takes is to make her his disciple. He explains his ideas so that she may become him.

The story of Lou in Nietzsche's life is relatively straight-forward. He tried to make her part of him and failed. After her departure he compensated with an artistic pregnancy, as it were to show he could do without her in securing a spiritual heir. She had a passionate affair with a version of him on paper. Powerful characters, turbulent souls, high intellects both, they had a huge impact on each other. It hastened and indelibly marked their most important current projects, Nietzsche's *Zarathustra* and Lou's *Struggle for God*.

Nietzsche's infusion of others with his own traits or aspects of his willed life however seems much more complicated in the case of Heinrich Köselitz. Here he succeeded because the younger man loved him.

Nietzsche knew what he was doing with such a relationship, for it was one of the most important mechanisms of his self-overcoming. After the break with Wagner, he was driven like a clever lonely child to create the company he needed. Life had to get easier to bear, so he invented out of Köselitz a friend, Peter Gast, and a music, Peter Gast's compositions, which he could praise unequivocally. Peter Gast came into being as the musician of genius who would thrust Wagner into the shade so long as he changed his name to something more acceptable to a general

138

European public. Nietzsche chose the name, used it publicly and projected Gast — or even sometimes Pietro Gasti — as a second Mozart, writing of him obliquely in *The Wagner Case*: 'I know only one musician today who can still cut an overture out of a single piece of wood, and no one knows him . . .' To create Gast was to create a musical friend, an absolute object of admiration and the token of a desirable future culture, as once Wagner had been. The situation of Peter Gast in European society was also an analogue of Nietzsche's own situation of unjustly unrecognized obscurity, against which he could then agitate, using all the contacts remaining to him from his Wagner days.

In a letter to Overbeck in October 1882, Nietzsche himself drew the parallel between the creation of Gast and his self-overcoming.

> Köselitz is the musical justification of my entire new practice and rebirth — to speak for a moment quite selfishly. Here is a new Mozart — I have no other feeling beyond that: beauty, heartfeltness, cheerfulness, fullness, an abundance of invention and the lightness of contrapuntal mastery — such qualities have never been found together before and I am on the point of being unable to listen to any other music. How poor, artificial and theatrical all that Wagner stuff sounds to me now!

He then sustained the simple Peter Gast dream for the rest of his life, despite Köselitz's conspicuous lack of success. On 14 April 1888 he observed from Turin to Fuchs that Köselitz was 'the only musician who makes music for me which seems today to be impossible: profound, sunny, loving, in perfect freedom within the rulebook'. Two weeks later Köselitz received direct praise:

> Your music! It has grown together with my idea of spring [. . .] Whenever one of your tunes comes into my head I hang on to my memories for a long time, with prolonged gratitude. Nothing has allowed me to experience so much rebirth, uplift and relief as your music. It is my good music *par excellence*, for

which inwardly I always put on cleaner clothes than for any other.

Just as Wagner had once pictured Nietzsche, Nietzsche now viewed his younger friend Köselitz, as a kind of musical Siegfried. Köselitz declared he felt more for Nietzsche than he had ever felt for his father. The evidence suggests these feelings were not of a sexual nature but lasted until Nietzsche's death. Is it possible that this replication of Nietzsche's relationship with Wagner, with Nietzsche's role changed to the stronger, paternal one, was not evident to Nietzsche himself? Nietzsche invented the very phrase 'superabundant substitutes' for real life. The age gap between master and disciple was halved by ten years. Köselitz, born in 1854, was only ten years younger than Nietzsche. But otherwise the bond between them seems to have been a perfect inverted analogue of the Nietzsche–Wagner relationship. In Tribschen Nietzsche put his own interests in abeyance to write Richard's publicity and run errands for Cosima. When Köselitz shared a house in Basel with Friedrich and Elisabeth, for nearly two years he acted as the master's secretary. The setup was not personally thrilling, as Tribschen had been. The young man found the arrangement stifling, while Nietzsche found the lad from Danzig poor physical company: 'clumsy and plebeian'. For his whole life he insisted on addressing him only with the formal you. But they got on so well at a physical distance that the postal friendship became a defining force in both their lives for over a decade. Nietzsche shared his musical life most fully with Köselitz, sending him notes on concerts he had attended, books and thoughts. The relationship flitted past, a mere shadow after the great, brief intimacy with Wagner. Yet it was life-saving. The arrangement resembled an arranged, deliberately unromantic marriage; and Nietzsche's notion of Gast's music, like Bizet's, a kind of opium to ensure his dreams.[15]

This kind of re-enactment, of suspended truth, of delight in falsehood, standing as it does at the centre of Nietzsche's complex psychology, I do believe became the basis for his philosophy.

Emotionally his balance was precarious. He was as neurotic as he claimed the Dionysus-worshipping Greeks were.[16] 'Despite all this I must in the years to come *invent* something with respect to my future and set myself in a position where I can be more *sure* of myself,' he wrote to Overbeck in December 1882. As Nietzsche often implied, human beings need delusions to live. We understand, as he did, that so much in Nietzsche's emotional world was happening beneath the level of full consciousness. In analysis he might have articulated it. Instead he found security in imagination. The personal uncertain element became caught up imaginatively in the works, to which the personal key was not then supplied, Brandes noted.

Nietzsche's psychology dictated a world view over which philosophers surely wrestle unnecessarily, for it was not destined to be a direct contribution to their subject. Nietzsche was an emeritus heretic, obsessed with his own problemsHn the letter to Overbeck from which I have just quoted he drew together many of the threads we have so far seen him spin between his life and work. He listed his intentions to recover from crisis and they mainly consisted in living out his own fiction. He would be hard against himself. He would invent his future. He would guard against too much solitude (by inventing friends, in practice). He would intoxicate himself with visions of happiness. 'I would like some Bizetism around me in every kind of form. I need the idyll for my health's sake.' He would also take real drugs, opium and chloral, to sleep.[17]

The confusion of Nietzsche's inner life, between his view of himself and things around him, which in an emergency so quickly acquired a fairy-tale strangeness even without resort to opiates, suggests a form of continuing autism. Notions of wilful deceit, mask, illusion and metaphor not surprisingly occupy a vital place in his philosophy. In the end we are bound to ask if Nietzsche's seminal contribution to modern philosophy is not the coincidental result of his complex, unevenly weighted, maladjusted character exaggerating the world for us, in order to show it in one of its true lights. In his case it is certainly true that there are no philosophies, only philosophers.

Dishonesty towards himself runs through his letters in extraordinary counterpoint to the ruthless honesty of the philosophical questioning. The minor deceits grow into the larger paradoxes of *The Wagner Case* and the cosmic convolutions of *Twilight*. His assertions of the untenable should be compared with Wittgenstein's of the unsayable. Like Wittgenstein he stresses the complexity of 'knowing'. His body, his whole being, are the bread and wine of modern philosophy, though that does not make it blessed, and Nietzsche, the man so wanting to overcome himself, remains a psychological problem.

Another aspect of not wanting to be understood surely contained the idea that it would be painful for the analytical reader to see through the published words to an utter incapacity for life. The *Übermensch* had no *ressentiment*, but Nietzsche the man was full of it, pretending retrospectively that Lou's ugliness had secretly revolted him, and backdating his hatred for Ree who had enjoyed a little more success with her. The antagonism was briefly comparable with his obsession with Wagner, though at least he managed to forget Rée quickly. Worse, far worse, was the petty hatred he allowed finally to surface against Lou in mid-1883. It coincided with his reconciliation with the sister he knew to be vengeful and venomous, and suggests both a weakness in the *family* – Elisabeth at least acknowledged that they were all hasty and vituperative – and also that he couldn't cope without their support after so much in his life had gone awry.[18] His personal vulnerability was unwaveringly desperate. It led to his distasteful written attacks on women, but they flowed more from the pen of an inadequate than a misogynist. His crass pseudo-worldliness covered his lack of real knowledge.[19]

Nietzsche's letters are marked by petty feuds and silences. In July 1888 he took furious umbrage against poor Fuchs who feared public knowledge of his association with the wicked Nietzsche might deprive him of a church organist's job he desperately needed, in order to feed his large family. Carl Spitteler, the Swiss critic who had previously responded positively to his work, also stirred Nietzsche's fury with a critical article.[20] At the end of the month, when in fact his spirits were quite good, he wrote to von Meysenbug, a woman at once motherly, witty and wise: 'Greatness of soul is needed even to tolerate my writings. I have the good fortune to embitter against me all that is weak and virtuous.'

She came back to him very quickly with a rebuke for that self-aggrandizing pity. She knew his value and tried to remind him of it:

It is a mistake or a paradox for you to say that you have the good fortune to have against you all that is weak and virtuous. The truly virtuous are not weak at all, rather they are the really strong, as the original concept of *virtù* even says. And you yourself are the living contradiction of that, for you are truly virtuous and I believe your example, if people really knew about it, would be more convincing than your books. For what is virtuous? To bear life steadfastly with all its misery for the sake of a great idea or an ideal, and with the exercise of mind [*Erkenntnis*] to deliver it from the unfreedom of the blind will into the freedom of self-determination. This is what you have done and in another form you have achieved the same as the saints did of an earlier world view. That these days in Germany people kneel before the idols of power is indeed sad, but the time will come when even the German spirit will wake afresh. And if it doesn't? Then the further development of humanity will pass to other branches of the human race, as you yourself are already experiencing in Denmark and America.[21]

Nietzsche was incapable of taking such a letter to heart. He needed reassurance but, being 'above all answerable to his work', he could accept no source for it other than himself. July leaked cold into the soul with self-questioning and gloom.

But slowly it passed and August was a better and thoroughly productive month. At last it felt like summer. Sils filled with guests – sixty alone in 'his' hotel – and Nietzsche, walking and working, and rowing on the lakes with Fräulein von Salis, was finally able to reap all the stimulating benefits he expected of a short-term change of habits. 'Something new is waiting at the door . . . this new discovery will be just right . . . that is what happens to me with dishes, ideas, human beings, cities, poems, music, doctrines, ways of arranging the day and lifestyles,' he wrote in *The Science of Joy*.[22]

In fact the stimulus came from two university professors of kindred interests, a musicologist called Karl von Holten and the theologian and one-time colleague of Overbeck's, Julius Kaftan. Holten, also a pianist at the Hamburg Conservatoire, evinced towards Nietzsche more than just a polite kindness and left upon him a brilliant impression of wit and benevolence. Discovering his enthusiasm for the music of Gast, von Holten learnt 'the love duet' from his opera *The Lion of Venice* and one morning in the conversation room of the Alpenrose gave Nietzsche a personal recital, obliging him with six encores. Nietzsche presumably supplied the score. Nietzsche liked Holten all the more because he was no admirer of Wagner, though clearly Holten was eager to please and Nietzsche was easily flattered. They spent many hours discussing professional musical questions, such as whether a definitive performance was possible or even desirable and whether, as Nietzsche had opined in *The Wagner Case* and may even have modified in the light of these conversations, the microscopic attention to detail manifest in Wagner's music, at the expense of larger structure, was not the wrong path for the music of the future.

Towards the end of the month after Holten left, Nietzsche spent more time with the Kaftans, from Berlin, whom he had first met in Basel. Kaftan was a devout Lutheran and a specialist in Christian ethics, but though they greatly differed in opinion they evidently discussed theology, among other subjects, without rancour on their outings. One day Kaftan was greatly moved by Nietzsche's suddenly stopping in the Fextal and explaining how illness had determined the vision he felt compelled to expound to the world. Kaftan felt this profound and enigmatic man, who so obviously needed people to talk to, could not be accused of merely wearing the mask of gregariousness. On another walk to Sils Baselgia, Nietzsche gave Kaftan a tantalizing glimpse into his preference for 'things close at hand' when he carefully explained to him a recipe. A recipe! Kaftan, who reminded himself this was a professor of philosophy speaking, failed to respond with sufficient seriousness, whereupon Nietzsche became quite angry. 'He gave me a lecture, saying what a crime it was to neglect the care of the body,' recalled Kaftan.[23]

So he was a cook then? A philosopher? A joker? An artist? Nietzsche's letter of 29 July 1888 to Fuchs rightly dissuades his friends from seeking a single definition:

I have never been characterized, neither as a psychologist nor as a writer (including as a 'poet'), nor as the inventor of a new kind of pessimism (Dionysian, born of the strength that enjoys seizing the problem of existence by the horns), nor as an immoralist (– the most accomplished form hitherto of 'intellectual integrity', which once it has itself become instinct and inevitability, can treat morality as an illusion). It's thoroughly unnecessary and not even desired that anyone should take up sides for me; on the contrary, a dose of curiosity, with the ironic guardedness one would bring to a strange growth would seem to me to be an incomparably more intelligent approach to me – Forgive me! I'm writing some naïve things here – a little recipe for getting myself happily out of an impossible situation.

Nietzsche held a socially conservative life together, while as an *immoralist* he meditated on life's appearances. While he suffered in solitude he meditated on joy and community, and the philosopher removed the conflict between traditional opposites. If all was appearance then what things were called and what they looked like uniquely mattered. His own days were not rich in appearances. Could they give him enough to feel this was sufficient life? The problem was in construing sufficient life as deep. When he wrote of the difficulty of stopping men pressing for profundity his own needs and foibles were uppermost in his mind. He declared that surface phenomena, as they became familiar, all too readily grew in the human mind into 'essences' and that the only possible counter-move was the constant conjectural challenge of artistic creation. Still ultimately created objects too would become absorbed into the establishment of unquestioned and revered things. How can we stop ourselves, as human beings, creating totems? How can we resist absolute judgements and objects? How to remember that reality is only a transient scheme of things? Nietzsche's campaign against certainty was the finest, least bombastic form his self-overcoming took, capitalizing on the necessity which made his own whole life into a scheme in his head. Only an unsympathetic commentator would find any of these marvellous, heuristic contradictions constantly alive in him hypocritical.[24]

I so much want to understand his attitude to society. He was always a difficult critical spirit, but it was mainly illness made him unsociable. He most wholeheartedly enjoyed human company in the early days around the Wagners and his well-known dandyism in Basel suggests acceptance of the social game. Even later, during the Lou affair, though his social world had crumbled, he could, aged thirty-seven, still see the way back. The documents surrounding the events of that summer speak volumes for his prickly personality, liable to fall into silence and self-deception with emotional panic, but capable of great devotion to his chosen idea. In Tautenburg he was the shy, pent-up professor trying to be alone with his rare discovery, a desirable woman, while his sister, redundant as a chaperone, stalked the village, and the chambermaids gossiped, all of them amassing evidence against his liaison. The local authority interrupted his thoughts to have him, a famous son of the region, bestow new names on the benches along its pretty forest walks. Nietzsche in Tautenburg, a younger relative of Nietzsche in Sils and Turin, was a serious citizen of the world temporarily stranded in a provincial hell; a tragic hero surrounded by comic characters who would destroy his dignity. It is one of the most accessible and attractive pictures we have of him.

Still after that season of 1882 the confirmation of lack of love hardly improved his grip on society, already menaced by illness and impoverishment. Moreover, he was already so much the shabby outsider in his thoughts, brilliantly qualified to analyse society for the subconscious content of its signs. In 1888 he very modestly told Julius Kaftan society made it difficult to resist being a satirist. Given that society was the context in which on paper Nietzsche so fiercely attacked women for their affectations and their vanity, it was clearly difficult not to appear furiously mysogynist too. The 'mysogyny' indeed was the form his satire often took, and it exposed the deepest contradictions in Nietzsche. Intellectually he admired dissembling and the un-graspable; in feminine social practice he evidently couldn't bear them. Now he suggested truth, now life might be 'a woman'. It was as if women embodied both the society where his place was uncertain and the truth philosophy was unwise to try to embrace. They were everything he didn't have, though philosophically he had turned that negative possession into a cause for celebration.

So he kept attacking women in *The Science of Joy* the proofs of which, because of his eyesight, he was passing to Köselitz, even while, because of his sexual blindness, he approached disaster with Lou. But apart from its embarrassing invective against the distaff side, that marvellous book about the surface of things showed no sign of myopia. Way ahead of its time, it called for a semiotics of life instead of a metaphysics of good and evil. Nietzsche suggested men and women should be wise to the surface of life and forget about what for so long had been regarded as serious and deep. For life had no depth. One might comment though that the wishing away of depth was itself profound and pathetic; also that in its ability to infect some minds it was dangerous.

An arrow from *Twilight* reminds us of Nietzsche's very personal goal:

Even the bravest of us rarely has the courage for what he really knows . . .

Nietzsche knew more about himself than any other human being, Freud suggested. But his very human limitation was that he could not overcome *all* he knew. And what perhaps he claimed to know best was the experience of death in life, which was almost too much to bear.

He longed for a full life, the kind of life he experienced in Wagner's music, the kind of life which, *pace* Kant, he thought a philosopher, who was also a real person, should lead, and which personally he had glimpsed while being uniquely and wholly himself in love with Lou.[25] To the extent that his longing for life was transvalued I believe it was Nietzsche's radicalism as a philosopher of desire which none of his contemporaries could grasp and which is still understated today. A remarkable paragraph in *The Science of Joy* approaches knowledge as the twitchiness of the skin, as the desire to possess, though I use my own words here. Nietzsche begins with the sensation of music and moves into a general description of what it is to accept the existence of the other, then to desire it, then not to be able to live without it. Given what Lou said about Nietzsche's inability to tolerate the difference between himself and other people it is all the more touching that he should cherish the possibility of such loving, poised between tolerance and longing, openness and the risk of loss, and that he should draw the analogy between human life and the art form which made him happiest.

One must learn to love – this is what happens to us in music. First one has to learn to hear a figure and melody at all, to detect and distinguish it, to isolate it and delimit it as a separate life. Then it requires some exertion and goodwill to tolerate it despite its strangeness, to be patient with its experience and expression, and kindhearted about its oddity. Finally there comes a moment when we are used to it, when we wait for it, when we sense we should miss it if it were not there; and now it continues to compel and enchant us relentlessly until we have become its humble and enraptured lovers who desire nothing better from the world than it and only it.

But that is what happens to us not only in music. That is how we have learned to love all things that we now love. In the end we are always rewarded for our goodwill, our patience, fairmindedness and gentleness with what is strange; gradually it sheds its veil and turns out to be a new and indescribable beauty. That is its thanks for our hospitality. Even those who love themselves will have learned it in this way: for there is no other way. Love, too, has to be learned.[26]

This passage occurs as part of a general critique of theorics of knowledge in which Nietzsche allows himself to be illuminated by his admired Spinoza. Spinoza had said the act of knowing involved an act of laughter, an act of mourning and an act of cursing. Nietzsche homed in on those subconscious processes. For him the act of knowledge embraced subconsciously that mixture of moods he consciously favoured as a working method. Knowledge – and love – emerged out of a confrontation on the battlefield of the subconscious, which engages our powers to spurn and to ridicule, to welcome, cherish and mourn.[27]

Knowledge thus conceived dances into view and moves on.[28] It invigorates like a swift plunge into cold water. Fueled by desire, it is nevertheless not, or Nietzsche does not wish to consider it in terms of, specific sexual excitement. He makes this point explicit in the groundbreaking Second Preface to *The Science of Joy*. It is true that philosophy has misunderstood the body and ignored the role of desire in knowledge, but as a *wise* artist of life he will accept the beauty and energy of that desire, without probing deeper. He invokes the Greeks, but it is exactly here we see his nature as the first philosophical troubadour, concerned with love for the unattainable one,[29] knowledge of the unknowable, articulation of the unsayable and now illuminating the Provençal motto of *The Science of Joy*, '*la gaya scienza*'.[30]

Knowledge-as-desire illuminates Zarathustra's life-intoxicated bedding of the night. The fourth book of that work, containing Zarathustra's quixotic death-in-love, the *Liebestod* of Wagner's friend and Nietzsche's fictitious son, has been deemed critically inferior.[31] Nietzsche himself though would soon feel 'close to death with excitement' at rereading it, with the famous 'Midnight' song Mahler set to music.[32][33] The lines of that song break forth as the drunken Zarathustra's ecstasy mounts, climaxes and dissipates with break of day. When day tries to resume the embrace of night the now sober Zarathustra finds his ideal partner has become stupid, clumsy and insensitive. 'Don't touch me. Did not my world become perfect just now?' Nietzsche's tone here is a strange mixture of the elevated and the banal, mixing the high seriousness of the *Liebestod* with the comic, also faintly pathological defensiveness of one who wakes to find his night misspent. The occasion is both erotic and emblematic. There is quickly a shift into non-sexual meaning. Day is too painful. *Deep is its woe.* Zarathustra the spiritual leader will not be known and loved by this realm searching him for deep happiness. 'Leave me alone! Don't touch me!' Nietzsche speaks for himself and his philosophy: even hallowing desire he brings his public no answers.

Lest this cosmic translation of his thwarted sensuality and desire for company begin to seem too far outside the range of normal feeling, let me finally dwell on Nietzsche's descriptions of a possible real happiness between man and woman. The passages come in *The Genealogy of Morals* where Nietzsche sees himself functioning mainly as a psychologist. Nietzsche maintains that though philosophers have a generic grudge against sensuality, they have often, as in the case of Schopenhauer, been deeply sensual. He quotes with deep approval Stendhal's definition of beauty as the promise of happiness and invokes such healthy spirits as Goethe and Hafiz, who know that the precarious human balance between the physical and the spiritual life, 'between beast and angel', is only one more incentive to love.[34] 'Between beast and angel' picks up famous words of Luther, of whom

150

Nietzsche writes, from the midst of a fierce attack on religious asceticism, that his greatest merit was to have the courage of his sensuality. The passage then relies on style to reflect the way the beautiful in human nature is made grotesque by enforced sexual restraint. All too vividly conveyed, but painful to contemplate perhaps, the idea has been lost in translation.[35]

Nietzsche, frustrated himself, loathed the repression of the sensual as a supposed moral value, hence much of his invective against the church. The achievement of *The Genealogy of Morals* was to see this institutionalized repression, practised by the church, in political terms. Nietzsche's 'ascetic priest' and his 'ideals' spoke of totalitarianism in all but name nearly fifty years before the twentieth century invented it, and impressively anticipated Wilhelm Reich's criticism of 'the mass psychology of Fascism'.[36]

One of Nietzsche's achievements as a man was to retain wise judgement about love and love of life despite his long trial by deprivation. He has been suspected of tending to sado-masochism, in his mind, I suppose, but in the writing, when he does come to use a more impersonal, Schopenhauerian-type image of the sexual will driven by the desire to dominate another, it is more to escape a gender trap than to imagine the infliction of pain. Individual psychological needs differ, as do, because of those needs, the ways people relate to each other. At stake is more interaction than domination: there is no need to adjudicate in terms of good and bad, or worse still good and evil. Nietzsche stresses that the balance of a relationship can change, that strong and weak are relative concepts. Nowhere does he speak of masculine and feminine as having a specific tendency. His words give the sense of libidinous energy shared between the sexes in varying individual proportions and modes.[37]

He raged against women, yet ahead of his time, he defended their education and independence. Of those in her day Lou was one of the most extraordinary examples in Europe and Nietzsche worshipped her. He raged against women, and they fed his philosophical wit, occasionally brilliantly. What indeed if truth were a woman? How flattering! As a woman I am also amused by resonances I read into his concept of Eternal Recurrence. The German *ewige Widerkehr* surely suggests to anyone acquainted with German literature Goethe's salvationary notion of the *Ewig-Weibliche*. 'The Eternal Feminine leads us on', the closing line of Goethe's *Faust*, Part II, is such a suitable pun in English that the woman-shy Nietzsche would surely have rejoiced had it come his way. Instead his concept of eternity simply left male and female unspecified. More serious accounts of this vapid concept, even an attempt to found it mathematically, will be found in other books than mine. I take it as a vague, less effective duplicate of *amor fati*. In the sexual context Eternal Recurrence in fact meant Nietzsche would be subject to vengeful women into infinity. He once said the eternal recurrence of Elisabeth was the only aspect of his theory which caused him regret. He did have wit, strange wit.[38]

Nietzsche like all of us was probably more lucid and generous on paper than always in life. If there was a sexual problem implicit, as I have said, he was probably rather 'feminine' by nature. Some of the worst attributes he gave to women – pettiness, vanity, remorseless vengefulness and sexually frustrated bitterness – look like aspects of himself he perceived as feminine and was striving to overcome by offloading onto womanhood in general. Undesirable aspects of himself were often traits Elisabeth also possessed, so it was not difficult to picture them. The lack of personal sexual perceptiveness in Nietzsche's behaviour may also have derived from whatever about him was feminine or was the result of growing up in only female company. To say he was not perceptive about his own sexuality is not to allege he had no sexual instinct, nor that he was not perceptive about sexuality generally. In both cases, far from it. But in any case the result was ghastly. A foul-mouthed vengefulness of Elisabeth's kind seized him when he temporarily yielded to hating Lou. It is the ugliest documented moment in Nietzsche's personal life.[39]

One cannot overcome everything. Nietzsche's case might be

issued as both an incentive and a warning to those who enter Freudian analysis. The rages against himself, the tetchiness, the fear of madness, the violent imaginings, the mockery, made him crave a God who catered for such negative, self-lacerating emotions. A non-decadent Dionysian God would understand the plight of being caught existentially between animal and *Übermensch*.[40]

In Nietzsche's eyes illness, from which we might infer all forms of frustrated life, incited these negative emotions. God's lovely creature became a parasite and a parasite was a criminal against life.

Now the only way the 'criminal' could recover was will-to-power, self-overcoming. In this context Nietzsche admired certain real criminals for their apparent determination and strength of will. Their potency found an outlet, even with the horrible acts of Cesare Borgia. On such raw energy of self-belief a non-decadent civilization depended. Nietzsche shared these interests with Dostoevsky and Stendhal, and they would flare up once more in Turin just before Christmas, when he would look again to Thomas Galton, this time for confirmation of his idea that crime arose when a man was too powerful for the social milieu into which he was born.[41]

Nietzsche himself was that: too powerful for provincial Saxony, therefore eccentric, unpredictable, and potentially frightening. He had been light-hearted to Elisabeth earlier in the year, calling himself 'your philosophic – nihilistic – good-for-nothing of a brother', but the isolation into which life thrust him made those caricatures signs of real danger. Where could he warm himself, let alone espy greatness, except in imagination? In the beyond, however peaceful, the temperatures are glacial. But there was a refuge: beauty. I think one can see from passages like this that Nietzsche's warmth was actually protected by his fundamental instinct for beauty:

God knows it is possible to endure all kinds of misery – vile weather, sickness, trouble, isolation. All this can be coped with, if one is born to a life of anonymity and battle. There will always be moments of re-emergence into the light, when one tastes the golden hour of victory and once again stands foursquare, unshakeable, ready to face even harder things, like a bowstring drawn taut against new perils. But, you divine patronesses – if there are any such in the realm beyond good and evil – grant me now and again the sight of something perfect, wholly achieved, happy, magnificently triumphant, something still capable of inspiring fear! Of a man who will justify the existence of mankind, for whose sake one may continue to believe in mankind . . . The levelling and diminution of European man is our greatest danger because the sight of him makes us despond.[42]

Words can be effective. Words can move men. This was Nietzsche's hope and his will-to-power as he descended from the mountains, like Zarathustra to resume his work but in what will be for him a last *untergehen*. Through August he had in fact applied himself furiously, throwing tantrums and refusing to open fat letters from Fuchs which appeared beside his place at lunch, for how could a friend so insensitively tire with twaddle a great mind in a period of creation. *Twilight* was finished by 9 September, in time for his intended departure date a few days later.

In the event though, Nietzsche was delayed almost two more weeks by floods. The chamois hunting season began and he heard Herr Durisch depart in the early hours. Lying awake in bed he imagined his work tracking down humanity's rotten idols was a kindred adventure.

Nietzsche so wanted to be effective, whether as dynamite or a hammer. In Nice he once witnessed an earthquake. He saw his fellow men and women, winter guests on the Riviera, in their nightclothes, wrapped in blankets and huddled on the pavements. He hoped they would tremble that way when they read him. He sounds monstrous, though the situation, with danger passed, was probably tragicomic. Nietzsche was his own worst enemy in borrowing images unheedingly from life, and never quite making clear where the divide lay between moral reality and aesthetic play.

I sometimes wonder what people thought of him in the train, which after two weeks of delay in his travel plans, finally conveyed him back from Sils to Turin via Como and Milan. This strange man, given to disguises, who is he? Might he not be plotting the crime of the millennium against humanity? How can we know or judge from his appearance? He is the sick traveller, the eccentric German, with a travelling bag, a plaid blanket, a military air and a huge moustache. He may be a debilitated fool or a genius. In both cases he may have a bomb in his bag. He may be carrying an explosive secret likely to endanger lives, or change them irrevocably for the better. His revelation is timed to go off in the indefinite future and no one can vouch for its benignity.

And the incorruptible Professor walked, too, averting his eyes from the multitude of mankind. He had no future. He disdained it. He was a force. His thoughts caressed the images of ruin and destruction. He walked frail, insignificant, shabby, miserable – and terrible in his idea of calling madness and despair to the regeneration of the world. Nobody looked at him. He passed on unsuspected and deadly, like a pest in the street full of men.

Joseph Conrad, who knew the real nature of Nietzsche's work, ended *The Secret Agent* on this resonant Nietzschean note, showing what those who called themselves Nietzscheans might become.[43] Nietzsche himself had a horror of what he called nihilism.

The real danger lies in our loathing of man and our pity of him. If these two emotions should one day join forces, they would beget the most sinister thing ever witnessed on earth: man's *ultimate* will, his will to nothingness, nihilism [. . .] One who smells not only with his nose but also with his eyes and ears will notice everywhere these days an air as of a lunatic asylum or sanatorium. [. . .] It is the diseased who imperil mankind, and not the 'beasts of prey'.[44]

155

But the very way he conceived of that nihilism was a wrongdoing, which poetry does not excuse. Also he often decried what was raging as a threat within himself, as a piece of self-prescription. He was wrong to equate with Christianity and the Christian value of pity those forces which would wilfully destroy humanity out of gratuitous resentment. ('Nihilist' rhymes with 'Christian' – in German at least – he mused frivolously in *The Antichristian*.) He associated nihilism with illness, his own illness and the cultural decay of all Europe. He campaigned against the whole of Christian and humanist moral philosophy and the politics of socialism because of the forces which threatened to destroy him personally: pity and sickness. He encouraged a new intellectual conscience to show the traditional Christian moral conscience to be far from good in its origins and aims. That was a brave act of intellectual cleansing but it left a gaping moral hole.[45][46] Nietzsche provided no notion of moral responsibility. With fanatical regard for his beloved and bloody Renaissance he pointed out that to have regard for the consequences of an action was not the business of an immoralist.[47] Once again, Nietzsche can too easily appear to be playing an aesthetic game with life in his head, like a character out of Pirandello.[48] His legacy to us is to be an insoluble problem, a man whom it is impossible to call good or evil, since he has the potential for both.

On the way back to Turin that night of 20 September his train met the flood waters which though now passable were still high. He enjoyed that emergency, so much so one could be forgiven for thinking weather was the only thing that happened in his life these days:

My journey had difficulties and brought the most severe tests of patience: it was midnight before I arrived in Milan. The most alarming thing was a long foot-crossing at night in Como over flooded terrain over a very narrow little wooden bridge, lit by torches! It might have been made for me, given that I'm blind as a bat![49]

Back in his compartment, his heart palpitating a little, Nietzsche sat locked inside himself, with that love of drama, of sensation, of the extraordinary, the tableauesque, locked in beside him. Because of the confinement of his fantasy within his head he was relatively harmless while he still existed in the present continuous. A real nihilist would have destroyed life for the pleasure of the spectacle. But it is a relief to know that, after a night in Milan, for the foreseeable future Signora Fino and her daughters and the waitress in his favourite trattoria would be keeping an eye on him back in Turin, for despite all his outward discipline, he was inwardly unpredictable.

9

ECCE HOMO

Behold this man. But who was he? 'I am one thing, my writings are another,' he would assert, impossibly, seeking through his last writing to define himself. *Ecce Homo* would be an essay in selfhood.[1]

> Listen to me! for I am thus and thus. Do not above all confound me with what I am not!
>
> I am, for example, absolutely not a bogeyman, not a moral monster . . . But you only have to read this writing.[2]

Rarely would a slim book capture so directly the richness and anguish of solitude, the many mansions of inwardness, the auto-erotic electricity, and the relentless drive to be known. Nietzsche showed that a modern man first becomes witty when he recognizes his obscurity and can enjoy the fact that, 'I am a nuance.' *Ecce Homo* contains not only an autobiography, but what it means to be an autobiographer. In a letter of late October Nietzsche speaks of his preoccupation with 'an uncannily solitary act of transvaluation'.[3] The transvaluation in his case is a rising from the dead, an account of the idealized dead father as he is imagined to have lived in the son, and thus a rendering of most important things at a great rhetorical distance. It is an auto-obituary.

This man wearing a crown of thorns did not come back to Turin as a terrorist but as a lover and a liberator and a spokesman for passion. He was a philosophical troubadour who after the death of God found his vocation in singing of things near at hand; now he was to map the survival of the human individual, whom godlessness had locked inside his imagination; he was to unwrap the human package suspended between animal determinacy and the self-overcoming. Revealed as a vision of solitude is the idea that humanity is a tension between mental agility and physical destiny. 'To live alone one must be an animal or a god – says Aristotle. There is yet a third case; one must be both – a *philosopher*.' Nietzsche's image from *Zarathustra* is a further variation on Aristotle. It is the famous one of the tightrope walker 'between animal and *Übermensch*', inspired, said his sister, by the travelling circus that every so often relieved the tedium of a childhood in Naumburg.[4]

Nietzsche's desire to confront the tension is his legacy to us. The working is contained in *The Science of Joy* and *Zarathustra*; in *Beyond Good and Evil* and *The Genealogy of Morals*; and in the last books, *Twilight, Antichristian* and *Ecce Homo*. These works are continuous, despite the changing focus indicated by the titles. To them the *Dionysus Dithyrambs* and *Nietzsche contra Wagner* are personal, and in the case of the poems, raw appendices, giving extraordinary access, if not always in artistically satisfying form, to Nietzsche's psyche.

Ecce Homo shows how a modern man can defend himself against those disintegrating forces which threaten his personality and his life. Nietzsche, modern to the core, counsels psychological insight, for moral and social prescription only mislead spiritually becalmed men and women further. He urges self-determination while simultaneously underscoring the chaos of existence: the individual must create himself though he is existentially worthless. Nietzsche's humility here has been much overlooked. He offers himself, an entity literally made through writing, as an example. Coming to write *Ecce Homo*, which with few notes suddenly takes shape in autumn 1888, he realizes that his lot has more than personal interest; that his way of coping with his talents and misfortunes is exemplary for the human condition.

A draft for the *Dionysus Dithyrambs*, deciphered by his mother, ran:

> I sought my heaviest burden
> and found myself.[5]

Nietzsche changed this in his fair copy of 'Between Birds of Prey' to:

> You sought the heaviest burden
> and found yourself
> a self you cannot now detach from you.

Nietzsche writes in the first person because he considers his loss of belief, loss of country, disappointment in love, loss of professional belonging and employment, poor health and loneliness can show us how to live. A conscious parallel with Luther recurs in the last writing, suggesting Nietzsche even feels he is initiating a new spiritual age. The title 'Ecce Homo' is its echo. 'I can do no different. God help me. Amen.'[6]

Yet Nietzsche cannot be a spiritual leader like Luther. His modernity is the sum of how warily he approaches the transmission of ideas, the creation of ideals and dictates, the pitfalls of writing and reading. In the game of literature he is both batsman and backstop, ever ready to catch himself out. Much turns on the word *Gleichnis*: metaphor or parable. The relating of parables is the activity which allows Nietzsche to compare himself with Christ as an example but not as a supplier of truths. He tells his readers, once they have absorbed his words: 'Now lose me and find yourselves; and only when you have all denied me will I return to you.'[7] He will teach us and yet he won't. The maze of caveats in Nietzsche is a rhetorical maze, which dispassionate readers today follow through as a kind of game. But to teach self-overcoming was not a game. To say *what* it was strained his rhetoric until he lost control of his destiny.

For advice on how to live a strong and fruitful life a few points from *Ecce Homo* may be summarized, albeit unsatisfactorily, for it is a work of art, not a self-help manual. Wise, clever, Nietzschean men and women (who may write good books and become a destiny) look inwards to find self-understanding; they are prepared to be out of season; they cultivate self-discipline; they belong only to themselves; and they deal with the world out of strength, not out of weakness.[8] The last point is crucial to understanding what Nietzsche meant by self-overcoming, by getting beyond inner conflict and dreaming (born of idealism) and beyond resentment (born of 'Man from Underground' impotence).[9]

Ecce Homo is neither philosophy nor psychology, but poised somewhere between the two, wanting both to elucidate and to heal. It speaks to those liberated from religious dogma yet not materialist; to connoisseurs of life who do not see in the perfectability of human nature a desirable goal. It is a poetic answer to the Darwinist Spencer and the Socialist Marx even in their own time. Nietzsche's spiritual survivors are deep, independent, abrasive, noble loners with a love of language and a sensitive ear; they are sceptical, critical yet passionate readers of great artists and thinkers. They do not think anything in particular because they have listened to 'the genius of the heart, who makes everything loud and self-satisfied fall silent and teaches it to listen, who soothes rough souls and gives them a new desire to savour – the desire to lie still as a mirror, that the deep sky may mirror itself in them'. 'Consciousness is a surface [which] has to be kept clear of any of the great imperatives.'[10]

This modernism of Nietzsche's – because it is intended as typical it may still be named with an otherwise tired word – is at odds with and yet strangely in tune with Turin, where it last flowered. The city had a stateliness and grandeur which reminded Nietzsche of the centuries he preferred to his own. Its unified architecture perhaps echoed something of the Greek spirit he as a modern man could only imagine. The civic ambience was certainly aristocratic and beyond the mentality of Nietzsche's perceived herd. Almost fifty years later the Piedmontese writer

Cesare Pavese, 'born in Turin in spirit', characterized the city in terms which suggest Nietzsche even helped tease into awareness its twentieth-century identity:

> City of dreams, with its aristocratic perfection composed of ancient and modern elements; city of the rule, with its absolute absence of material and spiritual wrong notes; city of passion, with its benevolent propitiousness to leisure; city of irony, with its good taste in life; exemplary city, with its tranquility rich in tumult. City virginal in art like a young woman who has already seen others make love and for her part has allowed no more than caresses until now, but is ready to take a st~p further if the man be found . . .[11]

Nietzsche enjoyed the implicit invitation to flourish in this complex world. To this last privileged environment for him as a writer we must return him now.

He drew from the Piedmont capital a sense of establishment and enjoyed its formal occasions, so it was disappointing, because his return from Sils was delayed, to miss a great wedding joining the houses of Savoy and Buonaparte.[12] Whether that sense of the workings of establishment was as theatre backdrop to the drama in his inflamed mind, or whether he enjoyed those workings for themselves, is difficult to say in the autumn of 1888, but it was clear Nietzsche loved pomp, the way he relished a series of state funerals between October and Christmas. First Antonelli, architect of the Mole, died; then the body of Count Robilant, the Italian Ambassador to England, was returned and buried, and finally Turin took ritual leave of Admiral Carignano on 18 December.[13] Nietzsche watched the funerals from his balcony in Piazza Carlo Alberto, and in those minutes may have felt like the Dionysian Greeks, whose 'ever more intense *craving for beauty*, for festivals, entertainments, new cults', he had speculated just two years before, 'grew out of a lack, a deprivation, a pain'.[14] Processions were something Nietzsche could admire in the painting of Claude, and as a young man had most vividly imagined in the choral movement of Beethoven's 'Dionysian' Ninth Symphony, 'where multitudes bowed awestruck into the dust'.[15] Nietzsche harboured a deep desire for epiphany. His spiritual condition spoke for bewildered would-be god-worshippers marooned in a godless age. *That* condition we might imagine we can hear in the funeral marches in Mahler, who was part of Nietzsche's musical legacy. Public ceremony fitted with Nietzsche's love of operetta and of masque and was the aesthetic foundation of his sense of community. His religious need to feel community in this theatrical, Dionysian fashion was what had long determined his ambivalent position towards secular theatre, and especially towards Wagner and the *Festspiele* of Bayreuth. He never found what he needed in the modern world outside his own head, but he was more able to enjoy contemporary pomp abroad, at the Nice carnival, and now in Turin, than in Germany, where Bismarck's imperial gaudies disgusted him.[16]

Haunted by the ghost of pomp and circumstance, embraced by the absent community, is how the painter de Chirico explicitly interpreted Nietzsche's Turin, with the city rendered as a giant still life, across which the occasional pin figure walks or bowls a hoop. 'Spring in Turin' shows the statue of Carlo Alberto and the Carignano Palace outside Nietzsche's window. A surreal breeze brushes these symbols of stately tradition, absolute power and the quality of reason, giving the impression the key to civic life has been lost, even while the buildings of the city still stand. About the whole there is an awesome beauty and fascination.[17]

Nietzsche understood the life of man as pin figure. When his books arrived from Nice, he reread his two most pictographic and communal books, *The Birth of Tragedy* and part of *Zarathustra*. Where once, Nietzsche imagined, the Dionysian was a rich, expressive communal culture, now, thin and almost invisible to the naked eye, it dwelt only within individual consciousness:

'I live in my own light, I drink back into myself the flames that break from me . . .'[18]

From the time of *Zarathustra*, Nietzsche's individuals live in an eternal present, absorbed in their own inner light. Eventually the light goes out. This 'abyss of the future', this *time being* was the modern condition under which *Ecce Homo* was written, and one in which death became the new and only god of life: a non-Christian promise of eventual delivery.

Nietzsche versified this death in one of the *Dithyrambs* called 'The Sun Sets'. To glow in his own light was rapture and rapturous fatalism, *amor fati*. *Ecce Homo* simultaneously praised Russian soldiers lying down in the snow when the battle overwhelmed them, and admired fakirs able to sleep for weeks in a ditch. Nietzsche's last passion for hibernation recalls Schopenhauer, an enduring inspiration for his 'pessimism of strength'. His toying with long sleep must also make us think of Brünnhilde. To think of her still sleeping is to contemplate a condition untouched by the pain of human individuality and sexual awakening. In *Ecce Homo* Nietzsche drags all that is significant about his past into the eternal present, swelling its rapture. He invites us to see the whole course of that life as something he willed. In the marriage of will and fate, *amor fati*, lies redemption, beautifully expressed with a citation in *Ecce Homo* from *Zarathustra*:

I walk among men as among fragments of the future: of that future which I scan.

And it is all my art and aim, to compose into one and bring together what is fragment and riddle and dreadful chance.

And how could I endure to be a man, if man were not also poet and reader of riddles and the redeemer of chance!

To redeem the past and to transform every 'It was' into an 'I wanted it thus!' – that alone would I call redemption.[19]

Only Nietzsche, be it under new pressure of autobiographical inspiration, ever-present inspiration from Wagner, or no longer able to stave off the delusions of syphilis, sees his fate as more than individual, for after his death (just as after Siegfried's and Brünnhilde's), the present gods will slide into eclipse, and the next dawn will illuminate a new human age. Syphilitic megalomania certainly seems to creep in. 'Only after me will there be *grand politics* on earth' sounds the fateful note of false apocalypse. We begin to lose the Nietzsche we love.[20]

Nietzsche was sinking yet agitating to be translated and known in the autumn of 1888, as his letters to August Strindberg, Brandes, Helen Zimmern and the editor of the *Journal des Débats*, Jean Bourdeau, testify. He was sane too when he noted in passing, and with punctuation making the comment obviously ironic, that Turin had experienced earth tremors on 13 November, just as Nice had trembled while he was staying there: evidence enough that the world shook in his presence. He was sane in knowing a curtain was descending before him, or the horizon rising, for the last time.

The autumn in Turin was colder than usual but bright and dry. The cold in his old room at Finos prompted him to order a charcoal-burning stove from a firm in Dresden, called Nieske. When the novel fuel arrived its near-weightlessness fascinated him, the Finos remembered, but before the Nieske stove could follow the Prussian authorities had certified its type dangerous. Nietzsche got his money back and put a gas stove on the purchase list for the end of November, but that appliance would never have a Turin owner called Nietzsche.

On this, technically his second visit, Nietzsche appreciated the convenience of Turin all the more: being close to a university, to libraries and theatre again, and he lapped up the benefits of a town centre without the noise. Curiously such a city figured in his dreams long before he knew Turin.

Architecture for people who think – it needs to be made clear, probably as a matter of urgency, what above all our big towns lack: tranquility and broad, extensive, roomy places for reflection, places with long, high-ceilinged cloisters for bad or all too sunny weather, where the noise of carriages and people shouting can't penetrate and where finer manners would forbid even the priest to pray out loud; buildings and gardens which as a whole would express the sublime idea of stepping aside to commune with oneself. The time has passed when the church has a monopoly on reflectiveness, when the *vita contemplativa* always had first to be the *vita religiosa*: everything the church built expresses that idea. I don't know how we can let ourselves be satisfied by its buildings, even divested of their ecclesiastical purposes; as houses of God and showhouses for otherworldly activity these buildings speak a far too rhetorical and inhibited language for us godless to be able to think our thoughts here. We want to have ourselves translated into stone and plants, we want to go walking within ourselves, when we wander through these cloisters and gardens.[21]

Turin, broad, extensive, roomy and tranquil, was a place where he could translate himself into stone and plant and walk plunged in contemplation. For some weeks he had still toyed with moving on to Nice, but by the third week in November he knew he would winter in Augusta Taurinorum, working simultaneously on *Ecce Homo*, the final version of *The Antichristian*, the *Dionysus Dithyrambs* and *Nietzsche contra Wagner*.[22]

He preferred as usual to be alone. Contacts he had made in spring he avoided by frequenting the unfashionable Café Livorno on his long walk from Piazza Carlo Alberto along Via Po and then right at the river as far as the Parco Valentino. Loescher's bookshop, where he might have bumped into Pasquale d'Ercole, who might have wanted to talk about Hegel, was definitely excised from the routine. Generally his days became stricter than ever.[23] He made lists, as he had long done, comprising rules for the smooth running of the human machine Friedrich Nietzsche. Wait for tea to *cool* before drinking it, avoid *all* alcohol, crowds, reading, writing letters, wear warm clothes in the evening, eat rhubarb from time to time, have a napkin at breakfast, remember notebook. The only god was to produce.

He liked the Finos and intended to make them a present of the Nieske stove after he left. They, who surely would have called it the Nietzsche stove, found him eccentric. His days ran like

166

clockwork (too much like the days of 'academic ruminants' even for his own best taste, but Lord Dionysus, he was struggling). Nor could the intelligent Finos square the professor's passion for silly operettas with his great seriousness. Nietzsche could be kind, they saw, and his kindness mitigated against his oddness. He gave caramels to the children and played duets with sixteen-year-old Irene. Still Signora Candida was bothered by his playing the piano alone in the dark, and all of them were struck by his odd manner of producing sound from the keyboard, by striking chords alone, between long periods of silence. The other daughter, Giulia, spied on him one day. Liking her less when he heard her creeping around outside the closed door, Nietzsche shouted out: 'Little brute!'[24]

How could they understand? He experienced the sunset of his conscious life through metaphors of ripe fruit dropping from the tree. Turin suggested compatible harvest colours: brown and gold and amber, all the colours of his last 'desert'. Fruit ripened and fell from the tree on Zarathustra's 'Happy Islands the imagery of which, in another blazing reminder of Nietzsche's affinity with Expressionist painters, recalls Gauguin.[25] In *Ecce Homo*, luscious figs drop in the north wind, and Nietzsche for his readers is both motive breeze and collectable fruit.[26] Nietzsche's letters of the time were hardly less lyrical. 'All around is autumn and clear sky and afternoon.' 'The purest October light every-where ... I am the most grateful man in the world, in an autumnal mood in every good sense of the word; it is my great harvest time.' 'Day after day dawns here with the same unlimited perfection and sunshine; the leaves on the trees are a glowing yellow, sky and the great river a delicate blue, the air of supreme purity – a Claude Lorrain in a way I had never dreamed of seeing him.'[27]

Back in *Ecce Homo* the mood united with music:

> ... what I actually want from music. That it be serene and deep, like an afternoon in October. That it be individual, easy-going, tender, a sweet little woman, base and charming.[28]

167

This was Nietzsche, who knew so well how to be combative, and who would soon flare up violently in the struggle to stay alive; this was Nietzsche at peace, liking his unreal women sweet, brainless and round: round little mouths with sharp white teeth that would (in 'Among Daughters of the Desert') chew him like a date. His 'clever' mind worked like a drawstring bag, holding, uniting and protecting his favourite dreams in these last peaceful days. On his birthday, as an emblem and pendant to *Ecce Homo*, begun that day, he condensed his love of autumn into one of his most characteristic non-violent and non-polemical metaphors.

On this perfect day, when everything ripens and not only the grape becomes brown, a shaft of sunlight fell on my life: I saw backwards, I saw beyond, I saw never so many good things all at once. Not in vain did I bury my forty-fourth year, had the right to bury it - what it possessed of life has been saved, is immortal. *The Transvaluation of All Values*, the *Dionysus Dithyrambs*, and, for relaxation, the *Twilight of the Idols* – all gifts of this year, indeed of its last quarter. How could I not be grateful to my whole life? And so I will tell myself the story of my life.

It is important for Nietzsche that we see him at peace because it helps him deny any part in Romantic striving. Nietzsche's desired self-image at least is no Manfred, no Faust. His is to be in our eyes a golden life, a literal 'still life', written by a maker perfectly poised in his final days to survey his achievements like fruit in a bowl.[29]

Nietzsche creates himself from before birth in *Ecce Homo*, and the new genealogical tree does not flatter his family, because what matters is ancestry by *Wahlverwandschaft* – elective affinity. With the exception of his father, he denies his close relatives in favour of Caesar, Alexander, Dionysus . . . As for acquired characteristics and habits, he maintains, though we know it to be untrue, that he was an instinctive atheist from boyhood. More true is his instinctive aversion from alcohol, though we know

168

from friends he wanted and tried to drink good (Barbera) wine, only refraining because it inflamed his head. Such untruths, big and small, lay bare the mechanisms of self-overcoming.[30]

The way some autobiographers turn on their home towns or their parents, Nietzsche most originally turned on German cooking as an early source of woe. His larger point was that the general discontent of his boyhood and youth might be blamed on an uncomfortable misunderstanding of the body which he absorbed from Christian idealism.[31]

> If I generally have no welcome memory of my entire childhood and youth, it would be foolish to bring to bear so-called moral causes – for instance, the incontestable lack of adequate company: for this lack exists today as it always did, without hindering me from being busy and cheerful. But ignorance in physiological matters, the accursed idealism – is the actual undoing of my life – the superfluous and the stupid elements in it, something out of which no good has grown, for which there is no compensation or antidote.

From the raw materials in Nietzsche's brief narrative emerges a vivid image of the lonely boy in Naumburg, eating heavy meals in company where the men who should have been his role models smoked and drank a lot of beer. They were no match for the angelic father of his false memory. Elisabeth expressly denies her young brother was fat, which suggests that he was, and that there was another dimension of physical unhappiness.[32]

The first time Nietzsche saw the Bay of Naples and experienced the antidote of Italy he wept for the years of lost early happiness.[33] In *Ecce Homo* he equally blamed Idealism for his early career as a philologist.

So when did the change come? When one day, into the pores of this unbearably culturally pressurized, physically depressing Germanic life, seeped Wagner's music, like a drug.[34] Nietzsche's emotional and sound worlds changed for ever. To have been young at the right time to appreciate the aesthetic revelation wrought by *Tristan* elicits from Nietzsche unparalleled gratitude.

But I still today seek a work of a dangerous fascination, of a sweet and shuddery infinity equal to that of *Tristan*. This work is altogether Wagner's *non plus ultra*; he recuperated from it with the *Meistersinger* and *The Ring* . . . I take it for a piece of good fortune of the first rank to have lived at the right time, and to have lived precisely among Germans, so as to be *ripe* for this work . . .

From the way Nietzsche writes about himself a shape emerges, which today, a hundred years on, is a kind of monument to self-discovery. It is a fine antidote to his lack of a superficially democratic political outlook that he provides men and women with an incentive to absolute self-creation, whatever the conditions of their origin. His reading habits and his eating habits and his favourite authors and thinkers, all examples of things near at hand, define *his* life.

The made self, the enabling product of self-overcoming, is the direct, exemplary result of will to power or *Machtgefühl*. *Ecce Homo* speaks of and exemplifies that process by which a man discovers himself already in the world. This for Nietzsche *is* philosophy. Grandly and passionately elaborated in *Ecce Homo* it is also inspiration.

Everything is in the highest degree involuntary but takes place in a tempest of a feeling of freedom, of absoluteness, of power, of divinity . . . one no longer has any idea what is image, what metaphor, everything presents itself as the readiest, the truest, the simplest means of expression. It really does seem, to allude to a saying of Zarathustra's, as if things themselves approached and offered themselves as metaphors.[35]

The inspired 'wise' and 'clever' man makes himself what he aspires to be. In Nietzsche's case he makes himself fearless, noble, without psychological murk, combative, untainted by Christian notions of sin and conscience.[36] But how does this self-projection fit into the lives and perceptions of other men? And how will it be mis/understood? *Ecce Homo*, in the matter of self-creation, knows both afflatus and undertow. Undertow, the place of a work and its maker in the world, the inevitability of misunderstanding, Nietzsche saw and foresaw was his greatest problem.[37]

> You sought the heaviest burden
> and found yourself
> a self you cannot now detach from you.

Malvida told Nietzsche his flesh-and-blood life exemplified what his writing, his self-making, sometimes destroyed. She failed to grasp that the theme of his philosophical life was his unwillingness to subscribe to ideals and his abhorrence at being taken himself for a hero or a tragic figure. She failed to understand that against those forces he built his art, which he described as a huge transfer of defensive energies into the creative sphere. He wanted to be understood as a tension, a tendency, a nuance. *Ecce Homo* was to exemplify that intermundial position, that being as potential. That subtle, profoundly personal sphere of the perilously poised ego in never-ending, dynamic making, *Ecce Homo* both inhabits and explores.

Nietzsche's is such an irritable soul. He knows 'an absurd susceptibility of the skin to pinpricks, a kind of helplessness in the face of everything small'.[38] He easily feels mistrustful and shunned, and thrust into deep solitude. Now he claims in writing that this vulnerability is the emptiness of resource left *after* creative achievement. In reality cause and effect in Nietzsche's life were not so clear. That self-discovery which became self-preservation in the face of hostile interpretation and the iron fist of tradition might well look like a turning away from life. It became a quest for an intellectually pure stance, equal to a perfect suspension of judgement in the face of the manifold ambiguities of language, the tricks of the human psyche, the distorting mould of grammar. It was also a quest for the emotionally pure life, in which *rancune* and *ressentiment* were distilled back into mere words; the genie of malevolent action rubbed back into the aladdin's lamp of ambivalent potential.

Nietzsche makes, as one does, profound excuses for inadequacy. Afflicted by too much insight into the psychology of others he is easily upset. This, both on and off stage, is understandable but an unappealing aspect of his argument against pity.[39] His yearning for purity in solitude looks like fear of contamination.[40] His explanation of creative habits bears directly on his emotional circumstances, harried by his sister's possessiveness, intrusiveness and destructiveness, and irritated by his mother's piety. Elisabeth was a great incentive to self-overcoming. He wanted, at least, not to be like that. He always struggled against the personal malice and animosity which threatened to seize his heart. (The real man could not deny he had a conscience.) He declared with renewed commitment in *Ecce Homo* that *ressentiment* was foreign to his *übermenschlich* ways. But he was at least as bad as most of us at conducting his life.

Still he is right to say his books are one thing, he another, which brings us back to our task as biographer of the autobiographer. The three elements demanding parallel consideration in the autumn of *Ecce Homo*: the book, the man made within it, and the man outside who is its increasingly infirm maker, underscore his range and his limits. He dwelled in Turin as artist, as psychologist and self-interpreter, and as fallible mortal. As the sunlit weeks went by, with their ecstatic days, art rearranged decay, psychology deepened it, but nothing stopped its real onward march.

The months of composition October and November saw various vexations which perhaps hastened that march. His mother unusually forgot his birthday, while his sister, provoked by *The Wagner Case*, greeted him with record spite. She revered the Wagners (as she revered the Christianity and Germany Nietzsche also loathed). Also, and surely fundamentally more important to her as a socially ambitious woman who had met her husband through initiation into the Wagner circle on her brother's coat-tails: was not Nietzsche cutting his one line to fame? (In fact by making himself famous as Wagner's opponent, he was assuring it, and already had never been so 'known' in his lifetime.)

My sister writes to me apropos of 15 October with extreme contempt, that I might finally start to make a name for myself. How lovely that would be! And the sort of rabble I chose to mix with, Jews who had eaten from every pot like Georg Brandes . . . At the same time she calls me her dear heart Fritz . . . It's been going on like this for seven years now![41]

Nietzsche by the time he paraphrased Elisabeth's birthday words in this Christmas communication to Overbeck may have rounded out her criticisms with morbid imagination. The invective against Brandes but not the aspersions against his lack of fame appear in the only extant birthday missive from Elisabeth. But the indication of Nietzsche's mood is clear: his sister is 'this stupid, vengeful creature', this 'vengeful, anti-Semitic goose'.[42] In mid-November he replied in exasperation, still seeking to maintain a sibling relationship called 'love'. But with illness weakening his resolve, and specifically syphilis bringing on its notorious tactlessness, the suppressed rancour towards Elisabeth and his mother bodied forth in prospective passages for *Ecce Homo* and, on the brink of final breakdown, in the Christmas letter to Overbeck. Another letter savaged Elisabeth and Förster as anti-Semites; a third attacked Förster directly. That Elisabeth, when she came to 'edit' *Ecce Homo*, suppressed and may have destroyed some such passages on the grounds that her brother was already sick is understandable, if not editorially justifiable. But the similarity between Friedrich's viciousness and her own must above all have embarrassed her.[43]

In fact, though I have divided them, the distinctions between art, biography and psychology wear thin in the Turin autumn. Nietzsche attacks his friends in equally vicious terms in both book and letter. He derides those very professors on whom he had so recently depended for company in Sils. The fools had not even heard of Stendhal. Overbeck is dried-out, sour and dominated by his wife; Köselitz is a flatterer, a stubborn ass and the embodiment of German heaviness. Almost no one close was immune from his febrile complaint.[44]

The exact role of external irritations, both in provoking his last writing and accelerating or even precipitating the final breakdown, is difficult to pin down. But irritations they certainly were, and one might say that syphilis worked against his art, redoubled his need for self-overcoming, because it put creative untruth out of reach. He ranted. He showed the weak and bad sides of his character. He was always wont to cast verbal aspersions behind his friends' backs, men or women, and was now incapable of concealing this less than *übermenschlich* conduct. Thus the number of hurdles to his complete dominance of the world mounted.

Of them one was not being answered by von Bülow concerning Peter Gast's opera, but far greater was the furore over *The Wagner Case*. The Wagnerian Richard Pohl's retaliatory article 'The Nietzsche Case' appeared in the last week of October. It was subtitled 'a psychological problem' and treated Nietzsche as mad. As close to the truth as it was not true, this strategem, though a fair riposte, was enraging. Pohl's text was also hurtful, as it contained a new disclosure that Wagner deemed Nietzsche's own music 'rubbish'. To add insult to injury Nietzsche's own publisher Fritzsch enabled its appearance. Nietzsche changed the concluding niceties of his next letter from 'sincere respect' to 'sincere scorn' and promptly began negotiations, not only to take his future work elsewhere but to buy back the rights to what Fritzsch had previously published. The result was the huge sum of 14,000 Swiss francs, towards which he began impossibly to save, though Meta von Salis, whose intellectual reverence was tinged with love, instantly gave him 1,000 Francs, and 'stupid' Deussen 2,000. (Von Salis would later buy Nietzsche and his sister Villa

Silberblick in Weimar, so that he had a home in which to end his days.)[45]

Since he was trying so hard not to let luetic depredations eat into his judgement, Nietzsche particularly resented the idea that he had *suddenly* changed his mind about Wagner and set out to refute it by collecting passages he had written about Wagner over the last twelve years. His anger gave so much urgency to *Nietzsche contra Wagner* that for several weeks he toyed with holding back publication of *Ecce Homo* to allow the little pamphlet to make its impact. Jibbing against the most basic misunderstandings of his purpose he began to doubt even those who wrote of him with insight. By Dionysus, did he have to SPELL OUT the Bizet DEVICE to Carl Spitteler:

That I attach my conversion [from Wagner] to *Carmen* is of course a bit of mischief on my part – I trust you won't doubt it for a minute. I know the envy and what a storm of rage *Carmen's* success provoked in Wagner . . .[46]

He pilloried as pantomime stooges in *Ecce Homo* those rhyming Wagnerian acolytes Nohl, Pohl and Kohl who apparently had ganged up on him. With luck that boosted his spirits.

In October-November he was still relatively robust. A measure of self-overcoming was only missing entirely in his dealings with Malvida von Meysenbug. Not all her letter of mid-October survives, nor any subsequent correspondence. One wonders whether Nietzsche tore up her words in a rage. The remaining substantial portion of the mid-October letter is a firm but gentle expression of disagreement. To slander old friends was not right, under any circumstances, Malvida said, even while she imagined Nietzsche shrugging his shoulders and branding her an old Wagnerian. Much in *The Wagner Case* she agreed with, only not calling Wagner a clown.[47] Malvida didn't understand Nietzsche, and especially she did not comprehend that peculiar 'humour' by which he saw *himself* as a clown or Shakespearian fool (*Hanswurst*), and his gift to posterity a series of bad jokes. His first reply to her was imperious, 'brooking no contradiction', though no more symptomatic of a sudden decline in Nietzsche than a similar note to Rohde eighteen months before.[48] His second was reasoned and sad, written in an intermission of lucidity about his impossible intolerance: 'I have gradually broken off nearly all my human relationships out of a horror of being taken for something other than I am. Now it's your turn.'[49] But only two weeks later the reasoning had gone again, the impossible sadness became demented *hauteur*. 'I've suffered from being far too just this autumn, it will really do me good to do someone an injustice . . . The Immoralist'[50] He sat down and sketched a part for Malvida in *Ecce Homo* as Wagner's Kundry, 'one who laughs when the world is ending'.

Nietzsche knew very well the pathology of these troubled moments. Like the mix-up over trains in Sampierdarena, though they might also be prompts to self-overcoming, they invited illness to take hold. In his precepts for survival in *Ecce Homo* he inveighed against putting oneself in a position where the necessary reaction was self-defence; where altogether a man was forced to react to other stimuli, rather than create out of himself. But *The Wagner Case* and *Nietzsche contra Wagner* are both more reactive than creative. In them the authorial consciousness is hardly a still mirror for the deep sky.[51]

To the last fierce creative period, in which *Ecce Homo* was set down in a draft sent to the printers, though later recalled, Nietzsche attached the dates 15.10 to 4.11. In it, just holding the balance of sanity over insanity, he tried with characteristic bombast to cover up for lapses. 'Rude letters are with me a sign of serenity,'[52] he told Köselitz and later Strindberg, while he made rudeness a heroic topic in the autobiography.[53] Art, psychological observation of himself, and the problems of daily life, he laced together ever tighter, like the boot with the broken fastening which, as a fallen dandy, would be his last sartorial complaint over Christmas.

Art could no longer contain his life. The lace was fraying. Even *Heiterkeit*, cheerful serenity, was losing its meaning. He propped it up with visits to the operetta and listening to Rossini, of whom he now knew eight operas and loved *La Cenerentola* best of all. It was easier to live in a posturing, funny stage world where all the tunes were supplied than to face the increasing involuntary bizarreness of his behaviour in the real world. In Audran's *La Mascotte* once again he found that kind of Bizetism which eased his soul: 'the paradise of all delicate and refined things' was a quote from Audran himself. Disbelief was briefly and gloriously suspended; jolliness on stage kept him smiling, but the centrifugal forces of brain decay were already tugging his mouth out of shape.[54]

Ecce Homo, in aspiring to anti-heroism, makes light of terrible distortions backstage in its author's mental life, and there is evidence Nietzsche understood that, indirectly calling his own work an operetta. Just as Offenbach made a jolly story out of the Trojan War with *La belle Hélène* so Nietzsche transvalued the serious problems of his life, and *Ecce Homo* transvalued a serious genre (related to the *Bildungsroman*, the novel of self-development) by introducing apparent trivia. A small but telling example comes with his giving up alcohol. 'Water does the trick ... I prefer places where everywhere one has the chance to draw it from running wells (Nice, Turin, Sils); a little glass runs after me like a dog.'[55] This picture, with its ridiculous props, recalls the prizes at a fairground shooting stall. Neither glass, nor dog, nor simile has aesthetic charm or coherence. They make Nietzsche himself sound old-womanish. Yet we feel he is doing something significant in literature with the discordant, ugly material of his life. Nietzsche occupies this odd position of wanting to introduce 'low life' – things near at hand – into the high forms of literature and philosophy and frame them in new forms of rhetoric.[56] The effect is to highlight the pathetic distance between ideal projections of life and its real, physical condition. 'With [this] ... perhaps the *great seriousness* first arises, the real question-mark is first set up, the destiny of the soul veers round, the clock-hand moves on, the tragedy *begins* ...'[57]

With my body I create a new genre, he might have said: the

Dionysian tragic, the operettic-tragic. Nietzsche with his written-down physical life does what he hoped Wagner would do with music: restores the sense of tragedy as a collective experience. The transvaluation of selfhood, the reversal of Christian 'de-selfing', is his means.[58]

The Dionysian-tragic autobiography casts a redemptive lucidity over the necessary confusion and murk of everyday life without offering a solution. It describes a process of survival, even as its author is overtaken. A draft for the dithyramb 'The Sun Sets' says simply: 'You were running too fast/Now you are tired for the first time/Your happiness can catch up with you.' Nietzsche's tragedy would serve its audience not in an Aristotelian sense, purging their fears that they might be equally lonely, ill or mad, but in the Dionysian sense, recalling that these forces make up our lives, are the burdens we live with.

The title *Ecce Homo* may have come initially from an English book lying on Overbeck's desk. It may also have come from Cosima Wagner thus referring to *Parsifal*.[59] Nietzsche was always an intellectual magpie, a habit he could justify with the midas touch of transvaluation. All he assembled would acquire unity and meaning as his gold. In this case it did. According to St John's Gospel 19.5 Pilate appeals to the Jews before ordering the crucifixion with the words 'Ecce homo!', encouraging them to accept Jesus and allow his release.[60] 'Ecce homo!' Nietzsche mocked in *Twilight*. 'That's what the moralists say who would lay down an absolute prescription for human behaviour.'[61] The usage was lost, it lacked resonance, until at last he found a place for it to describe the triumph and the humiliation of his own too short life on the verge of final collapse. It has often, as has the whole book, been taken as a sign of Nietzsche's arrogance, his blasphemy, his megalomania raised to a new power by syphilis. But in fact it betokens humility. Nietzsche's last creation is a final humble fight for clarity, like a drowning man coming up for air, and the boastful chapter headings belie what lies within. This is a man. These are his limits. Within them, as a writer, as a creator, he

178

discovered he could mine extraordinary power. Still he remained a mortal, fallible man.

Like Christ, as I have suggested, he offers himself as an example and a model. Some readers may still find that freely drawn parallel blasphemous. But Nietzsche's aim, even in *The Anti-christian*, was less destructive blasphemy than positive freedom, out of sympathy for the human plight. Here all those who believe he dismissed the virtue of pity, *Mitleid*, as a vice should look again.[62] The point of the title *Ecce Homo* is to encourage in all of us sympathy for the hidden pain of the individual; to explore man alone. This is how to survive as a spiritual man.[63] To the lonely he says implicitly: a lonelier man went before. Compensate by driving your life from within. Fill in that loneliness with the cross-hatching of self-definition. *Ecce Homo* is a record of Nietzsche's struggling to be that person whom Lou Salomé found so offputting because his goal appeared to her far from his immediate self; she was alienated by being plunged *in medias res* into his self-overcoming.

Yet finally, though he denied it, how could he not be striving? The field of reference demands that we compare *Ecce Homo* to Faust. There Goethe's whole enterprise is underpinned by the faith that 'a good man in his dark impulses is still well aware of the right path'. In Nietzsche's rejection of the Idealist tradition in its most acceptable form for him, in Goethe, there is a fundamental element of laughter at himself. Goethe's healthy 'naïvety' is out of reach. Nietzsche still aims at health; still at well-being. But his vision is to parody his way to a new 'great seriousness' by mocking every existing solemnity. Parody becomes a verb of motion.[64]

The opposition to Faustian striving follows from the rejection of the Lutheran context which gave it the highest value. Nietzsche tries to give it another context of value. Much of his work is concerned with removing what is of worth to him about German thought from German schemes of thinking which seem to him unacceptably Christian and nationalist and optimistic and rational. He does this by extracting from that classical philosophy whatever strikes him as more truly the business of psychology (processes of the 'mind', of religion, of art). This leaves him free to rename philosophy as a most modern tool, cleansing consciousness of unnecessary encumbrances to living. The outstanding Foreward to *Ecce Homo* explains:

Philosophy, as I have understood and lived it to this day, is a life voluntarily spent in ice and high mountains – a searching out of all that is alien and questionable in existence, of all that until now has been held in the spell of morality . . . How much truth can one mind take, how much truth does it have the courage for? That became for me more and more the real measure of value. Error (the belief in the ideal) is not blindness, it is cowardice . . . Every achievement, every step forward into knowledge, proceeds from courage, from being hard against oneself, out of cleanliness towards oneself . . . I don't refute the ideals, I just put on gloves in their presence . . . *Nitimur in vetitum*: in this sign my philosophy triumphs, for what was fundamentally forbidden until now was only the truth.

The counter-balance to this icy analytical ruthlessness is love of life. *Nitimur in vetitum semper, cupimusque negata* – 'We always strive for what is forbidden, and desire what is denied us' – comes from Ovid, *Amores*, III, iv, 17, and underscores the erotic, troubadour incentive to Nietzsche's drive to know. The sense is: I want to know and yet I will never possess knowledge as a finite object. The fundamental aspect of my being an individual is in my wanting and willing to make my way.[65]

In knowing and understanding too, I feel only my will's delight in begetting and becoming; and if there be innocence in my knowledge it is because *will to begetting* is in it.[66]

This is the *Machtgefühl* as the desire to live, Freud's Eros lauding it over Thanatos, the delight in knowing and creating, staving off

death. Nietzsche borrows Hölderlin's lines on Socrates as a lover
to say:

Who has thought deepest lives most fully,
Who has known life understands highest virtue,
And the wise in the end
Often lean towards beauty.[67]

10

DIONYSUS COMES TO THE RIVER PO

Nietzsche's art, which had become the art of life, fought a tremendous battle with sickness. He was like the outcast Trojan priest Laocoön, resisting the punishing sea serpents to the last breath. Thinking of the meaning of that classical statue, depicting terror and resignation, Nietzsche considered Laocoön's fate showed the Apollonian forces of life yielding to Dionysus. The statue could have worn his face. No wonder he called it pathetic.[1] His mental health late in 1888 was giving way; he was sinking into some putative collective unconscious. His last resistance was to use his *Apollonian* gift to depict the chaotic material of an individual life ending.

The terrifying mythical figure known as Dionysus Zagreus specifically betokened disintegration. Nietzsche gave Zagreus form, so that he could to the last see his fate as beyond himself. He went out to meet that fate as if he had finally met his Platonic other half, ideally loved. This was his last demonstration of *amor fati*, to shape his final destiny in the mould of the Orphic god who was destroyed and reborn.

It was a last artistic interpretation of himself, and we understand from it the limits of his artistic impulse, that a sense of 'not-self' was hard won. He wrote even as a young man that other people were as shadows in his Platonic cave. He alone was real.[2] Artistic interpretation was the only way he could conceive of an 'other', a not-I. Thus a Turin Zagreus was born.

The form-giving Apollo lingered long enough into late December for Nietzsche mentally to play through a sequence called 'Dionysus Zagreus comes to the River Po'. We no longer have that fragment, alas, though it depended on the same artistic empowerment as enabled Nietzsche to collect the *Dionysus Dithyrambs* and assemble *Nietzsche contra Wagner*. The result was a sprinkling of strikingly pictorial minor last works, with Nietzsche drawing on resources which served him well from *The Birth of Tragedy* to *Zarathustra*. Four of the *Dithyrambs* were specific revivals from the *Zarathustra* period and all his December 1888 work seemed to spring out of *The Birth of Tragedy*. That work was visually explosive and in the words of his old professor, Ritchl, as thrilling as a cheap Parisian romance.[3] The continuity of Nietzsche's pictures showed a creative life beginning and ending at the same point. The blazing Dionysian of 1871 contained the mental chaos of his own demise. The horror of war, the glory of Greek tragedy, and the joy of Nietzsche's hopes in Wagner had not lost their effect since they stimulated the early work. War, Greece and Wagner still powered his metaphors and shaped the outpourings of his soul. It seemed some cycle inside him was complete. He found 'that everything was on target, from the beginning – that everything is one thing and wills one thing. I read "The Birth" the day before yesterday [20 December]: something indescribable, deep, delicate, happy . . .'[4]

Nietzsche saw his mind returning ultimately from the aphoristic–philosophical to the pictorial. So much judgement remained that one wonders how much he controlled the process. The return was certainly inwardly driven. My feeling is that he *was* in control, and used his situation to exemplify his philosophy, as if he were a *tableau vivant*. That hypothesis shapes my interpretation of the written pictures and vital gestures of his last days. The pictures qualify the earlier words, just as Nietzsche had imagined Christ returning to *deny* his teaching; and just as he had imagined bringing his Nietzschean Zarathustra into being to dissolve the rigid metaphysical dualism of the historical Zarathustra. In 1886, when, having just published *Beyond Good and*

Evil and embarking upon *The Genealogy of Morals*, he reached his apogee as a philosopher, he was correspondingly disparaging about *The Birth of Tragedy*. It was 'badly written, clumsy, embarrassing, overladen and confused with pictures, driven by feeling, sweetened here and there to a feminine degree, of uneven tempo, lacking the will to logical cleanliness, very convinced and therefore raising itself above proof . . . an exuberant and passionate book.'[5] But in *Ecce Homo* he boldly reembraced *The Birth of Tragedy*'s aesthetic values and amoral vitalism, and dusted off its definition of Dionysian tragedy. In those terms his own life was about to reach its tragic denouement.

The will to leave a picture of himself behind was overwhelmingly strong. Moreover it had to be a Dionysian picture, of a particular kind of tragic figure, whose import was positive, because he had overcome himself:

> . . . Not to purge fear and pity, not to rid oneself of a dangerous emotion by means of a pointed undoing of tension – Aristotle was wrong: but rather, beyond fear and pity, to be oneself that very thing, *the eternal pleasure of becoming, that pleasure which also includes in itself pleasure in extermination.* In this sense I have the right to see myself as the first tragic philosopher. [my italics, LC][6]

Ecce Homo was a self-portrait in this tragic vein. Yet it still had the limitations of a literary work. Using mostly the colours of the contemporary world, Nietzsche framed his autopicture with such philosophy and politics as furnished his unique self-justifications as a cultural revolutionary. He began that process of turning himself into a modern myth, which proceeded apace after his death. If the myth which then took shape was more violent, less subtle, and ignorant of his religious sensibility, the fault was partly Nietzsche's. Having associated 'the pictorial man' with fanaticism, he denied in *Ecce Homo* that he was a fanatic, though nothing was more true of his mode of operation in the last days. With pictures of himself as a warrior, an iconoclast and an inexhaustible ego he chased an image and won an idolatrous following.[7] These were his projections in life and he needed them to sustain his self-belief.

But he needed pictures of a different order to depict his life's conclusion. His greatest moment, sinking into eternal night, was going to be his Dionysian answer to Socrates' irony. The truly Dionysian pictures abound in the poetry. There the symbolic images are still autobiographical, but removed from historical time. They portray Nietzsche's emotional relationships and his will to Greek religion. They embody the history of a soul never fully unveiled to us. Nietzsche, like an imagined category of women he despised, was coy. The poems contain riddles to which wilfully he never supplied the key.

'Dionysus Zagreus comes to the River Po', however, which Nietzsche set down on a few sheets of grey-edged Turin paper around Christmas, was a picture in prose, and all too clear. It showed Dionysus wandering amongst a valedictory assembly of friends and family. It could have been Nietzsche's parting arrow shot into posterity. a scene echoing Odysseus's descent to the Underworld, and one which might have been painted by Claude. Only to this creation Elisabeth threw away the lock and the door as well as the key. She took exception to Dionysus's view of the family and, pretending the deed was done by her mother, destroyed those sheets of handmade paper.[8] It was another demonstration of family wilfulness, manifesting itself differently in brother and sister.

We can try to reconstruct. 'Dionysus Zagreus comes to the River Po' was written at just that time when Nietzsche's enthusiasm for *The Birth of Tragedy* reawakened to help him deal with his impending mental death, and rereading that book he found he had already rehearsed the steps he would take. Dionysus would come after the world had purged itself of all that was parasitical and distorted, that was Christian. This coming would happen to the sacerdotal majesty of something akin to Wagner's music, but which would be Nietzsche's own verbal music; and there would be a great midday when initiates met to consecrate their task. Nietzsche had always informed Wagner's music and Wagner's Bayreuth with his own vision: 'the vision of a celebration that I will yet experience . . .'⁹ Now at last he would detach it and stage his vision independently.

Elisabeth wrote:

At this period [surmised to be the last days of 1888] . . . he covered some sheets of paper with the wildest fantasies, mingling the legend of Dionysus Zagreus with the story of the Passion and with the history of people whom he knew. The god, torn to pieces by his enemies, rises again and walks along the banks of the Po, seeing all that he has ever loved, his ideals, the ideals of the present age, far beneath them. His nearest and dearest have become enemies, who have torn him to pieces. These three sheets, which were addressed to my husband in Paraguay, and to our mother, contain attacks upon Wagner, Schopenhauer, Bismarck, the Emperor, Professor Overbeck, Peter Gast, Frau Cosima Wagner, my husband, my mother and myself. He signed all his letters at the time 'Dionysus' or 'The Crucified One'. Even these notes contain passages of arresting beauty, but on the whole they are clearly the work of a fevered brain. In the first years after my brother's stroke [sic], when we all cherished the vain hope he might recover, these papers were all destroyed by my mother. She thought that Fritz, with his warm heart and admirable taste, would be deeply wounded if he ever came upon such writings in after-years. I made myself a copy from one of the sheets.¹⁰

Against this dishonest, tyrannical benevolence on the part of his sister Nietzsche struggled in life, only to fall prey to it in madness. Part of the Paraguay insert does survive, however. The fascinated Köselitz made a copy of Nietzsche's testimony, which was found in 1969. There Nietzsche wrote of the forces which tore Dionysus Zagreus to shreds:

When I look for the deepest contrast to myself, the

inexhaustible meanness of instinct, I find over and over my mother and my sister – to believe myself related to such *canaille* would be to blaspheme against my divine nature. The treatment I experience from my mother and sister's side, to this very moment, inspires me with a terror beyond words: at work here is a perfect machine of Hell, with infallible certainty as to the moment when I can be bloodily wounded – in my highest moments . . . for that's the time when all strength needed to defend oneself against poisonous worms is lacking . . .[11]

The Wagners were not such enemies. Nietzsche went on in this passage to praise them to the skies. Cosima was the most noble nature he had ever come across. Richard Wagner was the most closely related to Nietzsche in spirit any man had ever been. So when we think of Dionysus Zagreus being torn alive, we are asked to think of Nietzsche's blood-relative she-devils alone, inflated in his mind into representatives of the dishonest idealism and Christian piety which threatened all healthy life.

Nietzsche's original account of Dionysus Zagreus in *The Birth of Tragedy* provides another clue to his lost final vision.[12] The fragmented god, transformed into air, water, earth and fire, represents the torment of individuation, out of which with his smile he creates the Olympian gods and with his tears human life. He, of a divine marriage of sky and earth, is both mild ruler and wild demon, bringing with him the promise of his rebirth which will reunite the world and end painful individuated existence. His rebirth will happen through his being re-sired on Demeter, goddess of the earth and its fruits. This Dionysus who was always a potent symbol for Nietzsche's Yes to life must have been doubly glorious to configure in the autumn of 1888. Was there a better site in the world for his rebirth than the fecund Po in an exceptionally golden season? Nietzsche described again the setting in *Ecce Homo*: 'I have never experienced such an autumn, also never held possible anything of the kind on earth – a Claude Lorrain thought of into infinity, each day of equal, unbounded perfection.'[13]

It was perhaps a scene like this then which Nietzsche painted, with the same Titanic brushstrokes he used for the skyscapes, seascapes and mountain scenery of *Zarathustra*. He certainly kept thinking of that book in conjunction with *Ecce Homo*, telling Deussen *Ecce Homo* would illuminate *Zarathustra* for the first time whilst moving a step further: 'This book deals only with me – in it I finally appear with my world-historical mission.'[14] To emphasize the 'I' here makes clear the difference: Nietzsche himself has taken over from Zarathustra as that Dionysus who metamorphoses into stone and water and sky and is in love with eternity. He would paint himself into the landscape.

In dictionaries of mythology however the story of Dionysus Zagreus is more grotesque than beautiful, and though he does not retell it directly in all its bloody detail, it is unlikely Nietzsche ignored it, in part because he revelled in physical ugliness and gore: *Zarathustra* abounds in grotesque imagery, as do the *Dionysus Dithyrambs*. (It was an old trait. In Sils he begged young Miss Fynn to put something nasty like a frog into her pretty pictures and even brought one along to make her squeamish. But his love of ugliness may have been intensified by illness. Syphilitics in the later stages of decline lose that control we call good taste.)

The story of Zagreus is certainly grotesque. Zeus is said to have taken the form of a serpent to beget this son, whom he intended to rule the world. Anticipating his wife Hera's jealousy at this extra-marital adventure he entrusted the child to Apollo and the Curetes, who brought him up in the forest of Parnassus, but Hera managed to discover him. Zagreus tried in vain to escape by changing his form but the Titans pursued him, tore him to pieces and ate him.[15] (Only later at Zeus's request were the fragments reconstituted and the second Dionysus born.)

Nietzsche, when he wore the mask of the first tormented Dionysus, knew the young potential world leader was destroyed despite paternal hopes and a grand begininng. The complete myth taken to heart would simultaneously have reinforced his terrified vision of his female family, his flight into poetry, into Zarathustran metamorphosis, his flight from the Titans of illness, and his promise, beyond their destruction, of a new eternity in rebirth. That is one speculation, then, that so much of Dionysus's life, with its bloodiness and its energy appealing to Nietzsche, became the most suitable final mask for his own.

Dionysus Zagreus's conception by Zeus and Persephone may in particular be compared with one of the darkest and most ferocious images in *Zarathustra*, at the opening of Book III, when a serpent creeps into the mouth of a sleeping shepherd. Zarathustra comes across the tormented shepherd and begs him to bite off the serpent's head. When the shepherd does so he is transfigured into a beyond-human figure whose laughter excites Zarathustra's longing for eternity. Smiling and laughing are Dionysian instruments. The shepherd appears thus to have been remade by Dionysus in painful but extraordinarily fertile intercourse. He becomes *übermenschlich* and Dionysian. 'On Vision and Puzzle' Nietzsche calls this chapter. The shepherd's transformation accounts for 'the vision'. As for 'the puzzle', it has evidently something to do with the framework Nietzsche provides for this story, reflecting his own father's death. Zarathustra comes across a man lying on the floor in mortal danger and a dog barking. Was Nietzsche himself then born as Dionysus out of this terrible vision of dying which is at once an image of copulation? Zarathustra is shy of sexuality; his great interest in 'pregnancy' is relentlessly cold and cosmic. He speaks emphatically of 'him' who is pregnant in 'The Seven Seals' section bringing Book III to a climactic close. Lust for Recurrence drives Zarathustra to become pregnant with the lightning future. This is embarrassing reading. But it has an important psychological content. Nietzsche found a formula for procreation without a female element. Zarathustra keeps on singing in case we miss the point: 'I have never met a woman by whom I wanted children, unless it be you, oh Eternity.' In the image of the serpent entering the shepherd the female element is displaced to the mortal progenitor. The element of Christian parody is strong. God comes into the mouth of the loving shepherd, and begets a son. The 'puzzle' is Nietzsche's own rebirth as Dionysus Zagreus.

189

In *Ecce Homo* Nietzsche has witnessed his death and invented his ancestors; in Turin recently he has seen his own funeral. There is nothing to stop him being present at his own conception, growing up rapidly and now wandering the banks of the Po. This jungle of imagery from picture book to picture book is I think just a prelude to understanding Nietzsche's rabid Dionysian imagination in the last six years of his life.[16]

The fertility of that jungle affected Nietzsche's general view of his style.[17] He believed he was the master in verbal expression of myriad inner states and moods and tensions, for which he had found signs and gestures. He referred to his exemplary style in 'The Seven Seals'. 'Every style is good which actually communicates an inner state, which makes no mistake as to the signs, the tempo of the signs, the gestures – all rules of phrasing are the art of gesture. My instinct here is infallible.' We do not have to accept the claim to find it valuable testimony. The wording is musical and closely resembles what Nietzsche had praised in Wagner. 'Dionysus comes to the River Po' may have had some musical quality in the words and the general conception. The garden element and the theme of a non-Christian redemption suggest a faint parallel and challenge to *Parsifal*, Wagner's last work. I am aware of the absurdity of comparing three fragmentary lost pages with a grand music drama setting Christianity against Paganism. But the obscure, forceful, often ugly dithyrambs written at the same time as Zagreus were certainly strikingly Wagnerian, which implies no qualitative comparison with Wagner. They were mythical and would-be musical, poised between rebellion and inner retreat, and shot through with the sweetness of sleep – and eternal sleep.

A dithyramb originally described the song of Dionysus. It was an expression of intoxication and community, with Dionysus leading others in choral song. The choral element was what first inspired Nietzsche to see in Wagner's music a rebirth of the Dionysian, in which respect we may conjecture two things. Nietzsche may have noticed that descriptions of ancient festivals of Dionysus, which were singing competitions, uncannily resembled *Die Meistersinger*. That historically words in the dithyrambic form gradually ceded more and more importance to music may also have helped frame Nietzsche's views on the future of nineteenth-century art. One of his apparent arguments with Wagner was on precisely this subject, which dominated contemporary German music.

The dithyramb also bore, in its modern meaning of a poetic tone more than a form, however, a much closer personal significance for Nietzsche. It betokened wild howling, vehement expression. Nothing could have been more apt for a poet in love with the masks of self-intoxication and madness. What a way to rebel against being made chaste and virtuous by misfortune! The medium itself expressed a desire to be sensually out of control. Had Nietzsche used the form to greater artistic effect his poems might have become iconic for the modern condition, like Munch's *The Scream*, because they are a kind of howling after lost community.[18] All of Nietzsche's writing where the pictorial and the musical dominate over the discursive could be called Dionysian and dithyrambic. They sing, they laugh, they flash colour, they luxuriate in texture. That style has been hailed as exemplary of the modern, because it is essentially a lament for fragmentation.[19]

Of the nine *Dionysus Dithyrambs* of December 1888, 'The Fire Signal' is a recent creation, drawing on Nietzsche's love of water imagery to make of his soul a bonfire on a small island amid an ocean, signalling to every kind of solitude, past and future, for the last and deepest confirmation of his own being alone. It recalls Brünnhilde before she is wakened to save the world. Another new poem, 'The Sun Sets', tends towards the ecstasy of inertia, of a hopeless, wish-free motionlessness which is a calm sea, skimmed by the lightest of boats floating into the distance. Nietzsche drafts a letter to an unknown correspondent on 27 November, introducing these minor works. In general their themes were drawn from the landscape of elemental forces with which Nietzsche was obsessed: earth and sun, desert, fire, mountains. They were peopled by Dionysus and Ariadne, with a few extra walk-on parts.

I come out of a hundred abysses, into which no glance has yet dared wander, I know heights which no bird has flown, I have lived in ice – I have been burnt by a hundred snows: it seems to me that warm and cold in my mouth are other concepts.

The dithyrambs are certainly cold in an intense, declamatory fashion. The rich alliteration once again recalls Wagner's imitations of medieval German *Stabreime*. The lines seem oddly dead on the page, as if they did come from a faraway, unreachable culture carried into the modern world in fragments. In particular Nietzsche's imagining of love, which mostly amounts to lust, is often strained and peculiar, because of the introduction of the gastric process. In a deliberate transvaluation of idealistic love he places biting, chewing, digesting, self-nourishing, self-perpetuating – and excreting understood – at the centre of his real world, which is yet a quite unreal one. In his (pro)creative satisfaction he is a fruit cooked in its own juice. Or he wants to be a sweet, gleaming date full of golden promise chewed in a young girl's mouth and bitten into by her sharp, ice-cold, snow-white teeth. To be swallowed like Jonah would also be sweet, conducive to arrival in the ultimate oasis-belly. There is a memory of a rare real sexual encounter. 'Among Daughters of the Desert' is peopled by dancers, creatures flitting about in gauze, who closely resemble the women he encountered as a bewildered young man in that Cologne brothel. The picture is of lust buried under so many layers of fantasy that a cursory reading might leave only a sense of frustrated impotence.

The singer of 1888 was fantasizing; remembering his sexuality in the tortured forms it took but mostly dying. 'Among Daughters of the Desert', included in *Zarathustra*, acquired a new last verse in the Turin autumn:

The desert grows; woe the man who sees not deserts.
Stone grinds against stone, the desert coils and strangles.
The monster death glances glowing brown
And chews – his life in his chewing . . .
Forget not, man, burnt out by lust, you – are the stone, the
desert, are death . . .

Even without reference to the siring of Dionysus Zagreus, Nietzsche is obsessed with serpents. He knows them from the Bible (which he told his mother he reread in Turin) and from the statue of Laocoön.[20] Now their image merged with his sense of life as a savage process of eternal consumption. Serpents numbered among its instruments. Plagued by a sense of nothingness, of the rising desert, he welcomed, in a rare beautiful phrase from the 1883 period, the air with light gone out of it ('*bei abgehellter Luft*').[21] As if he were Dionysus Zagreus he saw signs in the sky – lightning, clouds, sunbeams – with myriad metamorphoses: a cloud, invisible (!) lightning, a girl's face, a purple dragon. But these were almost quaint diversions from the Buddhistic nothingness ahead. He remembered the experience of war which stimulated his concept of the Dionysian, and he lived in his love of Wagner's *Tristan*. Each of the dithyrambs describes a sinking to the ground, in exhaustion, in agony on the battlefield, in something akin to prayer.

The dithyrambs thus return Nietzsche to Wagner, revealing themselves as another taking up of the invitation to the young professor to take from Wagner whatever might be useful.[22] Nietzsche, having asked his mother to search out that Wagner dedication earlier in the year, now answered it in 'On the Poverty of the Richest'. That dithyramb repeated word for word also brought *Nietzsche contra Wagner* to a close, while the title page of that essay set the scene for the last act of his tragedy: 'Turin Christmas 1888'.

The music to which that tragedy plays out is, by Nietzsche's choice, Wagner's *Tristan*. At Christmas 1888 he cannot think beyond *Tristan* as a fascinating, capital work, peerless among all the arts.[23] *The Donysus Dithyrambs* are replete with Tristan's characteristic imagery of fire, light and dark, ships, breath (air), mouth and lips and its Buddhistic spirit. In the language of the *Liebestod*, an ecstatic sinking of two lovers into willed darkness, Nietzsche describes his own solitary departure alone. As a composer he has wrought a thematic transformation of the boldest Lisztian kind, taking the original notes and making them express a quite different sentiment.

That Nietzsche's endless rivalry with Wagner preoccupied him as his end neared is clearly shown in a letter to Avenarius on 10 December. As usual, in his mind he made Wagner think about Nietzsche what in fact Nietzsche felt towards Wagner. For with Nietzsche's music and Nietzsche's poetry there was a tragic flaw: it wasn't good enough. He was a great writer and an extraordinary human and intellectual phenomenon. But he wasn't a great artist. Indeed the truth was, the great musical god Dionysus was Wagner. Nietzsche only sang in his chorus, imitated his poetry, but couldn't bear to admit it.

> It's now ten years since I've been waging war against the corrupting power of Bayreuth – since 1876, Wagner has considered me his real and only opponent, the evidence of this is abundant in his later writing. The contrast between a decadent and one who creates out of a superabundance of strength, that is a dionysian nature for whom the hardest things are play, is of course palpable between us . . . We are as different as rich and poor.

That paragraph of self-deception became the dithyramb 'On the Poverty of the Rich', which also began 'Ten years gone -' in *Nietzsche contra Wagner*. Meanwhile Nietzsche attempted, in the same way he distanced himself from romantic love, to keep the ideal Wagner at bay by turning on the frantic gastric metaphors. Wagner was indigestible. But the problem was the sensual, loving, deprived Nietzsche kept heaping Wagner onto his plate.

Nietzsche's music was odd, and to some ears (like von Bülow's) life-destroying, much as his dithyrambic poetry was odd and cold. At only fourteen years old he identified as modern the pioneering use of strange imagery.[24] He disapproved then, but later made that modernity his own course. We might compare him with Liszt for his often hollow-seeming showmanship. Liszt sometimes evokes the same kind of repugnance in music as Nietzsche evokes in poetry. But the comparison is not only negative. In both Nietzsche and Liszt prophetic strokes of artistic genius can suddenly carry the audience into the next century.

Nietzsche as artist and man provided a kind of music then, to which Wagner supplied most of the human content. It was Wagner who showed him what love was, and in the end Wagner who showed him how, in imagination, to die. Wagner did that not only with his works but his life. Going mad, Nietzsche imagined Cosima was *his* wife. That claim was the end of the Cosima drama which had been going on in his head for a long time, beside the drama of Richard. An early French critic of Nietzsche's saw it as the great unwritten romantic novel of the nineteenth century.[25] There is a dithyramb called 'Ariadne's Lament', which in *Zarathustra* was spoken by a man. The theme was rebelliousness against an absent God which was at the same time dependence. In *Zarathustra*, the trembling old man who declaimed it implausibly, next moment metamorphosed in Zarathustra's mind into 'actor, counterfeiter, liar . . . magician', i.e. into Wagner himself. The poem made more sense as Ariadne's lament, when according to myth, her lover Theseus abandoned her. In the 1888 version Ariadne was Cosima, Theseus Wagner, and Dionysus, who appeared for the first time to save the betrayed woman, was Nietzsche. The constant in these two versions was Nietzsche's lament for lost love, his anger and his dependence. He shuffled the parts, but only ever succeeded in expressing in a dramatic monologue his longing for the lost companionship of the Wagners. Possibly he didn't even think of the mythical parallel for his romantic situation himself, but had watched it as if on stage. Elisabeth claimed the Ariadne/Theseus/Dionysus theme was the first introduced into the life of

Richard Wagner by Hans von Bülow, trying to cope with his wife's desertion. Von Bülow was Theseus, Wagner Dionysus. Nietzsche, arriving at Tribschen where Wagner and the yet undivorced Cosima were cohabiting, was a *spectator* of one of the great love affairs of the century. He then fell in love with the beloved himself and, in so far as it already seemed like fiction, rewrote the script. With Richard dead and Cosima alienated he played through all the parts to animate his loneliness.[26]

Out of his incapacity to live he created a formidable life. In 'On the Poverty of the Rich', answering Wagner's creative wealth and wealth of personality, but in truth borrowing them, he argued that Zarathustra was too full of what was rich ... that he drained the land around ... how could he expect love ... his task was to give to others and thank them for the taking ... he must thank them for making him poorer ...

> Du opferst dich, dich qualt dein Reichtum –
> du giebst dich ab
> du schonst dich nicht, du liebst dich nicht:
> Die grosse Qual zwingt dich allezeit,
> die Qual übervoller Scheuern, übervollen Herzens –
> aber Niemand dankt dir mehr ...
>
> du muss armer werden,
> weiser Unweiser!
> willst du geliebt sein.
> Man liebt nur die Leidenden,
> man giebt Liebe nur dem Hungernden
> verschenke dich selber erst, oh Zarathustra!
>
> Ich bin deine Wahrheit ...

I wonder. Cosima confided to her Tribschen diary that Nietzsche with his emotional and intellectual needs drained Wagner and Wagner didn't get enough love in return. Did she ever say as much to Nietzsche, in their twice-weekly meetings and correspondence? She certainly noticed the way his behaviour became sometimes unnatural, as if he were determined to resist Wagner's allure. A story she related about lending Nietzsche the score of *The Siegfried Idyll*, Richard's birthday present to her on Christmas Day 1870, also seems suspect. Instead of returning it as agreed, Nietzsche left it on the piano where he knew Richard would be irked to find it, not properly looked after, as if his wife did not care for her gift. Was Friedrich, not for nothing the tricky Elisabeth's brother, scheming to foment marital strife? I think it highly possible, given a similar ploy to annoy Wagner a few years later, when he left a Brahms score open on the piano.[27]

The memories were rich. But nothing new would come to Nietzsche now, his capacity for new imagery being as moribund as his capacity for new experience. Necessarily *Ecce Homo* was retrospective and *Nietzsche contra Wagner* could hardly have been more than an assembly of old materials. He could barely read, and he avoided people, just seeing the weather, the light and the food on his plate. The only life in Nietzsche's works was, actually as it has always been, his own. The vision was of himself dying.

Staring,
chewing,
one who no longer stands upright.
You seem to me grown together with your grave,
grownover mind . . .
And only recently so proud
On stilts with all your pride
So recently the hermit without God,
Who opened his house to the devil,
The scarlet prince of exuberance! . . .

Now
wedged
between two nothings
a question mark
a tired puzzle
a puzzle for birds of prey . . .

They will 'solve' you soon enough
Already they long for your 'solution'
They are already flying round you, they're puzzling
Over you, hanged man! . . .
Oh Zarathustra! . . .
Who knows himself! . . .
Who has hanged himself! . . .
[Between Birds of Prey]

We latecomers, of course, interpreting him, are like Elisabeth
and his mother, his birds of prey.

11

COLLAPSE INTO THE BEYOND

Nietzsche clung to the conventional notion of harvest ripening but his last autumn resembled the one in which I am writing now, in 1994. In this unusually propitious season some green leaves still clung to skeletal trees in December, and gave the passing illusion of an exceptional new cycle of growth. But the time signalled decay.[1]

Nietzsche's letters from October 1888 to January 1889 make painful, alienating reading compared with the lively human correspondence of earlier months and years. The whole personality has fewer and fewer chances to flourish, and responds with fury. *Ecce Homo*, between what is printed and what is discarded, is a record of the fight against soured interests. He still understood the difference between real life and the rhetoric of art; a striving for artistic effectiveness is evident in the excision of some passages.[2] But it was not true that he had no fanaticism, no hatred, no contempt, no arrogance, that he never felt wretched over his isolation. The mind driving *Ecce Homo* frantically disavowed any struggle, yet disinhibited by syphilis it couldn't contain itself. The attacks against Germany and the present age came neat and furious.

For fear of broadcasting *lèse-majesté*, Elisabeth destroyed vitriolic remarks directed at Kaiser Wilhelm II and Bismarck.[3] Nietzsche was left to hammer away at German Idealism and its consequences in the published *Ecce Homo*, and to dream of destroying the cultural age over which Germany had presided since the hated Reformation. That was enough. He was clearly raving:

For when truth steps into battle with the lie of millennia we shall have convulsions, an earthquake spasm, a transposition of valley and mountain such as has never been dreamed of. The concept of politics has then become completely absorbed into a war of spirits, all the power structures of the old society have been blown into the air – they one and all reposed on the lie: there will be wars such as there have never yet been on earth. Only after me will there be *grand politics* on earth.[4]

A violent declaration of loathing directed at the church followed.[5] Written in November or early December 1888, 'The Law Against Christianity' was dated 'On the Day of Well-Being, the first day of the Year One (30 September 1888 according to the incorrect calculation of time)'. From that day priests and philosophers in the old faith would be imprisoned or starved or driven into the desert:

The accursed places where Christianity has sat on its basilisk eggs shall be razed to the ground and as despicable spots on earth become the terror of all the world after. Poisonous snakes shall be raised upon them.[6]

Such swollen language was the work of an at least intermittently disturbed mind. Hysteria made Nietzsche stage his own effect upon life as ushering in a *Götterdämmerung*. The snakes writhed in his consciousness like the spirochaetes curling around his brain tissue. (Students of syphilis in Nietzsche's day more often compared the twisting bacteria to spermatozoa, linking beginning and end in a man's hapless fate in being a man, but he was never a realist.) Nietzsche had a tame serpent in Lou. She became Zarathustra's friend when he resisted her bite. But otherwise, for a mind imprinted with the Gospels, the snake was a malign power. It helped paint a wild picture. Drawing on the residues of his unconscious, Nietzsche's sloganmongering was fateful for his bad myth.

The views themselves had not changed. The irreligious and anti-German sentiments were only those Nietzsche had long harboured, of a more virile and robust culture arising to take the place of Christianity. Nor were his views necessarily mad. To see in German profundity and national identity a destructive germ was prophetic. But illness too easily made the products of his sharp pen seem out of control.[7]

The role syphilis played in heightening his pronouncements may be glimpsed through a comparison with his fellow sufferer, and ultimate madman, the French writer Guy de Maupassant. The dying Maupassant believed people would soon read him in China and England and Russia and that he was the son of God. As the brain loses mass, the result of tertiary syphilis, the human consciousness seems to effervesce in megalomania. Nietzsche called himself 'the leading person of all millennia'. Like Christ he would change the calculation of the calendar. Turiners already revered his importance, as if he were a prince, and, as he observed, perhaps he was a prince. Women admired him in the street while across the world people were reading him and declaring for him. Overbeck worried about the letters he received from mid-October on.[8]

A leap forward into reckless disinhibition came with the drafting of letters to the Kaiser and Bismarck in the first week of December. Reading the *Journal des Débats* in Rosenberg and Sellier's bookshop or the Fino reading room gave him political objects to which his bad faith could cling. On Boxing Day 1888 Nietzsche further drew up a memorandum to European embassies urging the formation of an anti-German league. 'I want to fasten the Reich in a straitjacket and provoke it into a war of despair. My hands won't be free until I have the young Kaiser and his entourage in my hands.' A war of ideas, financed with Jewish money, and which would destroy Christianity, was now his reiterated hope. It was the vision of a dangerous fanatic precisely because of that notion of war.[9]

Yet again it was the language and the overestimation of his own power, not the notion of containing an anti-Semitic Imperial Germany which had already shown itself aggressive to Europe's cost, that branded Nietzsche demented. Moreover through the fumes of insane anger real and just causes of personal resentment were visible.[10] Never had Nietzsche sounded so revolutionary as in those moments when he recollected the harm done to an unfulfilled humanity by priests, by the ideal of chastity, and by racial and class barriers that ignored intrinsic human worth. Even in his lifetime Nietzsche suffered from being tarred unjustly with the anti-Semitic brush. He held that against Bernhard Förster's Germany. The only nation against which he did feel racial prejudice was Germany. Imagining Bismarck's *Kulturkampf*, a struggle for the Imperial and Protestant domination of German culture, aimed at him, he pictured his fate in fittingly extreme Russian terms. Censorship threatened. If the Germans could invent a Siberia, whither to banish him, they would.[11]

The fierce language, the graphic pictures resulted from the way this intellectually oppressed situation touched his combative imagination. There was a constant revolutionary aspect to his notion of himself as a volcano, endorsed by that long association with Wagner's Siegfried.[12] But like Siegfried's attempts to change the world, Nietzsche's were better suited to the stage, from where he might influence individuals through art. Early in his career of antagonizing the Second Reich he was even vexed to be taken literally. Having written his *Warning to the Germans* that national aggression and philistinism might run them into the ground, rather than endorse their military triumph, he was approached in 1873 by the Socialist International as a potentially sympathetic member. It need not astonish us, who know that before 1918 he would also be called a revolutionary in Russia, but it is a telling story for his coming misunderstanding.[13]

In sum, political concerns, when wrapped in apocalyptic language, do lend an air of insanity to Nietzsche's metaphors.

'After the abdication of the old god I will reign,' he incanted to Fuchs.[14] But he still had wit, and the evidence of disintegration was, in Giorgio Colli's words, just a smudge.[15] The compensation for the intimate reader of both work and correspondence is to sense continually how Nietzsche is resisting illness, and therefore to allow pathos to suffuse those moments and passages which make thoroughly resistible reading.

He still argued subtly for Wagner against Germany[16] and explained rationally that much of his disappointment came from Wagner's pandering to the Reich. To his musical concerns he remained apolitically loyal. In his last month, surrounded by evidence of Wagner's popularity, be it with a Wagnerian-style opera which failed in Turin, be it with the new production of *Tannhäuser* which opened at the Teatro Regio on 26 December, he produced no explosion of hatred.[17] Not only did he set down his admiration for *Tristan*, but also his love of *The Siegfried Idyll* and unspecified works of Liszt. His judgement was fit and good.[18]

Another way to appreciate the pathos of resistance is to infer its mental course from Nietzsche's pronounced passion for food in late 1888. For nearly two years after he collapsed his appetite continued to astonish his doctors in Basel and Jena. He was eating to survive, which generated metaphor after metaphor showing body and mind both clinging hungrily to a healthy life. *Ecce Homo* anecdotally connects Nietzsche's passion for food with self-overcoming, but the living evidence is in the letters.[19] Nietzsche so consciously attended to his food in Turin because on it seemed to depend his *Arbeitskraft*, his strength for work, which was all his life consisted in. Nor, besides music – not consumable – did he have other sensual joys. Around Christmas a Milanese dish of ossi buchi (veal on the marrow bone) with macaroni and broccoli in the Piedmont fashion (probably lightly boiled, then finished with olive oil and garlic and anchovies) made him declare he had never known what meat and vegetables could be. He ate in a grand two-storey trattoria with service so fine he would employ these people to cook and wait on him when he came to reign.[20] The view that if he ate well he would stave off madness reflected his insistence on biology over idealism. This was the physiological determinism or, jokingly, Reelism, he shared with his onetime friend Paul Rée, and which allowed him to speculate that hitherto philosophy, by not understanding mind and body as one, had gravely misunderstood the importance of the body. No philosopher has taken to heart more passionately Feuerbach's dictum that a man is what he eats than Nietzsche. But only the bizarre deceits of illness showed him a man who was flourishing and looked years younger in the mirror.[21]

He achieved an extraordinary measure of physical self-mastery, in contemporary and later medical views. A strong *physis*, carefully nurtured with food and exercise, resisted the onset of general paralysis and made his case of syphilis bewilderingly atypical. That he had an unusual body perhaps explains why he lost neither concentration nor artistic feeling almost to the end. Into December he was revising *Ecce Homo*, the manuscript travelling back and forth between him and Naumann the printer, and he was also assembling *Nietzsche contra Wagner*.[22]

The handwriting slipped before the mental grip. Already in June, because of his trembling, the manuscript of *The Wagner Case* was illegible, with Latin characters indistinguishable from Greek.[23] 'Soennecken's Rundschriftfedern', fat round-tipped nibs recommended by the local teacher in Sils, became his temporary salvation. (His physical dependence made him a pioneer finnicky modern consumer.) His strikingly beautiful regular script continued to decline, like a Bach fugue suddenly erring in tempo. The spacing and proportions became less regular. The delicate, intricate harmony unravelled. The letters grew larger and straighter, less distinct one from another, and phrases ended with dashes. (For this sad evidence we must be perversely grateful that Nietzsche had long given up his experiments with a typewriter.) In the end only his mother could read one of the early versions of the *Dionysus Dithyrambs*. Among the fragments she gives us one of such Rilkean purity and inwardness we can almost accept as beautiful the mind, bathed in illusory sunlight, slipping into darkness behind the thinnest shield of words:

Die Einsamkeit
plagt nicht: sie reift –
Und dazu musst du die Sonne zur Freundin haben[24]

Solitude is
not pain but ripening –
For which the sun must be your friend.

Nietzsche seems to have been aware of the encroaching madness but, to avoid the pathos of an acknowledged struggle, would not state it directly. He wore the operetta mask, telling Köselitz:

> You'll also find in my cheerful and wicked 'present state' perhaps more inspiration for 'operetta' than anywhere else: I enjoy so many silly jokes with myself and have so many clownish private insights that now and again I'm grinning for half an hour in the street, I know no other word for it . . .

Another attack of uncontrollable grimacing and weeping happened at a concert of 2 December. As he insisted, the outburst could be interpreted as extreme joy in the programme of Beethoven, Liszt and Goldmark, though the light music on the programme was an unlikely catalyst, and after this attack Nietzsche wrote straight to Köselitz, just as he had appended after the earlier street attack: 'Please come . . . '[25] On one occasion he referred to operetta as if *it* were syphilis and to be welcomed in those very terms: 'to be infected in body and soul by this little Parisian would be salvation for being German.'[26] These positive interpretations of unavoidable decay were all forms of *amor fati*. He was going out to meet his fate. Having contracted syphilis, he wished he had been sexually more adventurous along the way. The self-aggrandisement in his normal character also came into play, for always he had to swagger and boast to seem wholly a man. Hence the claims in *Ecce Homo* that he could take strong drink and that Lapsang Suchong tea, renowned for its powerful flavour of tar, was too weak for his taste. The most extreme example of swagger was his claim when already committed to the psychiatric clinic in Basel that he had 'twice infected himself with lues'. The active verb and the claim to a double infection were individually both absurd. But he wanted others to be in no doubt he was a potent and determined man.[27]

That appeal in a postscript to Köselitz to come and rescue him was therefore all the more poignant. There was silence on Nietzsche's part when Brandes, introducing Strindberg to him in a letter, added that Strindberg like all geniuses was a bit mad: Nietzsche spoke though of 'the tragic catastrophe of my life which begins with "Ecce"'.[28]

In his room at least he was safe. He enjoyed the idea of it as a temple as he had before enjoyed his room in Nice. That he did for once envision it as a temple and not the usual 'cave' augured well for his spirits. He felt exalted. On one occasion, while he was working, the jolly melodies of *The Barber of Seville* wafted gloriously up from the weekly concert in the Galleria Subalpina. He signed himself 'phoenix'. He extemporized for hours at the piano. Out buying fruit, he engaged in cheery conversation with the proverbially unforthcoming citizens of Turin.

As a foreigner he had some leeway, though his manner in the street must have been bizarre if he cried out that he was God come to earth in human form to bring men closer, or that he was the 'tyrant of Turin'. Not many would have understood his German and his Italian wasn't good enough to harangue an anonymous public effectively. But still. The Finos became suspicious when in a typical smudging of the distinction between imagination and reality he asked for his room to be decked out as a temple, with frescoes, so he could receive the King and Queen of Italy.[29] Presumably because he wished to play the natural aristocrat he told Burckhardt a few days later he would do this in his shirtsleeves. The last weeks were a confused swaying between the concepts he had long imagined for himself as guides to life, like cheerfulness, nobility and Shakespearian buffoonery, and their real embodiment in action. Moreover it was as if the man who once toyed with the pseudonym Felix Fallax – the happy deceiver – deliberately sought to confuse onlookers. He voluntarily donned masks so closely resembling the errant behaviour to which syphilis was driving him that it was hard to tell when he was acting, and when not. But there is this grace to his end: by making the predetermined gestures of sickness into the tragic face bequeathed to the world, the ordinary sick man could slip away and fade, off-stage, in peace.

That grace lay in cultivating the animal in himself as much as the *Übermensch* and is, I believe, one reason why he liked to refer to himself as 'a beast'. In July he had spoken of himself to Malvida as an animal who was constantly being hurt and who received no human word. He had pity for himself as an animal, for by the mark of illness he was one cast out of civilization and its comforts, though a creature of sensitivity and feeling.

One and possibly two animal stories have become inseparable from his self-staged end. The first is told only by Elisabeth Förster-Nietzsche, and, resting on the testimony of an invented correspondent of her husband's living in Turin, can at best be regarded as heuristic fiction. I call it that however because, though she lacked artistry, Elisabeth had the power to conjure up imaginary worlds and possessed a love of lies very similar to her brother's. This trait may account for why she felt so free to manipulate her brother's life story and the content of his works, for she herself was engaged in telling a story, based on that raw material. Wanting to convey the impression that 'Nietzsche at Turin showed a friendly interest in all whom he met' she described him coming to the rescue of a small dog which got its paw jammed in the door of a café where he went every day to read the *Journal des Débats*.[30] Inexplicably the dog's owner walked away without noticing, so her brother bathed and bandaged the injured paw with an expertise remembered from his days in the Prussian ambulance corps. The dog lay gratefully at his feet till his owner eventually returned to whistle him away. A few days later the dog returned with the washed and ironed handkerchief in his mouth, sought out Nietzsche, and with a brush against his leg and a little growl, thanked him. The story is preposterous, but we should ask ourselves why Elisabeth wanted to make it up. To reflect Nietzsche's kindness and closeness to animals, about which she had been told, is surely the answer. Unlike the other fictions involving a (surely rather too Spanish-sounding) 'Don Enrico', designed to show her brother's last outpourings of dislike towards her and Förster were misunderstandings, this one had no ulterior motive, other than to portray her brother's virtues in the most vivid light. Moreover, perhaps a little dog did one day run after Nietzsche in the streets of Turin, for whatever motive, which set that peculiar image of the canine drinking cup in his mind while writing *Ecce Homo*. Nietzsche invariably drew his imagery from real incidents.[31]

In any case we have the evidence. Nietzsche as Zarathustra lived most happily in the company of animals. Nietzsche as himself identified with the simple life of God's creatures, wrote beautifully of them in *The Science of Joy*, and faced his animal demise stoically. He demonstrated that identification memorably in the second, better-known animal story connected with his end.

On 3 January 1889 or thereabouts he tearfully embraced a mistreated nag in the street. The horse under duress was pulling a public conveyance on or near the Via Po. It may have fallen first or he embraced it and then fell himself, briefly losing consciousness. The accounts are various. Anyway Davide Fino, who came along soon after, confirmed such an event happened. Bystanders had called the police by that time. Fino may have been passing by chance, but as one well-known in the town, he is more likely to have been summoned. Nietzsche recognized him and allowed himself to be carried home. Elisabeth in her version of the collapse preferred to have her brother simply fall from an invented high pavement in Piazza Carlo Alberto. The parallel 'fall' suggests to me she knew of the horse story, but didn't use it because it made him look mentally unhinged rather than, as she intended in *her* story, the victim of a stroke.[32]

Nietzsche had other ideas about how he wanted to be remembered. In his embracing the horse several writers through the present century have seen a human being commiserating with an abused soul. Nietzsche rebelled against human cruelty and crudeness by hugging this horse who was his partner in metaphysical abjectness. The temptation to detect a symbolic and tragic gesture is compelling. Especially at the end, all too meaningful coincidences exist between the poses Nietzsche struck and thoughts he had already expressed here or there. In the case of the horse he had already dreamed the gesture the previous May and written it in a letter. It is possible too that he had read the passage in Dostoevsky's *Crime and Punishment*, where Raskolnikov, for all that he was a murderer, dreamed of throwing his arms around a mistreated horse.[33] When Nietzsche dreamed of the mistreated horse he felt pity; he wanted to weep. Now in reality some ultimate autobiographical urge made him embrace a real horse, and the shock of willing his own life to the last conscious moment, that momentary exciting flush of power, precipitated his collapse.

> Oh sink down upon me
> Night of love
> Make me oblivious
> to living.
> Take me up
> into your embrace
> release me
> from the world!

The words are sung by Tristan and Isolde in their ecstatic sharing of suffering. Nietzsche's last 'girlfriend' was the sun, but as Zarathustra his last companions were animals. Of animals, and our reasons for living with them, he once wrote:

> I want to have my lion and eagle near me so that I always have hints and omens that help me to know how great or small my strength is.[34]

With the fallen horse, suddenly struck by a vision of his own fate, he collapsed in an ecstasy of pity, 'dying' as God did according to Zarathustra.[35]

He had the ability to direct his actions, having lost from his reason only the restraint which distinguishes between what is appropriate in life and what is theatre. The two had merged. His life was now unbounded. I think this is why other writers have found the incident with the horse so symbolic and so moving.[36] Nietzsche, who witnessed Wagner's exemplary love of animals, and knew of Schopenhauer's fondness for them, spoke to the horse. The Czech novelist Milan Kundera wondered in *The Unbearable Lightness of Being* if Nietzsche did not beg this wonderful equine specimen to forgive Descartes for believing animals do not have souls. Kundera found Nietzsche's to be a symbolic gesture against the dominance, the arrogance of the human mind over nature, against blind worship of progress. The idea is convincing, even if in that case Nietzsche's gesture seems overblown. Schopenhauer, Wagner, Nietzsche: what more formidable trio could be found to challenge what remained in the late nineteenth century of faith in *cogito ergo sum*? Nietzsche, the man who asked, 'Has not all philosophy been a misunderstanding of the body?' finally managed to ask that very question with his body.[37]

The collapse came just after Christmas, when he was mulling over plans to rename as 'Ecce Homo' Antonelli's Mole landmark – then the tallest walled building in the world. The general order 'German will be spoken at my court' awaited worldwide dissemination.[38] He himself called the collapse the crossing of the Rubicon. He could see it but he couldn't stop it.

Possibly it was symbolic that the time was Christmas. A number of reviewers of Nietzsche's story have been lured along this path, for a religious interpretation would add a dimension to the story. (For in the end all his interpreters must create pictures of him, not only amass facts.) The days after Christmas were regularly the worst for Nietzsche's health. Did the rejection of God thereby intensify the illness?[39] The idea is plausible in so far as all conflict, all excitement, painful or pleasurable, seemed to exacerbate Nietzsche's condition, which physiologically was an inflammation of the cerebral cortex. It is both corroborated and belied by the inspired January of 1882 which saw the writing of the first book of *Zarathustra*. Nietzsche devoted a poem, 'Sanctus Januarius', to that explosion of mental activity.[40] There is no evidence Christmas retained its traditional significance for him, and yet for one obsessed now with death and rebirth, as Dionysus Zagreus and as Christ crucified, for one shouting out in the street that he was God come among men, what date could have been more significant than Epiphany, 6 January?

The possible pagan symbolic interpretation of Nietzsche's end, apart from the Zagreus legend, is less seductive. There were, one might say, the Ides of Sils, for meteorologically it had been a very strange year. That unusually Nietzsche was not ill on his return journey to Turin was another omen.[41] Turin itself meanwhile has a long reputation for magic and a disconcerting number of writers, from Tasso to Rousseau, J.M. Symonds to Primo Levi, have become depressed or gone mad there. Nietzsche has since become the most famous.[42]

He was anyway crazy with *Machtgefühl*. He wrote to Meta that he had taken power. He had become God and was resting after his creation of the world. The arrival of the potency he had been seeking all his sick life at last allowed him as Dionysus to woo his ideal woman Ariadne: as Dionysus he now wrote without restraint to Cosima Wagner.

The hovering tonality had resolved to a definite key at last. Burckhardt was in no doubt, but then he had always considered Nietzsche abnormal and said so in no uncertain terms: 'That Nietzsche fellow? He couldn't even have a healthy bowel motion.'[43] Köselitz on the other hand still didn't notice and even in the Basel clinic more than a year later suspected Nietzsche (who was such a bad actor, though he coveted the skill) was feigning. Brandes and Malvida were aware of trouble, but Strindberg, himself sick, was predictably oblivious.

The reality was that, besides Nietzsche's deliberate playing with masks, syphilitic madness still let through shafts of light. The last letters, signed 'Dionysus' or 'The Crucified One' contain pregnant particles of meaning in a puzzling jumble. They show reason breaking down into its component parts. Meaningful combinations of significant atoms of experience, apt references, occur ever more seldom, though the brain is obviously trying and only just failing to cohere. One letter to Hans von Bülow speaks of him, her former husband, as the first of Cosima's lovers, and of Nietzsche as the third. Nietzsche refers to Cosima as Veuve Cliquot-Ariadne, drawing a parallel between the widow who made the house of champagne boom after her husband's death and Cosima's management of the Bayreuth enterprise after 1883. That the wit of a 'madman' could still be sane and urbane must make us use that category with qualification. Nietzsche also found words and time out of the tiny repository of judgement left to him to forgive Malvida, remembering her goodness in adopting the Russian philosopher Alexander Herzen's motherless children. Only the injustice of anti-Semitism accompanied him into the darkness. I'll have them all shot, he promised the Overbecks, as part of my debt to you. As the Pope he would summon the Kaiser and Pastor Stocker to Rome and execute them. On a quieter note, lucid in perceiving what he had lost politically by going mad, he saw it was to Wagner's benefit in the debate stirred by *The Wagner Case*.[44]

His fragmenting mind had become a kaleidoscope. Out of it momentarily arose a beautiful metaphysical vision conveyed to Jacob Burckhardt.

> . . . for I, together with Ariadne, have only to be the golden equilibrium of all things, we have in each doing those who are above us . . . Dionysus.[45]

In the same note Nietzsche took the conscious step of switching from the formal 'you' to the intimate 'thou' in his relations with the revered older professor, who had endowed him with his love of the Renaissance. He reverted to the polite form in a final letter, though signed off 'with sincere love'. The last of his letters to anyone, it was uniquely long, a departing exercise in sanity from one who since the 31 December no longer knew his address. He struggled to describe his Turin life: the situation of his room, how much he paid in rent, his shopping habits, the broken state of his boots, his love of Turin's old-fashioned quiet.

Madness broke through in the form of what he called 'bad jokes'. They suggested, as Cosima-Ariadne might have detected, reading those she received, that his identity was fluid across time. He was two contemporary French criminals, whose sensational trials had recently been heard in Paris and reported in the *Journal des Débats*. He was Count Robilant and Antonelli, therefore had twice seen his own funeral recently. Having been born in the Palazzo Carignano as Vittorio Emanuele, he had been King of Piedmont at its most powerful. Other incarnations included Buddha, Alexander the Great, Caesar, Voltaire, Napoleon, Alexander Herzen, possibly even Richard Wagner. Once he hung on the cross. Now he was reborn as Dionysus, who had created a world.

Does the lues-infected brain break down by undoing one logical fastening at a time? To these wanderings there is a lurking psychological consistency, not only because each figure mentioned had been significant in Nietzsche's life and thought, but because the desire to assume other identities had been detectably with him since he was a child. It helped him be 'the golden equilibrium of all things'.[46] Moreover what gave him the power to unite all these figures under a roof of selfhood was his vision of himself as an artist. He was choosing himself roles to highlight aspects of his character, and only in the last weeks did these roles venture into a wildly impersonal and inappropriate sphere. Still he seems so close to being himself.[47] In the last days of his conscious life Nietzsche met his maker who was that self.

The written fragments weave together dementia and humility. The last letter to Burckhardt, pinpointing those 'bad jokes', contains a brilliant vignette of his value to posterity:

Since I am condemned to entertain the next eternity with bad jokes, so I have set up my writing business here [in Turin] and it leaves nothing to be desired. I am very prettily placed and under no strain whatsoever.

Beginning 'I would in the end far rather be a Basel professor than God, but couldn't push my private egoism so far as to abandon the creation of the world for his sake' and ending 'You may make of this letter any use which does not lower me in the estimation of the citizens of Basel', this letter is a final plea for his worth as a Shakespearian fool to be considered.

For six months after it his ravings continued to make some sense. He said it was Cosima his wife who brought him to the Basel clinic, and called his restraining attendant Bismarck.[48] Once installed there he played magnificent music which reminded Köselitz, writing to Fuchs on 1 February, now of Wagner's *Tristan*, now of Beethoven. 'Interwoven tones of *Tristan*-like sensitiveness! Pianissimi alternating with the fanfares of trumpets and the sonorous sounds of trombones, Beethoven-like profundity and jubilant songs rising above it, then again reveries and dreams – it beggars description. Oh for a phonograph!' This surely was the music to which Dionysus processed on his return to the River Po. Four months later a visitor told Nietzsche of a trip to Spain. 'Ah, Deussen went there,' he said. 'But I am Deussen,' said the speaker. Back in Naumburg he was barely coherent, and grew heavy with immobility. He was happiest sitting in a church.[49] Between Turin and Naumburg we have the sense of a consciousness passing behind dark clouds, breaking through into the sunlight here and there, but eventually entirely concealed behind an impenetrable barrier.

The veiled existence he had already imagined, and though it is a greatly vilified hypothesis it seems to me quite possible that syphilis affected his imagination earlier, from the mid-1880s, whilst not undermining his art or his importance.[50] But it is hard to judge because again Buddhistic repose was like a mask Nietzsche could don voluntarily just as life was forcing him into stillness. Death in life was his religious and sexual ideal long before he sank into the vegetative state. Schopenhauer had taught him to love the idea of removal from the appetitive immediacy of human existence. Ever after he often fixed his gaze on a distant calm sea. The 'smooth sea, perfection' was a theme in *The Wagner Case*, audible to him in the music of both Bizet and Gast. Even that troublesome creature woman became beautiful when envisaged as a distant ship gliding over a glassy sea.[51] Water was what he remembered of so many places where he had been happy. The Wagners' Tribschen lay on Lake Vierwaldstätt, and when he went back there to show Lou his old love he cried. The lakes Sils and Silvaplana inspired his vision of an Over-Earth, while from the Genoa years he had recently recalled in *Ecce Homo* the view from Porto Fino.[52] To the same Ligurian sea was written a poem in 1882, reworked and sent to Lou Salomé in autumn 1883. Another year later Nietzsche named his third version 'Yorick-Columbus'.

> Lady, said Columbus,
> Trust a Genoese no more!
> He stares into the blue nimbus
> Drawn by the distant shore . . .
>
> The strangest world is now dear
> Genoa has sunk beneath the strand –
> Stay cold, my hand! Hold, my heart, steer!
> Sea before me – and land? and land?
>
> I must go there – and I trust
> Myself now and my grip.
> Towards the open blue sea thrusts
> my Genoese ship.
>
> Everything becomes novelty
> Space and time glitter way beyond
> And the most beautiful monstrosity
> – which is Eternity – looks at me fond.[53]

Overbeck arrived in Turin in the evening of Monday 7 January, prompted by a unique visit to his house in Basel from an alarmed Jakob Burckhardt the previous afternoon. Candida Fino meanwhile had been browsing through her lodger's meticulously kept and jealously guarded bundles of correspondence for some soul close to him she might alert, and she too sent a telegram to Overbeck. The two entreaties left the kindly theologian little choice but to depart immediately for beyond the Alps.

He found the Finos in confusion and Nietzsche sitting on the couch in his room, reading proofs of *Nietzsche contra Wagner*. The sick man recognized his friend, leapt up, embraced him and burst into tears.

The Finos described their lodger's behaviour since his collapse in the street. The howling racket and the interminable eccentric piano-playing kept them awake. Candida, peering through the keyhole, saw Nietzsche prancing naked round the room, enacting solitary Dionysian rites. She and her husband contacted the German consul and the police. A local doctor for the insane – Doctor Turina – came to examine the patient who cried out: 'Pas malade! Pas malade!' Nietzsche was sedated when Overbeck first arrived, but when the medication wore off he resumed his autoerotic orgy. The gentle professor was horrified.[54]

Post-haste Nietzsche should be brought to Basel, Overbeck decided. There Overbeck knew the doctors, as did Nietzsche himself. The important man was Professor Doctor Wille – Doctor 'Will'. (The firm Nieske, Doctor Turina, Doctor Wille, finally the young Professor Miescher who would meet Overbeck and Nietzsche in Basel – for a storyteller trying to stick to the facts these names seem like taunts. Did Nietzsche's demise really belong to a devilishly ordained rhyme-scheme?)

Nietzsche was reluctant to leave. He loved the city of Turin as much in madness as in health. Overbeck also faced the problem of how to deal with him in transit, because he would keep singing, incomprehensibly talking to strangers, removing his clothes, falling into a rage, weeping. Someone, surely the German consul, found a suitable psychiatric nurse to travel with them. His name was Bettmann, and he was a German dentist resident in Turin. The qualifications didn't match in theory, but Overbeck was very grateful for Bettmann who evidently had great experience of the delusions of grandeur which accompany GPI (general paralysis of the insane), and only proved unacceptable when he asked an excessive fee for his services. (Elisabeth who, never having met him, dismissed Bettmann as a dubious money-grubbing character who probably stole a manuscript, was unfortunately inspired by the fact he was Jewish, and perhaps also worried at what he saw. She had to undermine his standing lest he told the world Friedrich Nietzsche, brother of the dignified and valuable personage Elisabeth, was a syphilitic lunatic given to unfortunate practices.)[55]

Bettmann described the great ceremony waiting to greet Nietzsche as a celebrity at the railway station in Basel. That persuaded the first tragic philosopher, the first and last Dionysian, to leave Piazza Carlo Alberto. But even then Nietzsche lingered outside and begged a last favour from his esteemed landlord: 'Dear Signor Fino, will you let me have your *papalina*?' He wanted Fino's triangular popish nightcap with tassle for the journey. When he put it on it must have made him look like a clown.[56]

So dressed he left Turin, the tragic philosopher who not only willed himself to be a clown but willed himself to bequeath that visual image to posterity. His message had to be certain beyond words.

He went to Basel, singing the Gondola song from *Nietzsche contra Wagner* as they rattled over the St Gotthard Pass.

> On the bridge just now
> I stood in brown night.
> Singing came from somewhere:
> Welled up in golden drops
> and vanished over the trembling surface.
> Gondolas, lights, music –
> the way led drunkenly out into the darkness . . .

To my soul, a violin
Invisibly moved, I sang
Secretly a gondola song,
Trembling and blissful at so much colour.
Was anyone listening?[57]

He went to Basel, playing Wagner, composing Wagnerian music.

Finally he went with his mother back to Naumburg, where he became unkind to dogs and anything that surprised him. Of the few words he uttered, the most frequent was 'elegant'.[58, 59]

After Franziska died in 1897, Elisabeth took him to Weimar. He lay in bed in a white robe and recognized no one.

NOTES

Nietzsche references are to sections of the main works which may be consulted in any edition. Works I have translated as *The Science of Joy* and *The Antichristian* are more commonly known respectively as 'The Gay Science' or 'The Cheerful Science' and 'The Antichrist'. More specialized references are to the *Kritische Studienausgabe* (*KSA*), herausgegeben von Giorgio Colli and Mazzino Montinari, 15 vols, Deutscher Taschenbuch Verlag and de Gruyter Berlin/New York 1967-77 and 1988. The correspondence, given by date, can be found in *Friedrich Nietzsche Sämtliche Briefe Kritische Studienausgabe* (*KSA*, Briefe), 8 vols, DTV and de Gruyter Berlin/New York 1975-1984. The letters of January 1889 appear in English in Walter Kaufmann *The Portable Nietzsche*, New York 1954. The letters to Brandes are translated in Georg Brandes, *Friedrich Nietzsche*, London 1914.

Frequent references are also given to the standard biography, Curt Paul Janz, *Friedrich Nietzsche* 3 vols, Munich 1978-9, to Carl Albrecht Bernoulli, *Franz Overbeck und Friedrich Nietzsche Eine Freundschaft*, 2 vols, Jena 1908, and to Anacleto Verrecchia, *La Catastrophe di Nietzsche a Torino*, Torino 1978

Nietzsche's works are abbreviated as follows –

> *BoT*: *The Birth of Tragedy*
> *HAH*: *Human, All Too Human*
> *BGE*: *Beyond Good and Evil*

Genealogy: *The Genealogy of Morals*
Twilight: *Twilight of the Idols*
EH: *Ecce Homo*
TWC: *The Wagner Case*

The translations are mine unless otherwise specified.

PREFACE

1. Leipzig University turned him down in 1883. Bernoulli, I, 368–9
2. Loved him for his love of life. In *The Intellectuals and the Masses* (1992) John Carey argues, in the view of the present author misleadingly, that Nietzsche encouraged the next two generations to hate the mass of humanity and will their extermination. Carey's book, based on translated sources, ignores the seminal scholarship of Kaufmann and other post-war critics revealing the human Nietzsche to readers confused by British anti-German and Nazi propaganda. He also makes persistent reference to *The Will to Power*, a book not to be found in *KSA*, and which Nietzsche never wrote. It was compiled by his sister from material Nietzsche did not intend to publish.
3. Nietzsche's closest friend, the theologian Franz Overbeck, analysed Nietzsche's attitude to Christianity and the Christian effects in his work. See, for example, Bernoulli, I, 409, for the comparison of Zarathustra to Christ, and even more substantial parallels with the Old Testament God. A senior contemporary of Nietzsche's at school was also reminded of Christ in the temple by Nietzsche as an adolescent. Elisabeth Förster-Nietzsche, *The Young Nietzsche*, 43

1

1. 'Apparently just . . .', 10.4.88
2. 'Not even old yet . . .', 14.4.88
3. 'Nietzsche heard . . .' Burckhardt also praised the cosmo-politanism of the Renaissance age as 'a sign of an epoch in which new worlds are discovered, and men no longer feel at home in the old', further encouraging Nietzsche to see himself as an explorer. See *The Civilisation of the Renaissance in Italy*, tr. S.G.C. Middle-more, ed. Irene Gordon (1960), 124; Nietzsche's homelessness briefly amounted to statelessness, but was never the evil it has become in the twentieth century.
4. 'I have now . . .', 11.11.87
5. 'In Genoa . . .', 7.4.88
6. 'The year-in . . .' 3.2.88 to Overbeck
7. 'took a room . . .' Verrecchia, *La catastrophe di Nietzsche a Torino*, is a pioneering and invaluable biographical study which contains the details of Nietzsche's stay. But the author's tone is mocking and the key concepts of Nietzsche's philosophy strike him as 'vague and nebulous'. The aim is to demythologize Nietzsche by revealing the conventional man behind the radical philosophy. Verrecchia uses local newspapers and eyewitness accounts to undermine the veracity of Nietzsche's opinions on Turin and events there and to question the motives for his enthusiasms. My comments are based on personal visits to Nietzsche's apartment, courtesy of Dino and Adriana Vallorani, and wanderings about the city.
8. 'Turin! . . .', 7.4.88
9. 'That one can see . . .', 14.4.88. 'The town has . . .', 10.4.88
10. 'So unrestrained . . .', *Conversations with Nietzsche*, ed. Sander L. Gilman, translated by David J. Parent (1987), 148
11. 'rugged and unbending . . .', 'Schopenhauer als Erzieher', 7, *KSA*, 1:408

2

1. 'Basically the man . . .', 7.4.88
2. 'analysed Schopenhauer's position . . .', *Untimely Reflections*, 'Schopenhauer as Educator', 3, *KSA*, 1:350ff.
3. 'A theory of masks . . .' See *Beyond Good and Evil*, especially [40], [230], [278], [289] and [290] and maxim 97: 'What? A great man? I always see only the actor of his own ideal.'
4. 'Between you and me . . .', 20.12.87
5. 'I have made . . .', 27.5.88
6. 'He was about . . .' For Nietzsche's physical appearance early in 1889 see Erich Podach, *Madness of Nietzsche* (1931), 183
7. 'manifold, mendacious . . .', *Beyond Good and Evil* [291], also note 3
8. 'Man is the animal . . .', *Beyond Good and Evil* [62]
9. 'A philosopher is . . .', *Beyond Good and Evil* [292]
10. 'Rohde said . . .', Janz, 2:447
11. 'Nietzsche was . . .', Janz, 1:55; 'He dredged up old excuses . . .' to Pasquale d'Ercole, 9.6.88; 'his only mask . . .', *The Lonely Nietzsche*, Preface, vi
12. 'pessimism of strength', 1886, *BOT*, Preface, I. Brandes said philologists he consulted welcomed Nietzsche's suggestion. Grimm, *Deutsches Wörterbuch* (1873), under 'Krieger' lists many instances of that word in the Lutheran Bible, generally signifying struggle for a desired result, in which case 'good' might be construed.
13. 'I am a brave . . .', 10.4.88
14. 'Köselitz's first impression . . .', Janz, 1:696
15. 'In truth . . .', Janz 1.222ff.; 'Help, Schopenhauer!' 3.11.67
16. 'A letter to Cosima . . .', *Cosima Wagner's Diaries* (I), 21.8.70
17. 'the terrifying . . .', 7.11.1870. 'What enemies . . .', 12.12.70.
18. 'The readiness to espouse . . .', cf., *KSA*, 1:566 ('Die dionysische Weltanschauung', 3). Nietzsche links the need to deal with 'the terror or the absurdity' of human life with Greek understanding of the wisdom of Dionysus; *KSA*, 1:40, *The Birth of Tragedy*, 4, speaks of *Urschmerz* and the Greek Apollonian outlook resting upon the veiled foundation of that suffering, a veil which the

Dionysian lifts; the Dionysian is repeatedly defined in Nietzsche's later works as an example from Greek culture pointing to the necessary psychology of a future healthy culture. *KSA* 6:160, *Twilight*, 'What I owe the Ancients', 5, is a model definition linked to Nietzsche's project to transvalue all values.

19. Arthur C. Danto, *Nietzsche as Philosopher*, 200. For another conscious illustration of Nietzsche talking to a mocking *alter ego* see *The Science of Joy*, Book 3 [255] and [262]. Walter Kaufmann's English edition provides invaluable notes to such 'jokes'.
20. 'Gibbon recoiled . . .' For a summary of attitudes to Turin's architecture, including Nietzsche's, see Edward Cheney, 'Architectural Taste and the Grand Tour: The Case of Guarino Guarini', *Bolletino del CIRVI*, 20 (iuglio–dicembre), 1989
21. 'He told Brandes . . .', 10.4.88
22. 'Despotism . . .', *Civilisation of the Renaissance*, 122
23. *BGE* [287]
24. *Civilization of the Renaissance*, 266–7. See also *BGE* [271] on cleanliness, where Nietzsche appears to be talking about individuals but might equally be talking about different cultures. The idea is that vast differences of spirit are conveyed in small details of the physical life and by extension the urban environment.
25. Verrecchia, 12

3

For a concise, authoritative account of Nietzsche's relationship with Wagner, see Caroline Schmidt-Löbbecke, Curt Paul Janz, *Friedrich Nietzsches Wagner-Erfahrung*, Sils Maria, 1986. Dietrich Fischer-Dieskau, *Wagner and Nietzsche*, London 1978, is also useful. *The Wagner Case* is referred to as *TWC*.

1. 'That was a man . . .', Schmidt-Löbbecke, p.99
2. 'We arrive . . .', 9.11.68 to Rohde; also translated in *The Young Nietzsche*, 188–92
3. 'In a poem . . .' 'Whatever with pains I have collected . . . I give it

to my Nietzsche. May it be of some use to him!' Wagner's dedication of the nine volumes of his collected works to Nietzsche on All Souls Day 1873. *The Young Nietzsche*, 365. Nietzsche explicitly remembered on 21.6.88 and 17.11.88 letters Wagner had written to him from the same time.

4. 'At Tribschen . . .', Fischer-Dieskau 33–4. 'We loved . . .', 27.4.83 to Köselitz. 'The only living persun . . .', *Cosima Wagner's Diaries* (I), 5 Jan. 1871
5. 'Bereits bereut!' *TWC*, Epilogue
6. 'The unnaturalness . . .', *Cosima Wagner's Diaries* (I), 15 July 1871. '. . . seemed to drain the composer . . .', ibid., 3 Aug. 1871
7. 'Star friendship . . .', *The Science of Joy* [279]
8. 'He who has . . .', Schmidt-Löbbecke, 66
9. 'Heaven on earth', 5.5.75 to his mother and sister. On the disturbing beauty of Wagner's music compare Bryan Magee, *Aspects of Wagner* (1988), 37: 'One might put this in Freudian language by saying that the singer's is the voice of the ego while the orchestra is the voice of the id, so that together they expand consciousness beyond all its normal limits into a total self-awareness of which we are otherwise incapable. Wagner knew that he was articulating what in others was repressed and that therefore there was an abnormal wholeness about both himself and his work.'
10. 'The hardest sacrifice . . .', 20.7.80 to Köselitz. Nietzsche 'was never the same man . . .', *Conversations*, 50, 53
11. 'Discussing with Brandes . . .', 27.3.88. 'Nietzsche avowed . . .', mid-April 1886 to Fuchs (*KSA*, Briefe, 7:688). See also *BoT*, 'Attempt Self-Criticism', 7; 'Ways out of the labyrinth . . .', *TWC*, Epilogue
12. 'Richard Wagner in Bayreuth', 9, in *Untimely Reflections, KSA*, 1:491–5
13. 'I wouldn't know . . .', *Nachlass*, Summer 1875, *KSA*, 8/11 [42]. Nietzsche, compiling these notes towards 'Richard Wagner in Bayreuth' had linked Wagner with the Dionysian in *BoT* as the artistic means to face the pain and absurdity of the world without succumbing to pessimism. See also Fischer-Dieskau 69–70; 130

14. 'The creaturely life . . .', *Nachlass*, Summer 1878, *KSA* 8/30 [155]. 'Neither to suffer . . .', ibid. [157]
15. 'What had here become creative . . .', *The Science of Joy* [370]. Wagner's was narcotic art but the Dionysian art was *instead of* a drug. See 'Die dionysische Weltanschauung', 3, *KSA*, 1:566
16. 'Redemption for the Redeemer . . .', *TWC*, Epilogue
17. 'To repeat . . .', *TWC*, 7
18. 'The outlook for art . . .', *HAH*. See also Arthur C. Danto, *Nietzsche as Philosopher*.
19. 'anvil-beating desire . . .', *HAH*, Preface, 3. The German original has *vulkanisch stossend* which is not 'volcanically erupting' as in the Hollingdale translation but a reference to the Roman deity Vulkan, associated with Hephaestus, the god of metalwork, with his workshops in volcanoes. Many direct references to Siegfried's heroic breaking away occur in Nietzsche's works and notebooks. His power is celebrated in 'Richard Wagner in Bayreuth', II, and put to a Nietzschean end in *Beyond Good and Evil* [256], where Siegfried is praised for being anti-Catholic and anti-Romantic. His qualities are those idealized by Nietzsche in the anti-Wagner struggle: he is 'too hard', 'too free' and 'too cheerful'. In other words by 1886 Siegfried has become an *Übermensch*.

4

On Nietzsche's music and music in his life, see *Der musikalischer Nachlass*, ed. Janz, and Luisa Moradei, *La Musica di Nietzsche*, with a preface by Mazzino Montinari, Padova, 1983.

1. 'tutto Carmenizzato . . .', 20.4.88 to Köselitz
2. 'For the thinker . . .', *The Science of Joy* [42]. See also [12]
3. 'Ariadne's role fell . . . to Carmen', *TWC*, 1
4. 'This music . . .', ibid.
5. 'What we Halcyons miss . . .', *TWC*, 10
6. 'failed now to give him' Wagner's music did once betoken sunshine for Nietzsche. See Chapter 3, note 13 above. Sunshine

certainly radiated from paradisaical Tribschen.

7. Nietzsche dropped from *The Birth of Tragedy* a section discussing the problem of music and words so as not to offend Wagner. Fischer-Dieskau comments on a disagreement always latent between Wagner and Nietzsche, 133, 188. The dropped fragment is available in *KSA*, 7/12[1], and in English translation as 'The Twofold Truth in Wagner's Aesthetics', Nietzsche's Fragment 'On Music and Words' in *Between Romanticism and Modernism* (London 1980). Carl Dahlhaus's commentary takes up the ambivalent quest for 'absolute music'.

8. 'Music had been a joy . . .' On Nietzsche's musical boyhood and his expectations that music express something beyond itself: Schmidt-Löbbecke, 13–14; *La Musica*, 6–11

9. 'The deprivation . . .', *La Musica*, 10. A letter to his Pforta tutor Robert Buddensieg, 12.7.64, spells out his early fascination with music's physical effects in conjunction with a sense of transcendence in the mind.

10. 'Paul Deussen recounted . . .' Janz, 1:137ff., while noting Deussen's memory was excellent, sees this as an unverifiable tale, lent a spurious extra credence by Thomas Mann's fictional reworking of it in *Doctor Faustus*. Its connection with Nietzsche's late poem 'Daughters of the Desert', first noticed by Brann, however, adds, in my opinion, to its likely truth.

11. 'Whether the young Nietzsche . . .' On Nietzsche's later limited and medically prescribed sexual experience with prostitutes, see Mazzino Montinari, 'Nietzsche and Wagner 1980 Addendum', in *Nietzsche in Italy*, Stanford 1988. This article adds a dimension to that other sensational myth of Nietzsche's biography, masturbation. Wagner, using the wrong word, *inferred* 'pederasty' from the effect of Nietzsche's eye trouble. Doctors of the day believed masturbation caused blindness. Nietzsche told Dr Eiser he practised 'nothing unnatural'.

12. 'Music conducting Nietzsche . . .', Fischer-Dieskau, 47

13. 'Schoolfriend Gersdorff . . .', *The Young Nietzsche*, 110

14. 'Hans von Bülow called . . .', *La Musica*, 14. 'Wagner even told . . .',

11.9.87. 'Nietzsche's music too ecclesiastical . . .', Podach, *Gestalten*, 90ff.
15. 'verbal instrumentalist', Fischer-Dieskau, 72
16. 'Themes from the author's own life . . .' For allusions to friends, etc., see R.J. Hollingdale's Introduction to *Thus Spoke Zarathustra* (Harmondsworth 1969). Fritz Martini in *Das Wagnis der Sprache* (1952) analyses Nietzsche's language.
17. 'A symphony . . . or . . an answer to Wagner', Schmidt-Löbbecke, 38, 46, 56–7, 2.4.83 to Köselitz.
18. 'closer and closer to music . . .', Schmidt-Löbbecke, 64
19. 'agreed with Rohde', 22.2.84
20. 'My style is dance . . .', ibid.
21. 'The Dionysian was . . .', Fischer-Dieskau, 73. 'Without music . . .', to Brandes 27.3.88

5

1. Carl Dahlhaus, *Schoenberg and the New Music* (1987), considers the non-necessary coincidence between musical and socio-historical change. However, composers such as Mahler and Schoenberg, Bartok and Stravinsky explicitly responded to violent and despairing moods in the new century. Mahler was profoundly inspired by Nietzsche's humour, as well as directed towards the use of folk-songs as a source of the Dionysian (Franklin, *Mahler Symphony No. 3*, p.51 and p.18). Richard Strauss saw the Wagner/Nietzsche debate as crucial in determining the modern aesthetic legacy, a view shared by Fischer-Dieskau (56, 73) and to be inferred from general histories of music, for example, Alec Harman and Wilfred Mellers, *Man and His Music* (1988). See also Schmidt-Löbbecke, 120, and Thomas Mann's imaginative creation of a Nietzsche/Schoenberg composite figure in *Doctor Faustus*. Artistic and spiritual problems foreseen and explored in Nietzsche's work, and the aphoristic, fragmented forms Nietzsche's works took, both found parallels in the content and form of the new music.

2. 'What Nietzsche had to say about Wagner . . .', *Genealogy*, 3. '*Beyond Good and Evil* had spelt out . . .' [255]
3. 'Poles of health and decadence. . .', *TWC*, Epilogue. On Wagner's manipulation of tired nerves, on the sleepwalkers' path to false serenity, as it were, see *TWC*, 5
4. 'Nietzsche did not state . . . but there were obvious implications . . .', *TWC*, 6, decries Wagner's phoney religiosity, and section 11 links his power to appeal to the mass, to the age of the demagogue and the rise of militarism.
5. *HAH*, 1:212, 'Old doubts over the effect of art': 'Plato could still be right when he says that through tragedy one becomes generally more fearful and emotional . . . what right has our age to offer an answer to Plato's great question concerning the moral influence of art at all?' Nietzsche's argument against Wagner closely resembled Plato's against the degenerate effects of art and the unreliability of artists, especially as set out in Walter Kaufmann, *Tragedy and Philosophy* (1968), 1: [5–6]. Iris Murdoch, *The Fire and the Sun*, 'Why Plato Banished the Artists', also serves to set *TWC* in context. Plato's puritanical objections to the theatre exactly parallel Nietzsche's to Wagner's theatricality. See, summing up this issue, Lesley Chamberlain, 'Why Nietzsche banished Wagner', *The Times Literary Supplement*, 4 Nov. 1994.
6. 'Everything that has ever grown . . .', *TWC*, Afterword. Nietzsche attacked *Parsifal* for indulging in counterfeit dealings with the beyond at the expense of life. This counterfeiting took the form of a sop to the senses, a wafting of incense in Wagner's music, and a corresponding hatred of mental clarity.
7. Christianity equally represented counterfeit dealings with a fake 'beyond', Nietzsche would argue in *The Antichristian*. The historicized, cushioned and optimistic 'Christianity' of David Strauss he denounced as an 'impious vulgarity of outlook ' (*ruchlose Vulgarität der Gesinnung*), *Untimely Reflections*, 1:7. His purity of mind, which was not puritanism, also objected to Wagner's false contrast between chastity and sensual pleasure.
8. 'Human beings . . .', *Genealogy*, 3:16
9. 'That torment . . .' In the same way as Plato took guidance from

beauty as furthering the highest good but suspected (beautiful) art of fostering moral and spiritual confusion (see Murdoch, *The Fire*, 17, 65), so Nietzsche distrusted all music, the art to which he was most sensitive, which undermined the human capacity to flourish. The consequences were restricting for art music, which might be preserved in small monastic brotherhoods or die away altogether, Fischer-Dieskau, 133, 164. 'Withering away . . .', see *HAH*, Book 1 [223]. 'The artist will soon be regarded as a glorious relic . . .' The problem for Nietzsche seems to have been the impossibility of a future authenticity combined with his rejection of an illusory, palliative music: see *TWC*, Second Afterword. At the same time he made illusion the basis of his written art, both sharing Plato's distrust of the written word (see Murdoch, 23) and striving to incorporate that very distrust in a new art form.

10. Kaufmann, *Tragedy* [6]
11. 'Nietzsche's own contradictoriness . . .' In *The Aesthetic Education of Mankind* (1795), which influenced Nietzsche during his writing of *The Birth of Tragedy*, Schiller spoke of two basic effects of art, energetic beauty and melting beauty (Letter 17), and two basic aesthetic modes of personality, tense and relaxed. Art corrected the dominant spirit of the personality – and ideally of cultural epochs – to maintain a dynamic equilibrium. A world too dominated by the cerebral is brought back to the material; an over-sensual world is urged to cogitate and find new intellectual forms. This antithetical thinking is evident in Nietzsche's early categories of the Apollonian and the Dionysian, but hardly serves his needs as a tense personality. He needs the 'melting' beauty of Wagner, even though it doesn't restore a balance; it destroys him. Thus his Dionysian, which gradually loses its Apollonian counterweight as Nietzsche's thinking becomes more his own, must have an effect both energizing and serenic, as the *Übermensch* maintains himself beyond conflict. The result is Nietzsche's cheerfulness, his *Heiterkeit*.
12. 'Forgive me . . .', winter 1884 from Nice.
13. 'His tight physical make-up . . .', see note 11 above
14. 'It is roughly . . .' Nietzsche, craving sweetness and tunefulness,

was extremely sensitive to a new brutalism in music he felt Wagner had unleashed, alongside the creation of great beauty. *TWC*, Afterword, contains an astonishing paragraph describing the night-time atmosphere in big towns. 'Walking through a largish town at night everywhere you hear musical instruments being raped with ceremonial rage mixed with an intermittent wild howling.' Wilfred Mellers in *The Twilight of the Gods* (1973) argued that The Beatles, with their tunefulness, ushered in a new age of Dionysian community through their popular music. The explicitly and aggressively sexual rock music which has succeeded them suggests that age was short-lived. Another form common to both art and pop music dating from the crisis in music Nietzsche identified is minimalism. Its harmonic stasis, with hypnotic effect, seems to be a deliberate and sinister eschewing of musical articulateness.

15. 'Some imagination . . .', Pierre Boulez quoted by Stephen Walsh in 'Problem Solved?', BBC Proms Guide 1994. Nietzsche also emphasized 'small' musical forms as the way forward (*TWC*, Second Afterword)
16. 'Eduard Munch painted . . .' See Arne Eggum, *Munch and Photography* (1989), pp. 84–8
17. 'By the same token . . .' See above, Franklin, *Mahler*, p. 18, and Nietzsche, *TWC*, 3: 'music needs mediterraneanizing . . .'
18. '. . . back to the Greeks . . .' Nietzsche's idea combines a traditional German love of the south and a new aesthetic enthusiasm for warm colours and exotic music with longstanding German thoughts, mediated through Schiller's theory of humanizing play, about the desirability of a Greek outlook. *KSA*, 7:3 [49], a notebook for *The Birth of Tragedy*, has: 'Man is first a human being when he plays, says Schiller; the world of Olympian gods (and Greek Antiquity) are representatives.'
19. 'until men became gods . . .' See note 18 above
20. 'The expression . . .', 2.12.87
21. 'aristocratic morality . . .', *Genealogy*, First Essay; *TWC*, Epilogue; Thomas Mann, 'Goethe und Tolstoi', (1921); *Gesammelte Werke in 12 Bänden* (Oldenburg 1960) IX; Dmitry

Merezhkovsky (1865–1941), 'L. Tolstoy and Dostoevsky' (1900) in *Polnoe sobranie sochinenii* (SPB-M 1912) v. VII

22. 'Kulinarismus . . .', Brecht, 'Kleines Organon für das Theater', Vorrede. Brecht also speaks, quite Nietzsche-like, of bourgeois theatre as 'a branch of the bourgeois drug trade'. See also Plato, *Gorgias*, 462, on oratory and cookery being branches of the same art of pandering. On Wagner's manipulativeness, see *TWC*, 8

23. 'He is at . . .', *The Science of Joy* [97]

24. 'We regarded . . .', *BoT* [24]

6

1. 'Funny but . . .', 17.7.88
2. 'Do you understand . . .', 14.4.88
3. 'Circling round this paramount problem', 18.2.88
4. 'My problem this time . . .', 23.5.88
5. '. . . had decided to concentrate' In late spring Nietzsche still drafted his forthcoming ideas under the heading 'The Will to Power'. At the end of the summer, however, 'The Transvaluation of All Values' looked like this in embryo: Book 1: The Anti-Christ. Attempt at a Critique of Christianity; Book 2: The Free Spirit. Critique of Philosophy as a Nihilistic Movement; Book 3: The Immoralist. Critique of the Most Fatal Kind of Ignorance; Book 4: Dionysus. Philosophy of Eternal Recurrence. *KSA*, 13:589.

   In the last lines of *Twilight* he explains it as a lifelong plan: 'and with that I again return to the place from which I set out − *The Birth of Tragedy* was my first revaluation of all values: with that I again plant myself in the soil out of which I draw all that I will and *can* − I, the last disciple of the philosopher Dionysus − I, the teacher of the Eternal Recurrence . . .'

6. 'Transfigured night . . .' *TWC*, Epilogue, 'Self-mastery morality . . . transfigures, beautifies, makes more rational . . .' ('*verklärt, verschönt, vernünftigt* . . .'), as opposed to Christian morality which

'impoverishes, drains of colour and makes ugly . . .' ('verarmt, verblasst, verhässlicht . . .)

7. 'I believe . . .', 29.4.88
8. 'One comes . . .' Beginning of December 1882. *KSA*, Briefe, 6:286
9. The psychology of a Redeemer, *The Antichristian* [30]
10. 'Basically . . .', 23.5.88
11. 'Because of their wealth . . .', 21.6.88
12. 'the need for more sausage . . .' 'Nietzsche ou les saucisses de l'Antechrist' is a superficial essay in an interesting context in Michel Onfray, *Le Ventre des philosophes* (Paris 1989)
13. 'Nietzsche said . . .', *Conversations*, 88; *The Young Nietzsche*, 243–4
14. 'Sils was once again . . .', 14.6.88. Nietzsche's views of Sils are collected in brochures available in the resort.
15. 'He would have walked . . .', 14.6.88. On the relationship to Epicurus, see *The Science of Joy* [45]. Kaufmann provides an excellent commentary.
16. 'Many writers and artists . . .' See the useful volume by G.T. de Beer, *Travellers in Switzerland* (1949)
17. 'I know nothing . . . Ober-erde' On the mountain landscape as inspiration for the *Übermensch*, compare in *The Science of Joy* the rising lake which refuses to flow into God any more [285].
18. 'Nietzsche knew well . . .' See Wilhelm Stein, *Nietzsche und die bildende Kunst* (Berlin 1925), pp. 19–20
19. 'Almost every day . . .', 4.5.88
20. 'One would have to be . . .', *Twilight*, 'Morality as anti-nature', 5. Being outside life is related to being 'untimely'. Of Schopenhauer's untimeliness Nietzsche drew a fine picture in *The Birth of Tragedy* [22], depicting him as Dürer's pale Knight from the painting *Knight, Death and the Devil*.
21. See Chapter five, note 16
22. 'All that is immortal . . .', *Zarathustra*, II, 'On the Happy Islands'. Nietzsche, like Freud, pursues well-being for the soul while avoiding religion. *The Science of Joy* [151] seems to me self-critical: his ultimate dependence on art returns him towards metaphysics. Arthur C. Danto, *Nietzsche as Philosopher*, 61, gives the scholarly view.

23. Zarathustra compared . . . See *Zarathustra*, II, 'On Immaculate Perception': 'loving and going under: for ages that has rhymed with the will to love: that is, with the willingness also to die. Thus I speak to you cowards!' The high mountains were therefore a place to overcome the affliction of disappointed love. The writing of Zarathustra helped Nietzsche overcome love of Lou Salomé. A curious parallel is suggested by the love of stones, which helped Goethe in his *Italian Diaries* recover from love of Charlotte von Stein.

24. For Siegfried's hammering, see chapter 3, note 9

25. 'Foreigners are astonished . . .', *BGE* [244]

26. Verrecchia has the full story of the encounter with d'Ercole.

27. 'Nietzsche's famous rejection of pity . . .' in *The Science of Joy* and *Twilight*

28. 'that morally stuffy front room . . .' R.J. Hollingdale, *Nietzsche* (1985), argues against this interpretation.

29. 'May be Dostoevsky . . .' Thomas Mann assumed so but Nietzsche claimed he hadn't even heard of Dostoevsky until February 1887. The coincidence remains puzzling, especially as the next section 'On the voluntary beggar' appears based on Tolstoy, whose views of religion Nietzsche certainly knew [*KSA* 14:754–6]. *KSA*'s editors comment: 'Nietzsche's reading [of Tolstoy] was knowingly concealed by the Nietzsche Archive.' Possibly Lou Salomé, a Baltic German who grew up in St Petersburg speaking Russian, talked to Nietzsche in 1882 of *Crime and Punishment*, a moment of intellectual intercourse which he then 'forgot'.

30. This, transferred to Communist Czechoslovakia, and complete with animal companions, is the spiritual plot of Bohomil Hrabal's, *I Served the King of England* (1989)

31. He retaliated . . ., *Twilight* [34–6]

32. '. . . disguised personal confessions', *Beyond Good and Evil*, [37]

33. 'Untruth a condition . . .' See also *The Science of Joy* [110] and [121]

34. 'radical modesty . . .', *Daybreak* [547]. *The Science of Joy* [351] attacks Plato and Pythagoras as proud and vainglorious. Nietzsche's 'modesty' chimes with the heresies of Galileo and Giordano Bruno. By the fifteenth paragraph of *The Wanderer and*

his Shadow he had advanced a plea for philosophical modesty on which rests his rejection of contemporary scientific positivism and preceding Christianity.

35. 'The inner world' . . ., *Twilight*, 3
36. 'Willing seems . . .', *BGE* [19]. While rejecting the supreme cognizant ego he was passionate that life could not be lived to the fullest, nor humanity strengthened, if we did not know the origins of that nexus called will.

7

1. 'English biscuits, tea and soap . . .' and Deussen's visit, see Peter André Bloch, *Das Nietzsche-Haus in Sils Maria* (1991)
2. Uncommon privileges . . ., Ben Macintyre, *Forgotten Fatherland* (1992), 122–3
3. 'Shots in the air . . .', 14.6.88 and 17.6.88
4. 'Superabundant substitutes' are the essence of the Dionysian position in the later Nietzsche. See *The Science of Joy* [370]
5. Ludwig Nohl, *Richard Wagner*, p. 95
6. Cosima is much maligned in Nietzsche literature. Her diaries present a thoroughly human picture.
7. '. . . longed for Cosima', Fischer-Dieskau, 121–2. *Cosima Wagner's Diaries* (I), April 1874: 'Nietzsche is tormenting himself. R. exclaims: "He should either marry or write an opera, though doubtless the latter would be such that it would never get produced, and so would not bring him into contact with life." ' Whether or not he noticed the passion for his wife, Wagner spotted Nietzsche's lack of sexual realism.
8. 'Wagner's homosexuality . . . real memories', Robert W. Gutman, *Richard Wagner* (Harmondsworth 1971), 447, 472, 608; Fischer-Dieskau, 53, 118, 122; *KSA*, 13:11 [27]; Schmidt-Löbbecke, 83–4.
9. 'had the character of a *levée* . . .', Carol Diethe, *Nietzsche and Women*, ms p. 100
10. 'a small flickering light . . .', 20.6.88. For Stöcker, see Crankshaw,

234

Bismarck, 380, and generally John Rohl, *The Kaiser and his Court*, Cambridge 1994
11. 'Nietzsche extracted . . .', *KSA*, 14:398; 'And one calculates . . .', *The Antichristian* [62]
12. 'His pharmacopoeia . . .', *KSA*, 13:14 [206]
13. '. . . rare example of genuine humour . . .', 30.6.88
14. '. . . destined him to madness', *Conversations*, p. 164; Janz, I:757
15. 'Theognis and Aeschylus . . .', E.R. Dodds, *The Greeks and the Irrational* (London 1951), p. 33. See also *Ecce Homo*: 'Human, All Too Human', 4. Leon Daudet saw syphilis playing the role of Fate in modern life. Quétel, *History of Syphilis* (1990), p. 174
16. 'dying and . . . genius', Quétel, 172–5
17. 'I need only . . .', *EH*, Foreword, I
18. '. . . the quality of compassion . . .', 14.9.84 to Overbeck. 'Since my childhood the sentence "my greatest dangers lie in pity (*Mitleid*)" has proved itself true over and over again. (It is perhaps the bad consequence of the extrordinary nature of my father, whom all who knew him reckoned more among the "angels" than among "men".'
19. '. . . fatherless teenager he saw himself to be . . .', 'Aus meinem Leben', Friedrich Nietzsche, *Werke*, ed. Karl Schlechta, III:16
20. 'without father and adviser', *KSA*, Briefe, 6:282
21. 'whom already . . .', *EH*, 'Why I am so Clever', 10
22. 'nightmare vision . . .', *Zarathustra*, III, 'On a Vision and a Puzzle'. Compare Isaiah 6:6–7
23. 'Like a child's dream . . .' *The Young Nietzsche* mentions a dog causing their father's fatal fall.
24. 'Freud . . . did not delve deeply enough . . .' Peter Gay, *Freud: A Life for Our Time* (1988), 45, hints at a kind of fear. Consciously Freud recognized Nietzsche as a vital precursor and hoped to find words in Nietzsche for things which remained silent to himself. Yet finding Nietzsche 'too concentrated' he only read him in small doses. Amassed reasons, legitimate but insufficient, for avoiding Nietzsche support Gay's interpretation. See also Paul Assoun, *Freud et Nietzsche* (Paris 1980): Part I shows just how important Nietzsche was as forerunner, inspiration and

pathological case-study to the psychoanalytic movement generally.

25. 'an early poem . . .', *KSA*, 11:322 (written in 1976); 'later set to music . . .', Arnold Schoenberg, *Acht Lieder*, Op. 6 (No 8. 'Der Wanderer'), *c.* 1910

26. 'Elisabeth later recounted . . . burning his hand . . .', *The Young Nietzsche*, 25, 81

27. '. . . saw Christianity as cruel and inhuman', Erich F. Podach, *Gestalten um Nietzsche* (1931), 16–17. Brandes told Nietzsche of their affinity, 11.1.88. On Kierkegaard's relationship to his father, see Patrick Gardiner, *Kierkegaard* (1988): 2–3. Conrad Bonifazi, *Christendom Attacked: A Comparison of Kierkegaard and Nietzsche* (1953) is a dated existentialist study.

28. '. . . frustration with the Hegelian legacy . . .', reflected in Nietzsche, *Untimely Reflections*, I, 'David Strauss'. For Kierkegaard, see Gardiner: 112

29. 'the Oedipus complex . . .', Sigmund Freud, *Studienausgabe* (1969–79), X: *Dostoewskii und die Vatertötung* (1928). Freud also picks out from *Zarathustra*, I, 'On the Pale Criminal', as a case-study in inherited Oedipal guilt. *Studienausgabe*, X, 'Some types of character from psychoanalytic work': 3. Jonathan Keates, *Stendhal* (1994): 306, 316, also shows how much, by their superfine intelligence, Nietzsche and Stendhal made good out of their inheritance, transcending traditional taboos and accepting chance. Both created original mixed genres to accommodate their supremely independent thinking.

30. Freud observed with symptomatic indirectness in *Observations on an Autobiographically Described Case of Paranoia* (1911): 'One of my patients, who lost his father early and in all that was great and sublime about nature tried to rediscover him, made me realize that Nietzsche's *Zarathustra* Part III hymn, "Before Sunrise", expresses the same yearning.' *Studienausgabe* VII: 179. Freud also associates Nietzsche's *Übermensch* with the collective father in the past (Assoun, 69), which suggests how Nietzsche conflated his idealized father with the dead God of Zarathustra.

31. 'The unresolved dissonances . . .', *HAH*, I:379

32. '. . . penned almost in envy . . .', *KSA*, I:408; *Untimely Reflections*, III, 'Schopenhauer as Educator', 7
33. Moradei, p. 8
34. 'Singing is . . .', *Zarathustra*, III: 'the convalescent'
35. 'life without music a mistake . . .', 27.3.88
36. 'The protestant priest is . . .', *Antichristian*: 10
37. 'Something odd and absurd . . .' to Brandes, 10.4.88
38. 'man of nothing . . .', 30.6.88, thanking Fuchs. The etymology of *szlachta*, combining high birth with military prowess, runs curiously parallel to Nietzsche's preoccupation with gut/Krieger, cf. Norman Davies, *God's Playground: A History of Poland*, I, 207
39. 'Nietzsche gave himself . . .', *KSA*, I:508ff. ('Richard Wagner in Bayreuth'); *KSA*, 2:15–17 (*Human, All Too Human*); KSA, 5:204 (*Beyond Good and Evil*, 8); KSA, 6:19–20 (*The Wagner Case*)
40. '. . . powerful individuals . . .', cf. *Beyond Good and Evil*, 199, and Kaufmann, *Nietzsche*, p. 224
41. 'The most spiritual . . .', *Twilight* [17]
42. '. . . post-Christian artistic vision . . .' The Christian aspect of Nietzsche is deeply out of fashion. Nietzsche in his indisputably Christian background is clearly visible in Bernoulli and sensitively approached in Frederick Copleston, *A History of Philosophy*, Vol. 7, Part II, 'Schopenhauer to Nietzsche'
43. 'One must test . . .', *Beyond Good and Evil* [41]
44. 'waiting to pounce . . .', *Zarathustra*, IV, 'Song of Melancholy', 3. '*Also/adlerhaft, pantherhaft/sind des Dichters Sehnsüchte . . .*', tr. Hollingdale, 'Thus eaglelike, pantherlike . . .'
45. 'better to attack one's own . . .', *The Science of Joy* [296]
46. 'artists of life . . .', *The Science of Joy* [344]; *Beyond Good and Evil*; 'The Natural History of Morals'
47. 'questions of spirit . . .', *Genealogy*, 2:16, and above, Chapter 1, in Genoa 'no longer having the courage to be cowardly . . .'
48. Oscar Levy, a German-born Jew and Nietzsche's first editor in English, in 1931, in the wake of the 1914–18 War, called Nietzsche 'the only innocent German', in contrast to the prophets of the German church-state. 'A disciple of Nietzsche belongs to no

country and has no right to defend one country, least of all that in which he was born.' *Thus Spake Zarathustra*, 6th edition (Unwin, 1932), Introduction. Suspect because of his origins and interest in Nietzsche, Levy was deported from Britain in 1921 and only some years later allowed to return. In the good Nietzschean spirit he published a journal, *The Good European*.

49. 'Then my instinct . . .', *EH, HAH*, 4

8

1. '. . . Adorno, visiting . . .' Theodor Adorno, *Ohne Leitbild* (1967), reprinted in *Über Sils und das Oberengadin*, Nietzsche-Haus-Sils Maria, nd
2. 'Hans Olde's photographs . . .', Eggum, *Munch and Photography*, London 1989, pp. 84–8
3. 'Lou Salomé regarded . . .', Pfeifer, *Dokumente*, 482–3
4. 'His fellow Kurgäste . . .' Janz, II, 601–30 covers the final summer in Sils.
5. 'Meta von Salis-Marschlins . . . observed . . .', Gilman, *Conversations*, p. 205
6. 'Women were his best . . .', Diethe, *Nietzsche and Women*, ms in preparation. 'Nietzsche's manifest unease . . .', H.W. Brann's analysis in *Nietzsche und die Frauen*, Bonn 1978, is compelling. On Nietzsche's friendships, see particularly pp. 169ff.
7. 'He wanted Lou . . . their non-affair . . .' See Pfeifer, *Dokumente*, esp. 125–86, 203, 239, and Rudolph Binion, *Frau Lou* (Princeton 1968), 1–119
8. Janz, II, 315; Gilman, 195, and *KGA*, Briefe, 3:6, p. 266
9. 'Nietzsche was reserved . . .', Gilman, *Conversations*, p. 167
10. Resa . . . used the word genius. English readers of Gilman will not recognize this from the translation 'genial' and 'geniality'.
11. 'not a trace of pathological megalomania . . .', Gilman, *Conversations*, p. 162
12. '"Grossenwahn" . . .', Pfeifer, *Dokumente*, 269, 473

13. 'He had no character . . .', Erich F. Podach, *Friedrich Nietzsche und Lou Salomé 1882* (1938), 114
14. '. . . he always needed to dominate', Hollingdale, 56
15. Podach, *Gestalten*, 85, observes Gast was a Wagner substitute. The fantasy took an odd toll on Köselitz, for whom Nietzsche was his only claim to fame besides a marching song written for the First World War. He was forty-six when Nietzsche died in 1900, and although he and Nietzsche only briefly lived side by side, for thirteen years he let himself be dominated by Nietzsche's needs. Then six days after Nietzsche was buried Köselitz married (Schmidt-Löbbecke, 8). Meanwhile historians of the Nietzsche archive, where Köselitz subsequently cooperated with Elisabeth to produce the first adulterated collected works, have been left wondering why this man allowed so much within his own memory to be deliberately falsified. Bernoulli (II:110) describes the man, who also brought a successful court action to have parts of his letters censored out of Bernoulli's highly reliable study, as a mixture of 'blind subordinacy and arrogant self-awareness'. Overbeck comments on Nietzsche's making a great effort to see this man as he wanted to (Bernoulli II:118). For Nietzsche's real views, for example of his clumsiness, see Janz, 2:353, 366, 376.
16. 'as neurotic . . .', *HAH*, 1, 214
17. drugs, opium and chloral . . ., Gilman, 163–4
18. 'Elisabeth at least acknowledged . . .', *The Young Nietzsche*, 330: 'Fritz knew only too well how characteristic it was of all three of us in the first flush of our indignation to say and write sharp and unpleasant things which a day or two later we scarcely remembered having thought or written.'
19. lack of real knowledge, Brann, 20–21, 189.
20. 'fury with a critical article . . .', to Overbeck 20.7.88
21. 'It is a mistake . . .', *KGA*, Briefwechsel, 3:6, p. 264 (12.8.88) The interpretation of Nietzsche's *life* as supremely Christian is also Copleston's.
22. 'Something new . . .', *The Science of Joy* [295]
23. 'He gave me a lecture . . .', Janz, II, 622
24. 'created objects too . . .', *The Science of Joy* [58]

25. 'a philosopher ... also a real person', 'Schopenhauer as Educator', 7 (*KSA*, 1:410). Uniquely and wholly himself in love with Lou ..., cf. Jan./Feb. 1884 letter drafted to Overbeck, *KSA*, Briefe, 6:471
26. 'One must learn to love ...', *The Science of Joy* [334]
27 '... to spurn and to ridicule, to welcome, cherish and mourn ...' This gave the lie to traditional rationalism, though not for Spinoza; cf. 'Thoughts are the mere shadows of feelings', *The Science of Joy* [179]
28. 'Knowledge ... dances into view and moves on', cf. *The Science of Joy* [381]
29. 'love for the unattainable one ...', cf. Murdoch, *The Fire and the Sun*, 37, on Plato on the attractiveness of the good, through its link with Eros.
30. 'Knowledge of the unknowable, articulation of the unsayable ...' Nietzsche anticipated Wittgenstein. Ray Monk, *Ludwig Wittgenstein* (London 1990), shows Wittgenstein ever-reducing the scope of what philosophy can sensibly *say*, whilst acknowledging for himself the *unsayable* truths of idealism. The following passage is doubly interesting in also marking Wittgenstein's 'break' with Schopenhauer. 'This is the way I have travelled: Idealism singles men out from the world as unique, solipsism singles me alone out and at last I see that I too belong with the rest of the world, and so on the one side *nothing* is left over, and on the other side, as unique, *the world*. In this way idealism leads to realism if it is strictly thought out' (p. 144). Nietzsche found his 'pessimism of strength', moving on from Schopenhauer, in a view of our entire world as made-by-art, not rational. He drew art into philosophy as a form of perception, in order to express the philosophically strictly unsayable, and in his own way to bridge the gap between idealism and realism. Understanding reality means inventing metaphors; seeing happening around us what we have already thought to ourselves. As metaphor reality is fleeting but sumptuously desirable. Nietzsche uses the apt image of 'lizard-moments' together with an echo of Faust longing to know the world in *EH*, Daybreak: 1: 'The art of making things which easily slip by without a sound, moments which I call divine lizards, stay still for

a little . . .' These are links I draw here for the first time, and to the best of my knowledge originally. Others between Wittgenstein and Nietzsche have been explored by Erich Heller in *The Artist's Journey into the Interior* (1966).

31. 'Knowledge-as-desire illuminates . . .', cf. Brann, Chapter 5, 'Dionysus ohne Eros', esp. 109, on Nietzsche's thwarted desire for plenitude.

32. 'close to death with excitement', 9.12.88

33. 'Mahler set to music . . .' Mahler was particularly fascinated by Nietzsche's shifting moods and his clowning. Adorno tellingly interpreted Mahler's music as 'futureless'. Franklin, 51, 34

34. '. . . only one more incentive to love', *Genealogy*, 3:2. *Ecce Homo* 75–7, is another statement of Nietzsche's unexpected wisdom: 'every expression of contempt for the sexual life, every befouling of it through the concept "impure" is the crime against life . . .'

35. Luther's 'between beast and angel' is translated in *Zarathustra* as '*Der Mensch ist ein Seil, zwischen Tier und Übermensch* – ein Seil über einem Abgrunde.' The passage in *Genealogy* speaks of 'tragic grunting and haste', though not all translators do. Studies of Nietzsche and Luther, like Nietzsche and Kierkegaard, have been neglected in recent years.

36. Wilhelm Reich, *The Mass Psychology of Fascism* (German edition 1933; 1st English edition 1946). Reich ironically shows Nietzsche used by the Nazis to encourage asceticism. It is not clear that he realized his own affinity with Nietzsche.

37. '. . . libidinous energy shared . . .', *The Science of Joy* [118] ('Benevolence'!). Nietzsche did not see individuals necessarily devouring each other in sexual relationships and was generally much more balanced in his views than Schopenhauer, from whom he mostly took only a palliative anti-female rhetoric. He was alert to Schopenhauer's powerful sexuality: *Genealogy* 3:6. Arthur Danto, p. 103, accepts Nietzsche's wisdom on sex yet seems to contradict himself when he suggests (p. 225) Nietzsche was unusually interested in the pain component of so-called sexual pleasure.

38. 'Eternal recurrence of Elisabeth . . .', *Ecce Homo*, 'Why I am so

241

Wise', 3, *KSA*, 6: 268–9 (this passage not included in the edition tr. Hollingdale)

39. rather 'feminine' by nature. Bernoulli I:272 (Overbeck's view), 289–90; Brann 169; Podach, *Friedrich Nietzsche*, 112. Elisabeth's manic tirades over the apparently hateful, sluttish and altogether disgusting Lou suggest she may have put words into Nietzsche's mouth when he called the loved one 'a monkey with false breasts'. But there was also a strong, lurid, tasteless streak in Nietzsche's imagination, a family trait (see note 18 above), which would eventually be exacerbated by syphilitic loss of tact.
40. 'a God catered for such negative, self-lacerating emotions . . .', *Antichristian* [16], also *Genealogy*, 2:23
41. 'a man was too powerful . . .', to Strindberg 6.12.88. See also Kaufmann, *Nietzsche* 224–5
42. 'God knows . . .', *Genealogy*, 1:12 [tr. Golfing]
43. 'And the incorruptible Professor . . .', *The Secret Agent*, final paragraph. Conrad himself did not document Nietzsche's influence. Geoffrey Meyers, *Joseph Conrad*, pp. 237–8
44. 'The real danger . . .', *Genealogy*, 3:14
45. 'a brave act of intellectual cleansing . . .' This theme runs as strongly through Nietzsche's philosophical work as it does through that of Wittgenstein who often spoke of 'tidying the room'. See *passim*, Monk, op. cit.
46. 'He campaigned . . . left a gaping moral hole . . .' Bernoulli in 1908 (II:5) had no hesitation in calling him a terrorist (see Kaufmann 113; Danto; Kofman, *Explosions*, I, 272–4; Steven E. Aschheim, *The Nietzsche Legacy in Germany 1890–1900*) (1993). James Joll, 'Nietzsche vs. Nietzsche', *New York Review of Books*, 11 Feb. 1993, is a useful summary of moral criticisms (though Joll still refers to Nietzsche as the author of *The Will to Power*.)
47. 'the business of an immoralist . . .' Nietzsche's lack of concern with the consequences of actions is interestingly explored in an unexpected context by Sarah Kofman, *Explosions*, I (Paris 1992), 271ff., 'Une nouvelle diététique'.
48. Luigi Pirandello (1867–1936) in, for example, *Il giuoco delle parti* ('The Rules of the Game')
49. 'My journey had difficulties . . .', to Köselitz 27.9.88

1. 'I am one thing . . .', *EH*, 'Why I write such Good Books', 1
2. 'Listen to me . . .' *EH*, Foreword, 1–2
3. 'An uncannily solitary act . . .', 30.10.88
4. 'inspired by the travelling circus . . .', *The Young Nietzsche*, 54
5. 'I sought . . .', Podach, *Gestalten* (1932), 31ff. See also *KSA*, 13:549, 557
6. 'I can do . . .', *EH*, 'Why I write such Good Books', 2. *Dionysus Dithyrambs*, 'Among Daughters of the Desert'
7. 'now lose me . . .', *EH*, Foreword, 4
8. 'out of strength . . .', *EH*, 'Why I am so Wise', 7
9. 'what Nietzsche meant by self-overcoming . . .', *EH*, 'BoT', 2
10. 'The genius of the heart . . .', *EH*, 'Why I write such good books', 5–6. 'Consciousness is . . .', *EH*, 'Why I am so Clever', 9
11. 'City of dreams . . .', Prosio, *Città nascosta* (1992), 12
12. 'a great wedding . . .', 13.9.88
13. The French theorist of Aryan superiority, Arthur Gobineau, had also died in Turin six years earlier. Elisabeth, as a follower, tried to create a historical link between this event and her brother's presence in the city by forging a letter. Verrecchia, 61 and 86, supposes a forgery, confirmed by its absence from *KSA*, Briefe.
14. 'ever more intense craving . . .', *BoT* (1886 Preface), 4
15. 'where multitudes . . .', *BoT*, 1. Alessandra Comini in *The Changing Image of Beethoven* (1987) begins her book with the day in 1902 when Mahler, conducting Beethoven's Ninth, formed part of a twentieth-century Viennese reenactment of Wagner's 1840 essay 'Pilgrimage to Beethoven' and also seemed to realize Nietzsche's description of the Ninth Symphony as a great communal occasion. The link from Beethoven to Mahler via Nietzsche is well documented. See example on Nietzsche, p. 292
16. 'Bismarck's imperial gaudies . . .', *Untimely Reflections*, 'The Confessor and Writer David Strauss', *KSA*, 2:204
17. '. . . is how de Chirico . . .', *Prosio*, 23–51. See also Cheney, op. cit.
18. 'I live . . .', *EH*, *Zarathustra*
19. 'I walk . . .', *EH*, *Zarathustra*, VIII (tr. Hollingdale)

20. 'Only after me . . .', *EH*, 'Why I am a Destiny', 1
21. 'Architecture for people . . .', *The Science of Joy* [280]
22. 'working simultaneously . . .' 'Podach, *Nietzsche Werke des Zusammenbruchs* (1961) [*NWZ*], 185–6, shows many passages were interchangeable
23. '. . . the routine . . .', Verrecchia, 212–16
24. 'Still Signora Candida . . . little brute', Verrecchia, 208, 216
25. 'Happy Islands . . .', *Zarathustra*, II
26. 'luscious figs . . .', *EH*, Foreword
27. 'In an autumnal mood . . .', 18.10.88, 19.10.88, 30.10.88
28. '. . . what I actually . . .', *EH*, 'Why I am so Clever', 7
29. 'no part in Romantic striving . . .', *EH*, 'Why I am so Clever', 10
30. 'aversion from alcohol . . .', *EH*, 'Why I am so Clever', 1
31. 'If I generally . . .', *EH*, 'Why I am so Clever', 2
32. 'which suggest he was fat . . .' The food he specified was dumplings and floury, overcooked vegetables. Elisabeth (who became a vegetarian with Förster) commented in *The Young Nietzsche* that such food, with a low meat content, was typical of their family but otherwise very unusual and unusually healthy. None of Nietzsche's strictures on food have any dietetic foundation.
33. 'The first time Nietzsche saw . . .', *KSA*, 9:607 (Notebook, Autumn 1881)
34. 'When one day . . .', *EH*, 'Why I am so Clever', 6
35. 'Everything is . . .', *EH, Zarathustra*, III
36. '. . . The inspired "wise" and "clever" man . . .' See those sections of *EH*, especially 'Why I am so Clever', 1
37. 'his greatest problem . . .', *EH, Zarathustra*, III and V
38. 'an absurd susceptibility . . .', *EH, Zarathustra*, V
39. 'his argument against pity . . .', 22.2.83
40. '. . . fear of contamination', *EH*, 'Why I am so Wise', 8
41. 'My sister writes . . .', to Overbeck, Christmas 1888. See also Elisabeth Förster-Nietzsche to her brother 6.9.88, *Kristische Gesamtausgabe*, Briefwechsel, 3/6: 294–6
42. 'This stupid vengeful creature . . .' The resentment went back to 1882. After she meddled in and muddied his relationship with Lou

Salomé he retaliated, without posting the letter: 'I do not like the kind of souls of which you possess one, my poor sister, and I like them least when they go in for moral bleating: I know your pettiness.' September 1882 *KSA*, Briefe, 6:267. See also to Malvida von Meysenbug, beginning of May 1884 [ibid.:500] and drafts to his mother and sister Jan./Feb. 1884 [ibid.:467–8]

43. 'suppressed and may have destroyed . . .', Kaufmann, *Nietzsche*, 443

44. 'Nietzsche attacks . . .', *KSA*, 14:507

45. 'He began impossibly to save . . .', Janz, II, 639–48. 'Von Salis would later buy . . .', Diethe, op. cit., 89

46. 'That I attach . . .', 19.11.88

47. 'Malvida said . . .', *KGA*, Briefwechsel, 3/6:330

48. 'a similar note to Rohde . . .', 18.10.88, 19.5.87

49. 'I have gradually . . .', 20.10.88

50. 'I've suffered . . .', 5.11.88

51. 'Knew well the pathology . . .' Podach, *Madness*, 95, blamed the family, to me excessively. Neither recent upsets nor longstanding tensions prompted the final physiological crisis, though possibly they hastened it.

52. 'Rude letters . . .', 30.10.88 and 8.12.88

53. 'Rudness a topic. . .', *EH*, 'Why I am so Wise',5

54. 'tugging his mouth . . .', 2.12.88. Vorberg, *Über Nietzsches Krankheit* (1933), 28, compares 'these symptoms of psychopaths as well as schizophrenics and paralytics' with the poet Lenau. The terms are fierce but the study, opposed to Förster-Nietzsche's whitewashing, was still essentially sympathetic to the creative artist in Nietzsche. See also Quetel, 160–61.

55. 'like a dog . . .', *EH*, 'Why I am so Clever', 1

56. *Nietzsche contra Wagner* described Wagner's last work, *Parsifal*, as a parody of the tragic. Talking about Wagner he seemed again to talk about himself. Podach, *NWZ*: 204, develops the idea of *The Wagner Case* as operetta or Satyric drama. It moves in the direction of Menippean satire with a mixture of prose and verse, establishing parallels with the 'low' Latin literature, for example, of Petronius. The irony is that Nietzsche's appropriation of low

forms in a new rhetorical context resulted in a form of highly encoded, ironic and some would say 'exclusive' modernism.

57. 'With this . . .', *The Science of Joy* [382]/ *EH, Zarathustra*, II
58. 'De-selfing . . .', *Entselbstung, EH*, Daybreak, 2
59. 'The title . . .', Verrecchia, 128; *Cosima Wagner's Diaries* (II), 25.12.78
60. 'according to St John's gospel . . .' Bernoulli, I:243, makes the point that Nietzsche found many more references in Christianity for his condition than he did in the Greek world.
61. 'Ecce Homo . . .', *Twilight*, 'Morality as Anti-Nature'
62. 'all who believe he dismissed . . .', *EH*, 'Why I am so Wise', 8
63. 'This is how to survive . . .', *EH*, 'Why I write such Good Books', 1
64. 'His vision . . .', *EH, Zarathustra*, II
65. 'fundamental aspect is . . . willing'. This theme can also be found in Wittgenstein's turning to religious faith inspired by Tolstoy. Nietzsche, like Plato, is supremely aware of the erotic tension in the quest for knowledge. Cf. Chapter 8, note 30, above.
66. 'In knowing and . . .', *EH, Zarathustra*, VIII
67. 'Who has thought . . .', paraphrased in *BoT* and *EH, BoT*, 2. The translation is mine.

10

1. 'Laocoön . . .', *KSA*, 14:58. Nietzsche was given a head of Laocoön by a female admirer of *BoT*, Bernoulli, I: 269
2. 'other people were shadows . . .', to Gersdorff, 5.10.72
3. 'as thrilling as . . .', *EH*, 'why I write such Good Books', 2. Substantial subject matter and thrills from *BoT* resurfaced in Thomas Mann's novella *Death in Venice* and found a happy visual translation in Visconti's 1971 film to Mahler's music. Thus Nietzsche found his way to the cinema screen.
4. 'everything was on target . . .', 22.12.88
5. 'badly written . . .', *BoT* (1886, Preface), 3
6. 'Not to purge . . .', *EH, BoT*, 3

7. 'With pictures of himself . . .' Nietzsche himself associated 'the pictorial man' with fanaticism, Bernoulli, II: 204–6
8. 'She took exception . . .', *KSA* 14:460–62
9. 'the vision . . .', *EH*, 'Tragedy', 4
10. 'At this period . . .', *The Lonely Nietzsche*, 392. Verrecchia, 196, rightly emphasizes the unique destructiveness of this act. Janz offers a slightly different interpetation of the donning of the Zagreus mask, 3:31–3
11. 'When I look . . .', *Ecce Homo*, *KSA*, 6:268; not available in the Penguin translation
12. 'Nietzsche's original account . . .', *BoT*, 10
13. 'I have never . . .', *EH*, 'Twilight', 3
14. 'telling Deussen . . .', 26.11.88
15. 'The story of Zagreus . . .', Pierre Grimal, *Dictionary of Classical Mythology*, 466
16. 'rabid Dionysian imagination . . .' Möbius, *Über das Pathalogische bei Nietzsche* (1902) argues for the first appearance of morbid symptoms in 1882. His thesis is more conjectural than its rapid dismissal by later scholars would suggest, and maintains from the first sentence that with or without sickness Nietzsche was a man of genius and (16–17) a fine writer. For Möbius one of the first signs of sickness was the image of the shepherd with the serpent in his mouth.
17. 'view of his style . . .', *EH*, 'Why I write down Good Books', 4
18. '. . . might have become iconic . . .' The Nazis did try to make the *Dithyrambs* iconic: wrong (*Übel*) can be justified if it edifies a god, Podach, *NWZ*, 360
19. 'all of Nietzsche's writing . . .', cf. *EH* 'Why I write such Good Books', 2
20. 'told his mother . . .', Podach, *Gestalten*, 31. Laocoön, see note 1.
21. '*Bei abgehellter Luft* . . .', strikes Möbius as nonsensical. Others of his examples, like comparing light to a cow, are more compelling. The overall aim, that Nietzsche should not be worshipped uncritically, was, in opposition to the Nietzsche Archive's false hagiography, admirable in 1902.
22. See Chapter 3, note 3. Wagner's positive view of the young

Nietzsche had recently been sent to his mother by an unknown correspondent, apparently encouraging their collaboration and in reproach for *TWC*, cf. 17.11.88. Nietzsche mentioned Wagner's old dedications for him twice over the spring and summer of 1888, in letters to Brandes and Knorz.

23. 'a fascinating, capital work . . .', 27.12.88 to Fuchs

24. 'identified as modern . . .' Nietzsche calls the music of Berlioz and Liszt 'Music of the Future' and finds it, like modern poetry, to have a brilliant iridescent style yet concealing often unoriginal or absent thoughts. *The Young Nietzsche*, 57-8, rightly highlights these early musings, reprinted in Schlechta, *Werke*, 111:34-5, and picks out Nietzsche's fondness for the Gretchen part of Liszt's Faust symphony (115)

25. '. . . early French critic . . .', Charles Andler, *Nietzsche* (1920–31)

26. Podach, *Madness*, 147. Andler's study is based on this platonic love of Nietzsche's for Cosima.

27. 'Was Friedrich . . . scheming . . .', Fischer-Dieskau, 58, 118

11

1. 'An exceptional new cycle . . .', *EH*, 'Why I am so Clever', 10

2. 'He still . . .', *KSA*, 14:506-7

3. 'For fear . . .' For her editing of 'Declaration of War', see *KSA*, 14:451-3. Alas for Nietzsche's misunderstanding this *Kriegserklärung* was a term Nietzsche took over from Malvida who had used it ironically, as did he. Cf. to Meta von Salis, 14.11.88

4. 'For when truth . . .', *EH*, 'Why I am a Destiny', 1

5. 'A violent declaration . . .' intended for either *Ecce Homo* or *The Antichristian: Gesetz wider das Christentum*, *KSA*, 14:448ff.

6. 'The accursed places . . .', *KSA*, 6:254

7. 'Nor were . . .', letters to Burckhardt, 13.9.88, and to Deussen, 14.9.88, contain the entirety of Nietzsche's 'mad' vision less fiercely expressed. His last sensible statement to von Meysenbug on Germany at the end of July gives an idea of his mental decline over five months.

8. 'the leading person . . .', Quétel, 163–8. Worrying letters were sent to Overbeck on 13.11.88, 26.11.88 and just after; 'as if here were a prince . . .', 11.12.88 to Deussen, 'a prince'.
9. 'A war . . .', to Brandes beginning of December; also 8.12.88 and 9.12.88
10. 'through the fumes . . .', draft to Brandes beginning of December.
11. 'censorship . . .', to Jean Bourdeau 17.12.88 (draft), Siberia 13.9.88
12. 'Wagner's Siegfried', see Chapter 3, note 19
13. 'approached in 1873 . . .' *Cosima Wagner's Diaries*, I: 1 Nov. 1873
14. 'he incanted . . .', 11.12.88
15. 'Giorgio Colli's words . . .', 'The Posthumous Fragments from the Beginning of 1888 to January 1889', *KSA*, 13: 663–8. Colli's words also appear in obscure translation in *Nietzsche in Italy*, ed. Thomas Harrison. Colli's text in Italian and English contains the valuable image of 'Just a smudge . . .', just a semitone out.
16. 'He still . . .', *EH*, 'Why I am so Clever', 5
17. 'No hatred . . .', Verrecchia, 157
18. 'works of Liszt . . .', *EH*, 'Why I am so Clever', 7
19. '. . . anecdotally connects . . .', *EH*, 'Why I am so Clever', 1
20. Nietzsche's passion for food only seems unsatisfactory when taken literally, for example by writers trapped in their own national culinary prejudices. Michel Onfray (*Le Ventre des philosophes*) and Verrecchia, a Frenchman and an Italian, respectively berate him for not taking their cuisines seriously. The clue to Nietzsche's sausage lies in his insistence on love of things near at hand, the usefulness of food as an anti-idealistic metaphor capable of expressing the joy of existence.
21. '. . . deceits of illness . . .', 17.11.88
22. '. . . revising . . .', 16.12.88
23. '. . . illegible . . .', 24.7.88. For moving specimens of Nietzsche's changing handwriting, accompanied unfortunately by a text biased to please Elisabeth Förster-Nietzsche, see Isabella Ungern-Sternberg, *Nietzsche im Spiegelbild seiner Schrift* (1902). Kaufmann also includes facsimiles. An absurd thesis that eyestrain caused all Nietzsche's woes was popular when syphilis was too

shameful to contemplate. Even Elisabeth Förster-Nietzsche was unconvinced. G.M. Gould, *Biographic Clinics* (London 1904), vol. 2
24. 'Die Einsamkeit . . .' Podach, *Gestalten*, 31. Colli classifies these lines as work towards the *Dithyrambs*, 'Die Sonne sinkt' and 'Feuerzeichen'
25. 'You'll also . . .', 25.11.88. Another attack . . ., 2.12.88
26. '. . . to be infected . . .', 18.11.88
27. 'twice infected . . .', Podach, *Madness*, 171, and W. Lange-Eichbaum, *Nietzsche Krankheit und Wirkung* (1946), 12. Lange-Eichbaum's source which gave him extraordinary details of Nietzsche's physical condition ('chronic genital excema') and incontinence, may be doubted: a Lepzig doctor told him first-hand of letters in which two doctors spoke of treating Nietzsche in Leipzig for syphilis in 1865. Möbius had also seen the letters, which were later destroyed. However, his evidence chimes closely with Montinari's 1980 presentation of new evidence from Wagner's Dr Eiser (in *Nietzsche in Italy*, ed. Harrison). Nietzsche, while (then) denying syphilis, said he had contracted some 'blemmorrhoeas' during his university studies (in Leipzig) and had practised coitum in Italy (Sorrento 1876–7) upon the advice of a doctor. Blunk *Nietzsche, Kindheit und Jugend* (1953), dates the syphilis from 1867
28. 'the tragic . . .', 16.12.88
29. 'cried out . . .', Verrecchia, 209, 'asked for his room . . .', Verrecchia, 206
30. 'the rescue of a small dog . . .', *The Lonely Nietzsche*, 381–2. Nietzsche's 'talking' to animals again recalls Siegfried, a character on whom he first presented a paper to his friends at school.
31. 'Don Enrico . . .', Verrecchia, 196–201
32. 'The accounts are various . . .', Verrecchia, 207–10
33. It is possible . . ., Janz, 3: 34–35.
34. 'I want . . .', *The Science of Joy*, 314. Janz, 3:34, is surely wrong to say Nietzsche didn't particularly like animals
35. 'an ectasy of pity . . .' He had written to Emily Fynn (6.12.88) saying he was no longer a creature in a cave but had emerged. He

was no longer the one to be pitied. As an 'Untier' (11.12.88) he could at last show pity for a helpless creature.

36. 'why other writers...' Milan Kundera, *The Unbearable Lightness of Being* (1984), 'Karenin's Smile'. See also Chapter 6, note 30 (Bohomil Hrabal, *I Served the King of England*). Hrabal's is a Zarathustran ending, depicting the point where individuals, in Kundera's words, 'step down from the road along which mankind, "the master and proprietor of nature", is travelling'. The Russian poet Vladimir Mayakovsky also wrote a poem in 1918, 'The Right Attitude to Horses', which closely mirrors these last events in Nietzsche's life, and though I have not and been able to prove a connection, see Lesley Chamberlain, 'The Right Attitude to Horses', *TLS* 1 March 1996.

37. *cogito ergo sum* . . . Nietzsche's contribution to the history of philosophy would be the reverse of the *cogito*: all that I am, my body, my psyche, my history, my enthusiasms, these are what make me 'think' as I do; thereby thinking is a secondary activity. Ecce homo! The philosopher should remember he is a man among men, and study unmediated life. Cf. Giorgio Colli, *KSA*, 13:665: 'Paradoxically the falling away of theoretical power [Nietzsche has exhausted his conceptual apparatus] does in the end lead to new theoretical formulations, in which behind outward brilliance and exuberance is hidden a profundity whose actual dimension has not yet been established. That the value of a philosopher or of an artist may reside in a personal element, less in comportment than in nature or character, suggests as a final goal the overcoming of literature, or mediated expression at least, in favour of a direct manifestation of wisdom, of the superiority of a physiological wisdom. This is the new doctrine, even if cut off at birth, that Nietzsche achieves in his last year.' Colli brings together Nietzsche's endurance and a primary thesis of the present book, that Nietzsche's attention to 'things near at hand' constituted his originality as a philosopher.

38. '. . . mulling over . . .', to Köselitz 30.12.88 (draft)

39. 'Did the rejection . . .' See Janz, 2:622, for Julius Kaftan's view, and 3:22, 35, for more general considerations.

40. 'a poem . . .', repeated in *EH*, 'Science of Joy'
41. 'very strange year . . .', 13.9.88; 'not ill . . .', 28.9.88
42. 'Turin has . . .' cf. Lesley Chamberlain, 'Elegance and Metaphysics beside the Po', *The Times*, 30 March 1996
43. 'That Nietzsche . . .', Bernoulli, I:52. I have supplied the obvious words omitted in 1908
44. 4.1.89 to Dr Wiener
45. 'for I . . .', 4.1.89
46. 'the desire to assume . . .', Podach, *Gestalten*, 12
47. 'so close to being . . .', Podach, *NWZ*, 180
48. 'called Cosima . . . and Bismarck', Podach, *Madness*, 193, 194
49. 'Interwoven tones . . .', *Conversations* [77]; 'Ah Deussen . . .', Podach, *Madness*, 216–17; 'Back in Naumberg . . .', *Conversations* [78]
50. This is Möbius's view.
51. 'woman . . .', *The Science of Joy* [60]
52. 'Porto Fino . . .', *EH, Zarathustra*, I
53. Yorick-Columbus, *KSA*, 11:328
54. 'autoerotic orgy . . .', Verrecchia, 211. Cf. also *KSA*, 12:47, 'the orgiastic soul'
55. 'grateful for Bettmann . . .' Janz 3:43–47, clears up the confusion surrounding the travelling companion
56. 'papalina . . .', Verrecchia, 216
57. 'Gondola song . . .', *Nietzsche contra Wagner*, 'Intermezzo'
58. unkind to dogs . . ., Podach, *Madness*, 218
59. 'the word elegant . . .', *Conversations* [77]

BIBLIOGRAPHY

Abraham, Gerald 'Nietzsche and Wagner' in *Romantic and Slavonic Music* London 1964

Adorno, Theodor W. *Ohne Leitbild Parva Aesthetica* Frankfurt am Main 1967

Ansell-Pearson, Keith 'Nietzsches Ubermensch' in *Journal of the History of Ideas* Vol 53, No 2 April–June 1992

Assoun, Paul *Freud et Nietzsche* Paris 1980

Bernoulli, Carl Albrecht von *Franz Overbeck und Friedrich Nietzsche eine Freundschaft* 2 vols. Jena 1908

Binion, Rudolph *Frau Lou Nietzsche's Wayward Disciple* Princeton 1968

Bloch, Peter André *Das Nietzsche-Haus in Sils Maria* Chur 1991

Blondell, Eric *Nietzsche The Body and Culture* tr Sean Hand London 1991

Bonifazi, Conrad *Christendom Attacked A comparison of Kierkegaard and Nietzsche* London 1953

Brandes, Georg *Friedrich Nietzsche* London 1914

Brann, Heinrich, W., *Nietzsche und die Frauen* Bonn 1978

Burckhardt, Jacob *Civilisation of the Renaissance in Italy* tr S.G.C. Middlemore ed. Irene Gordon London 1960

Carey, John *The Intellectuals and the Masses* London 1992

Copleston, Frederick *A History of Philosophy* Vol 7:II 'Schopenhauer to Nietzsche' New York 1973
Dalhaus, Carl *Schoenberg and the new Music* London 1987
Dahlhaus Carl, ed., *Between Romanticism and Modernism* London 1980
Danto, Arthur C. *Nietzsche as Philosopher* New York 1965
de Beer, G.R. *Travellers in Switzerland* Oxford 1949
Diethe, Carol *Nietzsche and Women* ms in preparation [1996]
Dodds, E.R. *The Greeks and the Irrational* London 1951
Eggum, Arne *Munch and Photography* London 1989
Fischer-Dieskau, Dietrich *Wagner and Nietzsche* London 1978
Förster-Nietzsche, Elisabeth *The Young Nietzsche* London 1912
    The Lonely Nietzsche London 1915
Franklin, Peter *Mahler Symphony No 3* Cambridge 1991
Freud, Sigmund 'Dostoejewski und die Vatertötung' (1928) *Studienasugabe* (Frankfurt am Main 169–79) X 267–286
Gardiner, Patrick *Schopenhauer* Harmondsworth 1967
Gilman, S. ed. *Conversations with Nietzsche A Life in the Words of his contemporaries* Oxford 1987
Greene, David B. *Mahler, Consciousness and Temporality* New York/London 1984
Gutman, Roy *Richard Wagner The Man, His Mind and His Music* London 1971
Harper, Ralph *The Seventh Solitude* (on Nietzsche, Kierkegaard, Dostoevsky) Baltimore 1965
Harrison, Thomas P. ed., *Nietzsche in Italy* Stanford 1988
Hollingdale, R.J. *Nietzsche The Man and His Philosophy* London 1985
Hirsch, Emanuel 'Nietzsche und Luther' *Jahrbuch der Luthergesellschaft* 1920/21

Hull, Isabel V. *The Entourage of Kaiser Wilhelm II 1888–1918* Cambridge University Press 1982

Janz, Curt Paul *Friedrich Nietzsche Biographie* 3 vols Munich 1978

Kaufmann, Walter *Nietzsche* 4th edition Princeton 1974

Tragedy and Philosophy New York 1968

Keates, Jonathan *Stendhal* London 1994

Liebermann, Kurt *Nietzsches Kampf und Untergang in Turin* Leipzig 1934

Lönning, Per 'Nietzsche and Christianity' in *The Dilemma of Contemporary Theology* New York 1962

Macintyre, Ben *Forgotten Fatherland* London 1992

Magee, Bryan *Aspects of Wagner* revised edition London 1988

Moradei, Luisa *La musica di Nietzsche* Padova 1983

Mellers, Wilfred *Twilight of the Gods The Beatles in Retrospect* London 1973

Möbius, Paul *Über das Pathalogische bei Nietzsche* 1902

Monk, Ray *Ludwig Wittgenstein The Duty of Genius* London 1990

Murdoch, Iris *The Fire and the Sun* Oxford 1977

Nehemas, Alexander *Nietzsche Life as Literature* London 1985

Onfray, Michel *Le Ventre des philosophes* Paris 1989

O'Shea, John *Music and Medicine Medical Profiles of Great Composers* Dent 1990

Pawel, Ernst *The Living Nightmare A Life of Franz Kafka* London 1994

Pfeifer, Ernst, ed., *Friedrich Nietzsche Paul Rée Lou von Salomé Die Dokumente ihrer Begegnung* Frankfurt am Main 1970

Podach, Erich F.

Nietzsche Werke des Zusammenbruchs Heidelberg 1961

Friedrich Nietzsche und Lou Salomé Zurich 1938

Gestalten um Nietzsche Weimar 1932
Madness of Nietzsche London 1931
Prosio, Pier Massimo *La Citta nascosta* Torino 1992
Quétel, Claude *History of Syphilis* Paris 1990
Schmidt-Löbbecke, Caroline and Curt Paul Janz
  Friedrich Nietzsches Wagner- Erfahrung (Sils Maria 1986)
Schoenberg, Arnold *Style and Idea Selected Writings* tr Leo
  Black London 1975
Stein, Wilhelm *Nietzsche und die bildende Kunst* Berlin
  1925
Sturrock, John *Autobiography* London 1993
Verrrechia, Anacleto *La catastrophe di Nietzsche a Torino*
  Turin 1978
Vorberg, Gaston *Über Nietzsches Krankheit* Berlin 1933
Wagner, Cosima, *Diaries* Vol 1 1869– tr. Geoffrey
  Skelton London 1978